Palgrave Macmillan Studies in Banking and Financial Institutions
Series Editor: **Professor Philip Molyneux**

The Palgrave Macmillan Studies in Banking and Financial Institutions will be international in orientation and include studies of banking within particular countries or regions, and studies of particular themes such as Corporate Banking, Risk Management, Mergers and Acquisitions, etc. The books will be focused upon research and practice, and include up-to-date and innovative studies on contemporary topics in banking that will have global impact and influence.

Titles include:
Yener Altunbas, Blaise Gadanecz and Alper Kara
SYNDICATED LOANS
A Hybrid of Relationship Lending and Publicly Traded Debt

Elena Beccalli
IT AND EUROPEAN BANK PERFORMANCE

Santiago Carbó, Edward P.M. Gardener and Philip Molyneux
FINANCIAL EXCLUSION

Allessandro Carretta, Franco Fiordelisi and Gianluca Mattarocci (*editors*)
NEW DRIVERS OF PERFORMANCE IN A CHANGING WORLD

Violaine Cousin
BANKING IN CHINA

Franco Fiordelisi and Philip Molyneux
SHAREHOLDER VALUE IN BANKING

Hans Genberg and Cho-Hoi Hui
THE BANKING CENTRE IN HONG KONG
Competition, Efficiency, Performance and Risk

Elisabetta Gualandri and Valeria Venturelli (*editors*)
BRIDGING THE EQUITY GAP FOR INNOVATIVE SMEs

Munawar Iqbal and Philip Molyneux
THIRTY YEARS OF ISLAMIC BANKING
History, Performance and Prospects

Kimio Kase and Tanguy Jacopin
CEOs AS LEADERS AND STRATEGY DESIGNERS
Explaining the Success of Spanish Banks

M. Mansoor Khan and M. Ishaq Bhatti
DEVELOPMENTS IN ISLAMIC BANKING
The Case of Pakistan

Mario La Torre and Gianfranco A. Vento
MICROFINANCE

Philip Molyneux and Munawar Iqbal
BANKING AND FINANCIAL SYSTEMS IN THE ARAB WORLD

Philip Molyneux and Eleuterio Vallelado (*editors*)
FRONTIERS OF BANKS IN A GLOBAL WORLD

Anastasia Nesvetailova
FRAGILE FINANCE
Debt, Speculation and Crisis in the Age of Global Credit

Dominique Rambure and Alec Nacamuli
PAYMENT SYSTEMS
From the Salt Mines to the Board Room

Andrea Schertler
THE VENTURE CAPITAL INDUSTRY IN EUROPE

Alfred Slager
THE INTERNATIONALIZATION OF BANKS

Noel K. Tshiani
BUILDING CREDIBLE CENTRAL BANKS
Policy Lessons for Emerging Economies

Palgrave Macmillan Studies in Banking and Financial Institutions
Series Standing Order ISBN 978- 1–4039–4872–4

You can receive future titles in this series as they are published by placing a stand-ing order. Please contact your bookseller or, in case of difficulty, write to us at the address below with your name and address, the title of the series and the ISBN quoted above.

Customer Services Department, Macmillan Distribution Ltd, Houndmills, Basingstoke, Hampshire RG21 6XS, England

Bridging the Equity Gap for Innovative SMEs

Edited by

Elisabetta Gualandri and Valeria Venturelli

With contributions from:

Fabio Braga, Luciana Canovi, Massimo Demasi,
Alessandro G. Grasso and Paola Schwizer

palgrave
macmillan

First published 2008 by
PALGRAVE MACMILLAN

Palgrave Macmillan in the UK is an imprint of Macmillan Publishers Limited, registered in England, company number 785998, of Houndmills, Basingstoke, Hampshire RG21 6XS.

Palgrave Macmillan in the US is a division of St Martin's Press LLC, 175 Fifth Avenue, New York, NY 10010.

Palgrave Macmillan is the global academic imprint of the above companies and has companies and representatives throughout the world.

Palgrave® and Macmillan® are registered trademarks in the United States, the United Kingdom, Europe and other countries.

ISBN-13: 978–0–230–20505–5   hardback
ISBN-10: 0–230–20505–4   hardback

This book is printed on paper suitable for recycling and made from fully managed and sustained forest sources. Logging, pulping and manufacturing processes are expected to conform to the environmental regulations of the country of origin.

A catalogue record for this book is available from the British Library.

Library of Congress Cataloging-in-Publication Data

Bridging the equity gap for innovative SMEs / edited By Elisabetta
    Gualandri and Valeria Venturelli ; with contributions from: Fabio
    Braga ... [et al.].
      p. cm.
    Includes bibliographical references and index.
    ISBN 978–0–230–20505–5 (alk. paper)
    1. Small business—Technological innovations.   2. Small business—
    Finance.   I. Gualandri, Elisabetta.   II. Venturelli, Valeria.   III.
    Braga, Fabio.
    HD2341.B75 2008
    338.6′041—dc22

                                                                  2008029947

10 9 8 7 6 5 4 3 2 1
17 16 15 14 13 12 11 10 09 08

Printed and bound in Great Britain by
CPI Antony Rowe, Chippenham and Eastbourne

To our wonderful partners, Carlo and Max, with thanks for all their understanding and moral support

Contents

List of Tables

List of Figures

List of Boxes

Acronyms and Abbreviations

AIFI	Associazione italiana del private equity e venture capital [Italian Private Equity and Venture Capital Association]
AIM	Alternative Investment Market
ATP	Advanced Technology Programme
BAND	Business Angel Netwerk Deutschland
BERR	(UK Department for) Business, Enterprise and Regulatory Reform
BIt	Borsa Italiana
BME	Bolsas y Mercados Españoles
BTU	Beteiligungskapital für kleine Technologieunternehmen
BVCA	British Venture Capital Association
BVK	Der Bundesverband Deutscher Kapitalbeteiligungsgesellschaften [German Private Equity and Venture Capital Association e.V.]
CDC	Caisse de Dépots et Consignations
CEFIN	Centro Studi Banca e Finanza [Centre for Studies in Banking and Finance]
CIS	Community Innovation Survey
DB	Deutsche Börse
DBAN	Danish Business Angels Network
DKK	Danish Krone
DtA	Deutsche Ausgleichsbank
DVCA	Danish Venture Capital Association
DUF	Dansk Udviklingsfinansiering
EBIT	Earning before interest and taxes
EBITDA	Earnings before interest, taxes depreciation and amortization
EC	European Commission
ECB	European Central Bank
ECF	Enterprise Capital Fund
EIB	European Investment Bank
EIF	European Investment Fund
ERISA	Employee Retirement Income Security Act
ERP	European Recovery Programme
EU	European Union

EVCA	European Private Equity & Venture Capital Association
FCPI	Fonds Communs de Placement Innovation
FCPR	Fonds Communs de Placement à Risque
FESE	Federation of European Securities Exchanges
FPCR	Fonds Publics pour le Capital Risque
FSA	Financial Services Authority
FSAP	Financial Service Action Plan
GDP	Gross Domestic Product
GEM	Global Entrepreneurship Monitor
IAS	International Accounting Standard
ICB	Industry Classification Benchmark
ICT	Information and communication technology
ICFC	Industrial and Commercial Finance Corporation
IPO	Initial public offering
IR	Investor relator
ISIT	Fraunhofer-Institut für Silicon Technologie
ISMES	Innovative small and medium-sized enterprises
KfW	Kreditanstalt für Wiederaufbau
LSE	London Stock Exchange
MAB	Mercado Alternativo Bursátil
MAC	Mercato Alternativo dei Capitali [Alternative Capital Market]
MBG	Mittelständische Beteiligungsgesellschaften
MTA	Mercato Telematico Azionario [Electronic Share Market]
MTF	Multilateral Trading Facilities
NVCA	National Venture Capital Association
PE	Private equity
PPM	Participation Guarantee Order Scheme
R&D	Research and development
RBAN	Regional Business Angels Network
RCAP	Risk Capital Action Plan
RDAs	Regional Development Agencies
Reg &: Off Mkt	Regulated and Official Market
ROE	Return on equity
RVCF	Regional Venture Capital Funds
SBA	Small Business Administration
SBIC	Small Business Investment Companies
SBIR	Small Business Innovation Research
SBS	Small Business Service
SCRs	Sociétés de Capital à Risque
SICAV	Société d'Investissement à Capital Variable

SEAQ	Stock Exchange Automated Quotation System
SETS	Stock Exchange Electronic Trading Service
SETSqx	Stock Exchange Electronic Trading Service
SMES	Small and Medium-Sized Enterprises
SWX	Swiss Exchange
TFP	Total factor productivity
Turn. vel.	Turnover velocity
VCT	Venture Capital Trusts
VDCIT	Venture and Development Capital Investment Trusts
WFE	World Federation of Exchanges

Notes on the Contributors

Fabio Braga has been a senior analyst at the Economic Research Department of Borsa Italiana, London Stock Exchange Group, since 2005. His research interests focus on capital markets and corporate finance. Before joining Borsa Italiana, he worked at the research department of Unicredit and spent a short period at Bocconi University and the Centre for Economic Performance, London School of Economics as a research assistant. After graduating in economics from Bocconi University, he earned a Master's degree in economics from the London School of Economics.

Luciana Canovi is a Lecturer in Finance at the Marco Biagi Faculty of Economics of the University of Modena and Reggio Emilia, where she teaches corporate finance. Her main research interests are finance for SMEs, the real option approach to investment valuation and the life cycle of the firm and financial constraints. Her research papers have been published by Italian academic journals. She is a member of Centre for Studies in Banking and Finance.

Massimo Demasi has been a senior analyst at the Industry Analysis and Business Support Department of Borsa Italiana, London Stock Exchange Group, since 2003. He was previously an intern in the Debt Capital Market Office of Unicredit Banca Mobiliare. His main research activities and responsibilities concern the analysis of Italian and international financial markets with a focus on market micro-structure, evolution of the exchange industry scenario (from trading to post-trading), and the corporate and business strategies of all major players. He holds a degree in financial economics from Bocconi University.

Alessandro G. Grasso is a postdoctoral scholar in market and financial intermediaries at the University of Modena and Reggio Emilia. His main research interests are private equity activities in Italy, the regulation of the financial system in the European Union and the economics of banking institutions, with a focus on intellectual capital.

Elisabetta Gualandri is a Professor in Banking and Finance and co-director of the MA course in corporate finance and management control at the Marco Biagi Faculty of Economics of the University of Modena and Reggio Emilia, where she is a member of the governing board of the

Centre for Studies in Banking and Finance. She is member of the Faculty of the PhD programme in financial markets and institutions at the Catholic University of Milan and a member of the governing board of ADEIMF (the Italian Association of Scholars of Economics and Management of Financial Institutions and Markets). Her recent research topics include financial regulation and supervision, capital adequacy and the New Basel Accord and the financing of innovative SMEs and public intervention programmes. She has participated in Italian and international congresses on these subjects, with a large number of published papers. She was appointed as an auditor of Banca d'Italia in 2007.

Paola Schwizer is Professor in Banking and Finance at the University of Parma. She is a Professor at the SDA Business School, Bocconi University, Milan and a member of the Faculty of the PhD programme in banking and finance at the University of Bologna. She is member of editorial boards of the *Journal of Management and Governance* and *Economia & Management*, and a member of the board of directors of Nedcommunity, a community of non-executive and independent directors, Milan. She is author of various publications in the field of banking and finance, on topics including regulation and competition in the banking system, the strategies, institutional structures and organisational models of banks and banking groups, and corporate governance and internal controls in banks.

Valeria Venturelli is a Lecturer in Banking and Finance at the Marco Biagi Faculty of Economics of the University of Modena and Reggio Emilia, where she teaches financial markets and capital budgeting at both undergraduate and graduate level. She graduated in economics from the University of Modena and Reggio Emilia and received a PhD in financial markets and institutions from the Catholic University of Milan. She is member of the editorial board of ADEIMF (the Italian Association of Scholars of Economics and Management of Financial Institutions and Markets). Her main research interests are the economics of banking and other financial institutions, regulation of the asset management industry in the European Union, finance for SMEs, valuation methods and the cost of capital. She is author of several articles in leading academic journals.

Preface and Acknowledgements

This book is for the most part the outcome of a research project fully funded by the Basic Research Investment Fund (Fondo per gli Investimenti della Ricerca di Base, FIRB 2003) of the Italian Ministry for Education and Research. The project sets out to evaluate risk capital instruments and financial sources for small and medium-sized enterprises (SMEs) and is part of a national project entitled 'Redesigning the financial infrastructure of networks of companies: in search of new financial, institutional and IT solutions to support competitiveness, innovation, corporate reorganization and risk management', the principal aim of which is to redesign the infrastructure which provides backup for the financial management of networks of SMEs in their various possible forms. Professor Luca Erzegovesi from the University of Trento is the national head of the research project, and our thanks go to him for his support of the entire undertaking.

For this book the editors, from University of Modena and Reggio Emilia, have coordinated the contributions of a team of researchers who specialise in different fields: banking, financial markets, risk capital intermediaries and corporate finance. Fabio Braga and Massimo Demasi from Borsa Italiana, London Stock Exchange Group, Paola Schwizer from the University of Parma, Luciana Canovi and Alessandro G. Grasso from the University of Modena and Reggio Emilia.

The editors' objective in preparing this book was to bring together various aspects related to the theme of equity capital financing for innovative SMEs (theoretical and empirical, institutional framework, role of financial markets and intermediaries and public sector intervention policy) by drawing on the different areas of expertise, experience and fields of activities of the contributors. The book is thus intended to be of use to readers of different kinds, including students, academics, practitioners and policy-makers.

During the drafting process we received helpful ideas and information from Professor Gordon C. Murray from the University of Exeter; our thanks go to him.

We are grateful for comments and suggestions from the members of a panel of invited experts at the workshop on the theme 'Risk capital financing for the innovative SMEs' held on 2 April 2007 at the Marco

Biagi Faculty of Economics of the University of Modena and Reggio Emilia, organised by CEFIN and the European Commission Representation in Milan. Thanks in particular are due to Andrea Landi, Professor at the University of Modena and Reggio Emilia and Massimo Marchesi from the European Commission Representation in Milan.

Finally, special thanks to Margaret Kearton, our English proof-reader.

Introduction

Elisabetta Gualandri and Valeria Venturelli

The contribution of small and medium-sized enterprises (SMEs) to job creation, innovation and economic growth is acknowledged and testified in developed countries, as well as in developing and emerging economies. Although it represents an extremely small proportion of the total number of SMEs in any given country, the subsector of innovative SMEs (ISMEs) has an even greater role in creating new jobs and enhancing technological development, with a major contribution to overall economic growth. This is particularly true for advanced economies, where growth in productivity is generated not so much by the accumulation of capital as by innovation and its diffusion by the knowledge spill-over mechanism and entrepreneurial capital.

In view of the strategic economic role played by the creation and development of these firms, an understanding is required of the factors that may adversely affect the growth of SMEs, and especially the financial difficulties which may prevent them from fulfilling their potential. Since SMEs, and ISMEs in particular, may face serious constraints due to market failures, these firms may be the victims of financing and equity gaps even in advanced economies.

Given this scenario, the book deals with the theme of the equity gap for innovative SMEs and the devices and instruments developed in order to bridge it.

The *main research questions* might be summarised as follows:

1 Is it possible to separate out and verify the financing constraints that affect the birth and development of ISMEs?
2 Is it possible to identify and perhaps measure the size of the financing gap in a reliable manner?

1

3 Is there a role for financial intermediaries and markets in bridging the equity gap? And if so, what is it?
4 Is public intervention feasible in solving this problem? If so which are the best practices developed at the international level by policymakers?

The main results can be summarised as follows:

1 There are financing constraints that affect the birth and development of ISMEs in particular, arising from market failures due especially to information asymmetry. Moreover, given the specific characteristics of firms of this kind, risk capital emerges as the most suitable form of financing, in a reversal of the traditional hierarchical financing structure.
2 An equity gap for young and innovative SMEs does exist. The measurement techniques developed to date have not been fully satisfactory due to their concentration on qualitative methods; in spite of this, they are useful for an initial rough quantification of the phenomenon. However, an improvement in quantitative estimation is required, and the model presented here is intended as a step in this direction.
3 The intermediaries which may contribute the most to overcoming the financial constraints facing ISMEs are venture capitalists and business angels; they also make a significant contribution to the growth of venture-backed firms. As far as financial markets are concerned, exchanges do not appear to be suitable for financing the initial growth stages, but are able to help remove financial constraints by providing investors with the guarantee of effective exit strategies. To this end the identification or creation of specific markets/segments on which these firms can be listed seems to be the right path.
4 The existence of market failures in providing ISMEs with adequate financial resources justifies the growing role of the public sector in providing equity financing. However, as the best practice developed at the international level shows, an effective public intervention policy must take all the instruments in the financial ladder into consideration and also include non-financial measures aimed at stimulating entrepreneurship. Moreover, a cost-benefits analysis assessing the fit between the objectives and results of public assistance schemes is necessary as a basis for the drafting of future policies.

Structure of the book

The book is divided into eight chapters.

Chapter 1 deals with the problem of defining innovation and innovative businesses and the factors influencing the mechanism for the spread of innovation, which fosters economic growth. For our purposes, innovation is considered in the broad sense of the term and therefore includes – within the individual firm – not only product, process and organisational innovation, but also institutional innovation which involves the production system. The nexus between innovation and economic growth is not straightforward; it is in fact a complex linkage, starting from the diffusion of innovation through the mechanisms of knowledge spill-over and the presence of entrepreneurship capital. Here, we define entrepreneurship that fosters innovation and growth as any action carried out with the main purpose of transforming ideas/knowledge into economic opportunities; it can be proxied by the number of start-ups. One of the main problems for this kind of firm is linked to funding opportunities; it is difficult for innovative firms to support their growth due to a problem in obtaining external resources, especially in the form of debt. Risk capital operators, and in particular venture capitalists, play a fundamental role in this context. Therefore the analysis shifts to the different roles performed by venture capital, which can be considered one of the determinants of economic growth. Directly, because it speeds up the transformation of inventions into new products and processes; indirectly, because venture-backed firms, typically small, high-tech companies, have higher growth rates in terms of employment, sales, investment and R&D expenditure.

Chapter 2 provides the theoretical framework for analysis of the financial needs and financial constraints of SMEs, briefly introducing the factors justifying government intervention to sustain the companies most at risk of credit rationing (new firms and small firms with innovative business plans) in the early stages of their development. The review of the financial literature clearly reveals that innovative small and/or medium-sized firms' access to external financing is restricted by capital market imperfections which can be attributed to various reasons, mainly due to problems of information asymmetry. Also significant are the effects of agency and transaction costs and fiscal factors, as well as the broader unsuitability of some financial systems for financing new businesses and the most innovative projects. The principal consequences of these market failures, which may impede the birth of new businesses and the development of innovative firms, may take the form of credit rationing, the excessive cost of loans, and the inadequacy of technical forms of financing to cover firms' financial needs, for reasons related to their life cycles and the innovative, high-risk nature of their production processes. Therefore, it emerges that in the hierarchy of sources of financing available to an innovative firm, equity capital financing is preferred to bank debt because it is less expensive and better suited to the circumstances. The application to innovative firms of the financial growth cycle approach, developed in corporate finance studies, leads to the conclusion that during the seed stage, internal sources (self-financing or funds made available by family or friends) will be used, followed as the firm grows by financing using funds provided first by business angels and later by venture capitalists. The market issue of shares is a means of financing used in the final stage of the firm's growth, when it has reached a certain size and also has a fairly high degree of notoriety. The use of loan capital in the sustained growth stage may help to improve the firm's net profitability. The inverted hierarchy of sources of financing generates a shortage of risk capital financing, especially during the initial phases of firms' life cycles: this is the so-called equity gap.

Chapter 3 sets out to define the concept of the equity gap within the broader concept of the financing gap. The focus is on ISMEs, for which these phenomena derive from market failures mainly due to information asymmetries. In these cases, a dual problem can be identified – both a finance gap and a knowledge gap. Thereafter, the problem of measuring the equity gap is introduced and the different methodological approaches developed (demand and supply sides; qualitative and quantitative) are presented. The most significant evidence with regard to the equity gap is examined, with a focus on the UK: it was here that the Macmillan Report, produced in the 1930s, provided the first proof of such a gap, and interesting surveys on this topic have been conducted since the 1990s. Our analysis of the different approaches developed in various contexts for the assessment and measurement of the equity gap for ISMEs focuses on their limits and level of significance. The main finding is that demand-side analysis is the less well developed, especially as far as the quantitative approach is concerned, due to difficulties in data collection and in the definition of a suitable methodology. In spite of the limitations of the various methods, they have identified some equity gap thresholds and some types of firms affected. The equity gap thresholds identified vary even within the same context depending on the point in the economic cycle, while in an international comparison the differences between the financial systems may explain the diversity of results. With all their shortcomings, these results are the starting point for policy-makers called upon to draft intervention policies to help overcome the problem, which demands action due to the importance of ISMEs in the present economic context.

In Chapter 4 we present the development of an original equity require-ment estimation model. The model enables the identification and verification of the causes which generate financial needs requiring cov-erage by equity, and estimation of the absolute and relative size of the investment required. The several versions of the model developed were applied to a sample of 167 growing Italian micro and small companies in the manufacturing and service sectors, with a high-tech innovation content. An observation of the sample's characteristics reveals that over-all investments per unit of sales are low and the role of self-financing in fuelling growth is absolutely marginal. Moreover, it is essential for firms to be able to transfer a large proportion of their financing require-ment to other non-financial enterprises. Given these findings, the firms' future demand for equity measured in monetary terms appears to be relatively low; on average, assuming a constant indebtedness ratio, the equity requirement is about €250,000. The results, and in particu-lar the tiny amount of the equity requirement discovered (though this cannot be taken as a specific estimate of the equity gap), may indirectly confirm the problem of a gap in the availability of risk capital for young innovative companies.

Chapter 5 uses an institutional approach to depict the intermediaries active in the risk capital industry, investigating the taxonomy of the players involved and their distinctive features. The focus is on the broad area of private equity, the lack of a common definition of which at the international level is underlined, in spite of a gradual standardisation of terminology in line with the proposals of the two longest-established investors' associations, the NVCA and EVCA. For the purpose of this study, private equity is an asset class which consists of equity investment in enterprises not listed on a stock market, and venture capital is, strictly speaking, a subset of private equity and refers to equity investments made for the launch, early development or expansion of a business. The main characteristics of the operators (business angels, incubators, corporate venture capitalists, closed-end funds, investment firms and merchant banks) which engage in risk capital investment are illustrated. They make up a composite universe; they differ from each other in the legal forms used, the aims pursued and the way in which the funds used are raised. The differences are due to a variety of reasons, including the diverse kinds of operators involved, and fiscal, organisational and legislative factors. Irrespective of the intermediary's institutional characteristics, the operating cycle of a risk capital operator always has the same features: an operator making an investment in risk capital implements a strategic plan with a beginning, duration and end. The operating cycle of a risk capital investor is divided into four main areas: organisational structure, fund-raising aspects, investment management and exit strategy. The investment management process highlights the important role of these operators as active investors in the enterprise, through the input of their managerial expertises.

Chapter 6 focuses on the size and type of the role of financial intermediaries in financing ISMEs in Europe and the US, with a closer look at the seven European states which together account for more than 95 per cent of the funds raised (the UK, France, Germany, Sweden, Italy, Spain and the Netherlands). In some cases the study surveys the years 2002–6, while in others it uses 2006 figures only. The principal parameters analysed are related to the trends in fundraising and investment allocation. In the first respect, the US market leads the way, although the gap is narrowing. With regard to the breakdown of the investments made, a predominance of buy-out operations and a concentration of venture capital investments in the expansion financing segment are found in both areas. An examination of the European context clearly reveals the pivotal role played by the UK, explaining the similarities with the US. Apart from the UK, Germany, Spain and Italy are among the European countries surveyed with the largest proportion of venture capital investments, but allocation is to different stages in the firm's life cycle. While in Germany and Spain the focus is on the birth and development of high-tech firms, in Italy there is a prevalence of expansion financing operations. From the analysis, it emerges that the differences among the countries stem from several institutional features. For instance, the development of specialised markets can facilitate exit strategies for operators; while the structure of the financial system helps to explain the amount and composition of the funds raised. When private equity is considered as an asset class, the rates of return are higher on average for buy-out than for venture capital operations, although the margin is not easy to quantify.

Chapter 7 analyses the relationship between financial markets and small and medium-sized enterprises. At the company level, going public is perhaps the most important decision a firm may take, but the process is complex and involves a wealth of issues. The role of equity markets in this process, in terms of the benefits accruing to firms and investors, is pointed out. In this context, the key aspects relate to the functioning of the primary market as well as the mechanisms governing trading on the secondary markets. As far as the primary market is concerned, the study focuses on the structure and characteristics of the main European markets and segments dedicated to SMEs. The decision by some exchanges to establish alternative markets for SMEs may represent a significant contribution to financial development; however, current evidence may only be preliminary since some time is required before these markets' relative success can be fully assessed. The choice was to concentrate the analysis on markets/segments dedicated to SMEs, since the history of new markets has tended to be one of early success followed by the fatal consequence of the bursting of the dot.com bubble. The fourth section deals with the process of going public, with a focus on the case of Italian small and medium enterprises during 2002–7, analysing the structure of the offer, the procedures for setting the offering price, and finally the role of professional investors. As far as the secondary market is concerned, section five approaches the topic from the investors' point of view, basing the analysis on the comparison between liquidity classes, using a sample of 4,891 companies divided into classes by 2006 year-end market capitalisation. The results indicate that SME caps are less liquid than larger ones; the introduction of special segments seems to be of help in closing the liquidity gap. At the end of the chapter, an appendix on the organisation of trading in the secondary markets is provided.

Chapter 8 analyses the role of the public sector in bridging the equity gap and the main measures adopted for this purpose (demand and supply sides, direct and indirect measures), focusing on the creation of public–private partnerships aiming at developing a private venture capital market. Public sector intervention in bridging the equity gap is motivated by the existence of market failures and these firms' strategic economic role as an engine for growth in modern economies. The objectives set and the approach developed to achieve them by the EU, subject to the constraints imposed by the regulations governing state aid, are identified. There is a growing perception that Europe's growth problems may be caused not so much by rigidities in the labour market as by weaknesses in capital markets, and in particular in the access to risk capital. To identify the drivers which ought to guide policy-makers, the best practices developed in the US, Israel, UK, Germany, France, the Netherlands and Denmark are analysed. The analysis suggests that first of all, the equity gap must be identified and measured (size/type of firms, affected/regional dimension). The drivers of public sector intervention should be based on an action plan which defines the target firms, the operational goals, the rules of the game between public investment and private investor, the set of instruments available for use and the duration of the schemes. In the case of direct measures on the supply side, it emerges that the guiding principle is that of risk/profit-sharing between public and private investors, moreover public funds should be managed in line with market mechanisms and by private managers. Since two types of gap – the finance gap and the knowledge gap – have been identified, incentive schemes on the demand side aimed at fostering entrepreneurship must be considered, together with intervention along the complete financial ladder of instruments. Finally, we stress the importance of assessing the efficacy and efficiency of public measures. To this end the role of OECD is important in taking the lead in establishing international benchmarks for evaluating the impact of government actions. These analysis serve a dual purpose: firstly they improve the follow-up of existing initiatives, and second, they spread the good practices identified to other countries.

1
Innovation and Economic Growth

Elisabetta Gualandri and Valeria Venturelli

Introduction

It is widely recognised that innovation is a fundamental driver for economic growth due to its role in increasing output and productivity. This is especially true for the advanced economies, which are increasingly reliant on innovation and entrepreneurship for their sustained growth (Bottazzi et al., 2001).

Technological change resulting from innovative activities, including investments in intangibles such as research and development (R&D), impacts positively in the long term on both employment rates and incomes. Therefore, at the macro level, a country's ability to innovate supports its long-term growth.

The most advanced economies are depending to an ever-greater extent on factors such as knowledge, information and high skill levels, and have a growing need for rapid access to these in the 'knowledge-based economy', of which innovation is seen as the main driver.

The reinforcement of innovation is one of the pillars of the strategy adopted to achieve the aim set by the Lisbon Council of Europe in March 2000: to make the European Union (EU) the world's most competitive, dynamic, knowledge-based economy by the end of the decade. The European Commission (2002) has already stressed that a lack of innovation is one of the key factors behind Europe's disappointing results with regard to growth in productivity.

Policy-makers, therefore, have a clear interest in adopting policies that create the conditions in which technological change can develop at the micro level in individual firms, through innovative activities and investments. R&D has a key role to play in achieving this, by enhancing a firm's capacity to absorb and make use of new knowledge of all kinds, not just technological knowledge. This chapter is structured as follows. First, we focus on the problem of defining innovation and innovative activities and on the factors influencing innovation. Then, we analyse the mechanisms by which innovation is spread through the economy, by means of knowledge spill-over and entrepreneurship capital, to influence economic growth. Finally, after pointing out that the financing gap is particularly large for new and innovative small and medium-sized enterprises (SMEs), we analyse venture capital as a further mechanism of economic growth.

Defining innovation

Firms innovate to achieve competitive advantages; and through their innovation processes and technological changes, they aim to expand their market share by achieving lower costs than their competitors, which result in lower prices or a higher mark-up, or a combination of the two.

Modern theories regarding innovation have been strongly influenced by the work of Joseph Schumpeter, who identified the dynamic process by which new technologies replace old ones, known as 'creative destruction', as the driver for economic growth. In his seminal contribution, Schumpeter (1934) introduced a classification of various types of innovation:

- introduction of a new product or a qualitative change in an existing product;
- process innovation new to an industry;
- opening of a new market;
- development of new sources of supply for raw materials or other inputs;
- changes in industrial organisation.

In view of the many possible types of innovation, the complexity of innovative processes and the different ways in which innovation occurs in different types of firms and industries, clear-cut definitions are not always possible and conventions have to be adopted. Consequently, the definition used in any study or survey may have an impact on the results (OECD, 2005).

Using the approach adopted by the 'OSLO Manual', for the purposes of this study we consider the process by which innovation occurs at the micro level – mainly technical innovation in products (goods and services) and processes (OECD, 2005). The innovation process includes all scientific, technological, organisational, financial and commercial changes which actually, or are intended to, lead to the implementation of technologically new or improved products or processes. In particular, technological innovation transforms scientific and technological ideas into new products and processes. In particular:

1 *Product innovation*: consists of the introduction of a product or service which offers significant improvements from various points of view, including technical characteristics, components, materials or the software incorporated. An innovation of this kind generally originates from an invention, scientific discovery or a new production or management technique. In the case of goods, new know-how or technologies, or new uses or combinations of existing know-how and technologies, are employed. In the case of services, this category involves the introduction of absolutely new services, or the improvement of existing ones, through the addition of new functions or characteristics.
2 *Process innovation*: consists of a change in the way in which a product is built or a service is delivered. An innovation of this type may lead to a reduction in production and/or transport costs, or an increase in the quality of the products or services concerned. As well as the production function, logistics, equipment and the methods of procurement of the inputs and software used may be involved.

As well as these main forms of innovation, there are:

• innovation in organisational models and processes;
• market innovation, involving the extension of existing products and services to new markets or customers;
• marketing innovation, with changes to design and packaging, product positioning, pricing and forms of promotion;
• management innovation, in which the management processes and culture are modified; and
• infrastructural innovation.

The innovation process may consist of a combination of these various types.

In the context of this book, innovation is considered in the broad sense of the term, and therefore includes product, process and organisational innovation (within the individual firm) and institutional innovation (involving the production system). So, innovative firms are those that introduce new production methods (process innovation) or create or sell new products for both the consumer and the intermediate markets (product innovation).

The nexus between innovation and economic growth

The nexus between innovation and economic growth is not straightforward; rather, we have to focus on the way in which innovation spreads and becomes established through the mechanisms of knowledge spillover and the presence of entrepreneurship capital. To this end the first step is to consider briefly the main theoretical framework developed on innovation.

The first attempt to link technology and economic growth can be found in Schumpeter's theoretical work.[1] Schumpeter initially considered innovation to be a factor external to the firm, the outcome of the invention, the work of individuals (a meta-economic phenomenon) and a complex of social and economic factors, including the presence of entrepreneurs capable of taking up the opportunities offered by inventions. He subsequently came to the conclusion that innovative activity is promoted by large firms and is endogenous to the firm, thanks to a dynamically creative/destructive process that influences economic growth. In the neo-Schumpeterian approach adopted by many modern economists,[2] innovation is still viewed as endogenous to the firm, but is now conceived in terms of the interaction between market opportunities and the firm's knowledge base and capabilities.

More recently, theoretical studies and empirical analyses have investigated the contribution to growth of the classic production factors included in neoclassical theory – namely, physical capital and labour – and have come to the conclusion that changes in the quantity and quality of these do not account for much of the variation in firms' growth performance and productivity. Total Factor Productivity (TFP) depends not only on the quantity and quality of the capital and labour available, but also on factors that are often difficult to measure, such as technological and organisational progresses, not to mention, in the recent past, information and communication technology (ICT). One of the main determinants of the evolution of TFP is the ability to create new productive ideas and improve the knowledge stock – patents, number of researchers, and investment in R&D (Bottazzi et al., 2001).

The most recent theories have highlighted the importance of knowledge in the innovation process and in economic growth thereafter. At the firm level, innovative opportunities are endogenously created thanks to investments aimed at creating new knowledge: R&D, enhancement of human capital through training and education, and university research. At the macroeconomic level, in the growth models developed by Romer (1986) and Lucas (1993), knowledge is assumed to spill over automatically and determine benefits for third party firms, with free access. Therefore, knowledge can improve the system's efficiency and productivity through the innovation process with the creation of new firms (Bottazzi et al., 2001).

However, the spill-over of knowledge may be limited by externalities affecting the decision-making process: uncertainty, information asymmetries and transaction costs. 'Knowledge filter' (Audretsch, 2007) is the term used to describe the gap between new knowledge with a potential commercial value and the knowledge actually commercialised. This filter may lead to differences in the assessment of the expected value of a new idea on the part of the firm which has developed it through its knowledge investments, and by an employee or a group of employees, especially those with experience in the R&D laboratories. When the firm decides not to develop and market new ideas, entrepreneurial opportunities may emerge, and the employee/group of employees may decide to create a start-up as a spin-off of the existing firm. In this way, entrepreneurship becomes the mechanism by which production factors take advantage of the knowledge spill-over to create and spread innovation, which leads to economic growth. This all-important growth is achieved through the creation of start-ups. Moreover, even if perceived entrepreneurial opportunities are present, knowledge spill-over may be prevented by a lack of early stage finance, leading to a financing gap.

Recent studies have investigated the concept of entrepreneurship capital, in the sense of the capacity for entrepreneurial activity. Entrepreneurship capital is made up of legal, institutional and social factors. A spatial dimension for this capital has also been identified: locations and geographical areas such as cities, regions and districts have been pinpointed as key factors in explaining knowledge production and spill-over, and therefore in determining innovation, technological changes and finally economic growth (Audretsch and Feldman, 2004). One emblematic example of this is Silicon Valley (Audretsch, 2007).

The possible causal link between entrepreneurial capital and the growth in the productivity of the production factors has been extensively studied.[3] Although there are considerable problems at the methodological level, the empirical evidence produced in recent years tends to indicate a positive correlation between small new firms and economic growth, for developed countries (Audretsch and Thurik, 2002; Carree and Thurik, 2003) and in terms of regional development within the individual state.[4]

In conclusion, economic growth derives from a number of factors. On the one hand, the physical accumulation of labour and capital; on the other, the creation and adoption of new ideas and the accumulation of knowledge. For advanced economies, growth in productivity is triggered not so much by the accumulation of capital as by innovation. Innovation spreads thanks to knowledge spill-over and entrepreneurship capital; economic growth is sustained because of the continuous creation and diffusion of knowledge. Moreover, several authors[5] have reassessed the role of SMEs, compared to that of large firms, as agents for change in a knowledge-based economy: 'smaller high-technology companies ... [are] the source of a majority of "radical" technological innovations and a disproportionately large share of employment growth' (Timmons and Bygrave, 1986, p. 162). As a consequence, the main focus should be the study of small new innovative firms as drivers of economic growth.

The nexus between innovation and financial resources

Entrepreneurship that fosters innovation and growth, in our context, refers to actions undertaken with the main aim of translating ideas/knowledge into economic opportunities, and can be proxied by the number of start-ups. One of the main problems for this kind of firm is linked to funding opportunities; it is difficult for innovative firms to support their growth due to the problem of obtaining external financial resources.

There is broad agreement in the financial literature and the direction of EU policy that the financing of SMEs' operations is a crucial factor, potentially capable of reducing their growth. Alongside the general problems of access to finance which are the main obstacle to entrepreneurial ventures and the growth of SMEs, the last few years have seen many studies underlining the significance of financial constraints for the firms most involved in innovative activities. As early as 1995 the European Commission's Green Paper on Innovation (p. 28) underlined the nexus between innovation and financial resources, stating that: 'Financing is the obstacle to innovation most often quoted by firms, whatever their size, in all Member States of the European Union and in virtually all sectors'. The Community Innovation Survey (CIS),[6] conducted in 1997, found that 56.2 per cent of the firms interviewed had postponed, abandoned or given up an innovative project due to various economic, organisational, legal and market-derived constraints. This rises to 71.8 per cent for innovative firms and falls to 43.9 per cent for non-innovative ones. The main constraint on innovative firms – their lack of appropriate sources of financing – restricts the business of 24.4 per cent of these firms, as compared to 20.2 per cent of non-innovative companies. Of the 22 per cent of all firms subject to financial constraints, 7.9 per cent postpone their projects and 10.4 per cent do not start them at all. These difficulties are faced above all by small enterprises (22.8 per cent), followed by medium-sized firms (21.4 per cent) and large companies (16.3 per cent) in innovative sectors.[7]

The importance of the consequences of financing obstacles for innovative SMEs means that closer analysis of these firms' financial structure policies is appropriate. Innovative projects have a number of features, linked in particular to information opacity, which make them especially difficult to finance using borrowed capital. Therefore, in the hierarchy of sources of financing available to an innovative firm, equity capital financing is preferred to bank debt because it is less expensive and better suited to the circumstances.

Moreover, as Berger and Udell (1998) show, the technical forms of equity financing depend on a firm's size and above all its stage of development; during the embryonic phase internal sources (self-financing or funds made available by family or friends) will be used, followed as the firm grows by funds provided first by business angels and then by venture capitalists.

Start-ups and innovative firms are often financed in the more developed countries through the intervention of one or a syndicate of venture capitalists. Venture capital in fact has emerged as an important intermediary in financial markets, providing capital to firms that might otherwise have difficulty in attracting financing, since banks are incapable of adequately financing innovative firms, and technology-based start-ups in particular (Gompers and Lerner, 2001). So, another question particularly relevant to the aim of this book is whether venture capital can be considered as a mechanism for growth. If it is, special attention has to be focused on policy measures intended to stimulate the creation of an active private market for venture capital.

In the current debate, the role of venture capital has been analysed along several research lines.[8]

In macro terms, several works have highlighted the economic impact of venture capital. The majority of studies are published or commissioned by the national and international venture capitalists' associations: the NVCA for the United States, the EVCA for Europe and the BVCA for the United Kingdom.[9] These studies' conclusions tend to emphasise the way venture capital fosters economic growth through job creation, the high growth rates recorded by venture-backed firms and international expansion. They also underline that venture capital is capable of significantly reducing the time needed to bring an innovative idea to market. Concentrating on the latest report published by the BVCA (2007), of the 489 venture-backed firms respondent to the survey, 91 per cent said that venture capital was responsible for the existence/survival of their businesses and had made more rapid growth possible. Moreover, during the five-year period to 2006/7, venture-backed firms increased worldwide employment by 8 per cent per annum, the sales growth rate was 12 per cent per annum, they increased corporate investment by 14 per cent and R&D expenditures increased by 12 per cent per annum. During the same period, for the same aggregates, the FTSE Mid-250 companies showed lower growth rates: worldwide employment 3 per cent per annum, sales growth rate 5 per cent, corporate investment 3 per cent and R&D expenditures 1 per cent.

At the micro level, several studies published during the last few years have estimated the impact of venture capital on corporate performance. The conclusions reached by the various authors are that venture capital encourages firms to innovate (Hellmann and Puri, 2000) and increases their likelihood of registering patented inventions (Kortum and Lerner, 1998). Other studies emphasise that the high growth rates recorded by venture-backed firms are due to a certain extent to the financial and managerial involvement of the venture capital organisation (Engel, 2002). It clearly emerges that the venture capitalist helps the firm to grow and enhance its professionalism through the provision of a wide range of services and the expertise it contributes to the company's management (Hellmann and Puri, 2002).

On this evidence, venture capital has to be considered as a link in explaining differences in economic performance; that is to say, venture capital can be defined as one of the determinants of economic growth: directly, because it speeds up the transformation of inventions into new products and processes; indirectly, because venture-backed firms, typically small, high-tech companies, have higher growth rates in terms of employment, sales, investment and R&D expenditure. Moreover, the involvement of venture capital in very small, young firms increases take-up of the knowledge spill-over generated by universities and larger companies (Romani and Pottelsberghe, 2004).

2
Access to Finance of Innovative SMEs

Valeria Venturelli

Introduction

This chapter surveys the theoretical literature on the financial constraints affecting small and medium-sized enterprises (SMEs)[1] and then briefly introduces the reasons supporting government intervention to sustain the companies most at risk of credit rationing: new firms and small firms with innovative business plans in the early stages of their development. The focus here is mainly on SMEs, although the financial constraints on innovative operations also affect larger firms (Hall, 2002; 2005).

Innovation is generally considered one of the main drivers of economic growth, both in terms of its impact on the individual firm's performance and at the aggregate level, through innovation's effects on a country's competitiveness and thus, in the final analysis, on the economic growth rate.[2]

The European Commission has attributed Europe's unsatisfactory economic growth to a lack of innovation; given the decisive role of innovative business, it thus becomes necessary to create a favourable environment for the launch and growth of innovative firms, especially SMEs, by removing the constraints which may reduce their numbers, among which problems relating to access to finance are particularly significant.

This chapter discusses innovative firms' difficulties in obtaining funds and is divided into three sections. In the first, the emphasis is on the financial sustainability of the growth of innovative new firms, and we trace the operating risk and financial risk profiles which can be associated with each of the different stages in these firms' life cycle. The second section investigates market failures related to the capital market imperfection correlated to the risk and profitability characteristics of the innovative project. The conclusion underlines the fact that financial theory provides evidence as to how different forms of financing contracts, financial intermediaries and the capital markets can reduce these imperfections. The third section discusses the usefulness of applying the financial growth cycle approach, developed in corporate finance studies, to innovative firms to find out whether the hierarchy in sources of finance is different for small innovative firms.

The distinctive features of innovative new firms

As explained in chapter 1, innovative firms are those that introduce new production methods (process innovation) or create or sell new products for both the consumer and the intermediate markets (product innovation). Innovation, taken here in the broad sense of the term, therefore, includes product, process and organisational innovation (within the individual firm) and institutional innovation (involving the production system).

The fundamental point is that small and/or new innovative firms have a high level of expected profitability, accompanied by a high level of risk. In addition, their riskiness and their need for financing depend on the stage reached, which in turn affects decisions concerning the firms' financial structure.

Conventionally, the process which leads from the birth of an innovative idea to the sale of the relative product on an industrial scale consists of four main stages, which differ substantially in rate of growth in sales, capital intensity and capability for self-financing (Bank of England, 2001). These are the factors which affect the amount of financing needed in each stage, the level of risk and the information opacity associated to the investment.[3]

In the first stage, known as the *seed stage*, where the innovative idea is conceived and a feasibility study on the innovative project may be undertaken, there is a great deal of uncertainty about the potential results, deriving from the risk of failure and the number of unknown factors surrounding the new idea. Financial needs are often limited to the expenditure required to make a technical and economic assessment of the investment plan. In this stage, the volume of sales is zero, as is the capital intensity. Furthermore, the extreme uncertainty concerning the expected outcomes and the lack of operating results make the use of external sources very difficult, rendering further development of the project dependent on the entrepreneur's own resources.

In the next stage, *start-up*, the idea becomes a reality: it is implemented and presented to the market. This stage, the most complex in the life cycle and the one in which the innovative idea is most likely to fail, requires a large amount of finance to develop the project (marketing studies, patents, and so on), provide production capacity and invest in operating capital. In the initial stage, costs continue to rise while sales are basically low, leading to growing capital intensity. This stage, therefore, involves both the highest level of operating risk and the need for large amounts of financing, which in most cases must be met from outside sources.

In the *early growth stage*, the level of operating risk gradually decreases, while the financial demand continues to be high, due to the need to fund a distribution network, the high capital intensity required for investments in production capacity and the rapid growth in operating capital. In this stage, the high rates of growth in sales allow an increase in the rate of self-financing, although not sufficient to cover all financial needs, and external sources are therefore still required.

In the *sustained growth stage*, the rate of growth in sales gradually slows. The need for funds is proportional to growth in sales, since the degree of capital intensity stabilises on values which are on average lower than the initial levels, while in the meantime profit levels and self-financing capacity improve. In this stage, external sources of financing are used to guarantee the firm's financial equilibrium.

Therefore, the growth process of innovative new firms is difficult to sustain in financial terms, especially in the initial start-up and early growth stages, when it is impossible to cover needs through the production of internally generated cashflows, and external sources of finance are essential. Moreover, these firms' use of some types of financing contract is restricted by their high operational and financial risks, lack of track-record and their inability to offer plentiful collateral because the majority of their assets are intangible.

Access to financing obstacles for ISMEs

As we have seen, it is difficult for innovative firms to support their growth due to a problem in obtaining external resources. This affects mostly small and/or recently established firms, which have higher combinations of risk and return.

Innovative firms' access to external financing is thus restricted by imperfections in the capital market – with the potential for genuine market failures – which the financial literature attributes to a number of reasons, including fiscal factors and problems of information asymmetry. Also significant are the effects of agency and transaction costs, as well as the broader unsuitability of some financial systems for financing new businesses and the most innovative projects.

Firms' choice of external financing sources is influenced by imperfections in the capital markets and the firm's phase in its life cycle. Market imperfections restrict the supply side of external sources of financing, due to factors that affect the cost and the availability of the different financial sources to the firm. However, we need to remember that owners/managers express preferences for particular forms of financing; thus the demand side shows a clear preference for some financial instruments, thereby confirming the pecking order theory.[4]

When analysing firms' decisions concerning their financial structure, the distinction between the two frameworks of reference, the demand and supply sides, is not always either easy or necessary since, as Hughes states, differences in the financial structure: 'are consistent with a chronic market failure constraining small firms to a sub-optimal position, or with a structure reflecting an optimal choice [expression of owner/management], or some combination of both' (1993, p. 17).

What is undeniable is that for innovative new firms adverse selection and moral hazard are accentuated, as are the problems of controlling and providing incentives for the entrepreneur's activities. Consequently, a different mix of contractual forms of financing is required, and this in turn affects the hierarchy of forms of financing, which also varies in response to the life and financial cycles of innovative new firms.

Therefore, constraints of a financial nature, which may stand in the way of the birth of new business ventures and the development of innovative small firms (discussed below), may take the form of credit rationing, the excessive cost of loans and the inadequacy of technical forms of financing to cover firms' financial needs, for reasons related to their life cycles and the innovative, high-risk nature of their production processes.

Asymmetrical information distributions may give rise to particularly tight financial constraints. In general, information asymmetries occur when economic players make their decisions on the basis of different sets of information. If the relevant information, the acquisition of which involves costs, is asymmetrically distributed, there may be a misalignment between the expected return on the innovative project and the cost of capital demanded by the financiers. In this case the prerequisites for a complete contract are not met.

In the financial literature, information asymmetry has traditionally been assessed on the basis of its effects on financiers' ability to make an *ex ante* evaluation of the risk/return characteristics of individual projects (adverse selection), or their inability to control the borrower's actions once the contract has been finalised (moral hazard).

In the case of innovative projects, information asymmetry arises because the entrepreneur/inventor has better information about the innovative project's nature and chances of success than the potential financiers. This is a good example of a 'lemons market', first described by Akerlof (1970), who examined the famous example of the used car market to conclude that the most immediate effects of information asymmetries are a significant reduction in trade and sometimes a real market failure, in which the best quality goods suffer most (adverse selection).

One possible solution to this problem may be provided by the parties that respond by passing on private information in their possession to the market by means of signalling (Leland and Pyle, 1977) on the part of the prospective borrower, or screening (Diamond, 1984) on the part of the prospective investor.

Reducing the level of information asymmetry *ex ante* through these practices becomes more complicated in the case of innovative projects. Signalling theory suggests that potential contractors with the most information to offer have an interest in signalling the quality of the proposed investment to the other party in order to overcome the negative effects of adverse selection. This mechanism is not particularly effective in this context, due to the ease with which new ideas can be copied.[5] Firms are reluctant to provide full information about a project's innovative content if this is their main competitive advantage (Bhattacharya and Ritter, 1985; Anton and Yao, 1998). For this reason, the entrepreneur may not have the necessary incentives to direct the available information about the firm's quality to the financier, and the possible detrimental consequences of divulging the idea reduce the quality of the signal.

Apart from the risk related to the use the financier might make of this information, in the case of some innovative firms the entrepreneur may be unable to signal his economic and financial situation to the financier effectively. This mainly occurs in small enterprises with a high degree of information opacity, where decision-making processes are generally informal (Brugnoli, 2003), there is no clear division between the firm's assets and those of the entrepreneur, and the main areas of corporate management are poorly developed (Caselli, 2001).

The project's quality can also be signalled through the entrepreneur's willingness to provide collateral (Bestre, 1985). However, this mechanism is again difficult to apply in the case of innovative projects, given the small amount of collateral the firm is able to provide, since most of its assets are intangible.[6] Moreover, any fixed assets it does possess are firm-specific as well as specific to the innovative project itself, and so their market value is fairly low. This is the basis for Williamson's (1988) conclusion that investments in R&D, which on average have higher sunk costs than ordinary investment projects, should be financed by equity.

An alternative way to deal with information asymmetries *ex ante* is the screening of investment projects, that is the project quality assessment undertaken by an intermediary, to ensure that financing is granted only to those considered most deserving. If the resources available are to be allocated in an optimal way, thus avoiding the assumption of risks which are unsustainable or higher than the contract levels, financiers must gather the information they need to assess the project's real risk and profitability levels. Sometimes, financiers may be incapable of interpreting the information supplied, especially in the case of innovative firms whose investment projects have a high-tech content.

The presence of large *ex ante* information asymmetries gives greater importance to the role of the various forms of contract and the different types of intermediary in reducing the information gap with regard to innovative projects.

When it comes to financing by means of debt contracts, the large information asymmetry accentuates the difficulties in defining an efficient pricing policy due to the problems in segmenting borrowers into uniform risk categories. This forces the lender to set a single average price for loans even though borrowers' risk levels vary, encouraging demand from the highest-risk firms and leading others to reject financing offers as too expensive. This is a potential cause of the form of credit system inefficiency known as credit rationing, which can be defined as the situation in which only some potential borrowers, apparently indistinguishable from others, do not receive funds (Stiglitz and Weiss, 1981). Compared to conditions of competition with full transparency of information, the incentives for banks to grant loans does not increase in direct proportion to the interest rate, since the effect produced by rate rises is an increase in the risk levels of the borrowers still in the market. This may lead to market failure if the best quality firms decide to use alternative forms of financing, on better financial terms.

This problem is particularly striking for innovative firms. There is a high degree of uncertainty concerning the returns on innovative investments, which are always something of a gamble; the likelihood of failure is high, but so too are the returns in the event of success. Because interest rates are fixed, banks do not receive a share of the high returns if the innovative idea proves to be a success, so when they set the price of the loan, they have a greater interest in including the high probability of failure, which may lead them to set high interest rates or decide not to grant the loan at all (Stiglitz, 1985).

The financial literature[7] has identified relationship lending as the means of overcoming the problems deriving from information asymmetry. Long-term relationships between SMEs and banks, with the granting of loans renewed over time, improve the efficiency of the financier's selection and monitoring operations (Diamond, 1984) and allow the acquisition of more detailed, confidential financial information (Fama, 1985; Ramakrishan and Thakor, 1984), and the reuse of this information for financial interactions repeated over time (Greenbaum and Thakor, 1995).

Relationship lending seems to be the mechanism best suited to cover the financial needs of SMEs with some degree of maturity, or which operate in traditional sectors where the prospects for growth are relatively modest (Landi and Rigon, 2006). The situation of innovative new small firms is different. Due to their lack of a track-record, the bank is reluctant to grant credit to the new firm; moreover, for this kind of firm, moral hazard is particularly acute.[8]

Innovative projects therefore have a number of features which make them particularly difficult to finance with debt (Himmelberg and Petersen, 1994); in spite of this, the effects of investors' difficulties in assessing projects' risk levels can also be seen in equity capital. However, unlike loan contracts, equity financing does ensure that the entrepreneur and financier share an interest in achieving high profits, since the financier participates in the life of the company and in its financial returns.

Nonetheless, the financial literature has identified disadvantages with share contracts compared to bank lending. Obtaining a bank loan also sends a positive signal to other financiers (Diamond, 1991), while the direct issue of shares on the market is seen as an indication that the entrepreneur is overestimating the worth of the firm, or even a sign of the inability to obtain credit. Myers and Majluf (1984) also interpret the issue of new shares as bad news. In their theory concerning the hierarchy of sources of financing, they report that internal sources are preferred to bank borrowing, which in turn is preferred to the direct issue of shares. This conclusion originates from the fact that when new shares are issued, entrepreneurs tend to protect existing shareholders to the detriment of future investors. Moreover, in the event of default on the part of the firm, the loss for the financier is lower in the case of a loan contract with priority repayment.

Innovative firms are in a different situation. The extreme variability of their results and the consequent riskiness of the project mean that the financier's likelihood of losing the capital invested is particularly high. Moreover, the equity contract provides an immediate solution to the moral hazard problem linked to the *ex post* variation in the risk profile of the project. In this case, the shareholder is enabled to monitor the firm's performance directly and constantly, thus narrowing the information gap.

It should be remembered that information asymmetry may still affect the relationship between the firm and the financier after finalisation of the contract, since once the financial resources have been obtained, the entrepreneur may be tempted to behave in his own interests rather than those of the firm and its investors. This problem, known as moral hazard, is particularly severe for innovative firms, which have high growth potential and high risk, and whose risk level may change – and increase in particular – after receipt of the funds. Moral hazard thus arises in relation to the financier's difficulty in monitoring the firm's operations (Diamond, 1984); it is more acute for innovative, new small firms, which have high growth potential and high risk, since once the financing has been obtained the entrepreneur may change his behaviour against the investor's interests, using the capital to support projects with a higher risk than those initially financed.

With regard to moral hazard, the focus is on possible conflicts of interest which might arise between the different categories of investors (shareholders vs. lenders) or between the investors and the firm's managers (Jensen and Meckling, 1976). There is no doubt that in innovative small firms where the owners and management are more or less one and the same, organisational structures are only embryonic and there is little delegation of responsibility, the most probable type of conflict of interest is between the two types of investors within the firm. Conflicts between investors and managers tend to arise in firms of larger average size.

The literature on agency costs and incomplete contracts views contractual forms of external financing as alternative means of regulating conflict of interest between the entrepreneur/proprietor and financiers. The type of financing contract to be used may therefore be chosen with a view to minimising conflicts of interest between investors and entrepreneur.

The use of debt capital which will leave the entrepreneur as the owner of the entire business once the financial costs of the loan have been paid provides excellent incentives for ethical behaviour. The debt contract maximises the incentives for good behaviour by reason of the financial charges on the debt, which are the same regardless of the firm's economic performance and reduce the cashflow available, and the fact that in the event of default the entrepreneur will lose control of the firm (Jensen and Meckling, 1976).

With reference to innovative firms, we have already underlined the significant problems of *ex post* information asymmetry, requiring monitoring of the debtor to ensure that he does not act in a way which increases the investment project's riskiness. The financier may ensure some degree of control over the management of the firm if the investment is made by means of a share contract. The associated ownership rights mean that its management can be influenced, through the appointment of the directors, for example. Moreover, the entrepreneur's efforts can be assisted by the financier's technical know-how, improving the prospective return on the investment. A share contract thus maximises the degree of control over the entrepreneur's performance. Moreover, the risk capital operators, who may be venture capital intermediaries, for example, support the innovative project's growth through their active participation in the firm's management, while also acting as consultants.

The significance of moral hazard for innovative firms explains why the use of risk capital provided by intermediaries may be preferable to loan capital, since the investor who joins the firm often has more information and know-how than the entrepreneur himself. However, there may still be advantages in hybrid contracts, by which the financier is able to decide whether to play the role of creditor or shareholder, depending on the profitability trend of the project financed. Contracts of this type include convertible bonds, warrants and mezzanine finance.[9]

The financing 'menu' of innovative firms

One of the main market failures examined in the previous section reveals that the hierarchy in forms of financing for new and innovative firms is the exact opposite of the one first proposed by Myers and Majluf (1984), which holds good for consolidated firms operating in traditional sectors. The financial hierarchy of sources of financing depends on the point reached in the firm's life cycle.

When an innovative idea is conceived (seed stage) and the financial resources needed are small, external capital is difficult to obtain, forcing the entrepreneur to use informal sources of capital, including his own and/or relatives' savings, or capital provided by business angels. In the start-up stages, the problem of the impossibility of observing the entrepreneur's actions to verify compliance with the contract terms is particularly acute and the use of risk capital becomes more appropriate. In other words, the lack of information about the project to be financed or of a consolidated history for the innovative firm, which is making its first appearance on the market, limits the availability of debt capital or renders it prohibitively expensive. If the entrepreneur does not have sufficient collateral to cover the loan, the bank may be forced to set a high interest rate even if it is willing to grant credit. Firms, therefore, apparently find it preferable to contact a venture capital intermediary, which will use its know-how to attenuate the information asymmetries and will not require collateral.

Therefore, in the hierarchy of sources of financing available to an innovative firm, risk capital financing is preferred to bank debt because it is less expensive and better suited to the circumstances.

This line of reasoning can be found in Berger and Udell (1998), who conclude that the hierarchy of sources of financing depends on a firm's size and above all its stage of development. Size and stage of development both affect the amount financing required. During the seed stage, internal sources (self-financing or funds made available by family or friends) will be used, followed as the firm grows by financing using funds provided first by business angels and then by venture capitalists.

The role of the venture capitalist is extremely important in the stages of the firm's growth where the risk of bankruptcy is high, since venture capital is able to provide the entrepreneur with valuable know-how in a series of specific areas.[10] However, some features of venture capital mean that it is not suitable for financing schemes still in the embryonic/seed stage or which require only very small amounts of funds. The latter case, the so-called 'small ticket problem', especially affects projects which are too small for financiers to see the prospect of recovering their contract and evaluation costs.[11]

The initial public offering (IPO) procedure is a means of financing used in the final stage of the firm's growth, when it has reached a certain size and also has a certain degree of track-record. Stock market listing is not only a means of obtaining capital directly on the market, but also indirectly favours access to the venture capital segment by providing operators with an effective and efficient exit strategy for their investments.

The use of loan capital in the sustained growth stage may help to improve the firm's net profitability. The principle of financial leverage states that within certain limits, the use of debt may have positive effects on the firm's profitability, thus increasing its worth and the wealth of its shareholders. According to Modigliani/Miller's Proposition II (1958), it is in the long term that firms improve their return on equity (ROE), since they increase their operating profitability and reduce the cost of their lending. In view of the size of the risk factor for innovative firms, financial leverage can only be used effectively in the later stages of their development. In the early stages of their life cycle the very high level of risk, together with their inability to provide inside collateral, makes the cost of borrowed capital so high that it is often unsustainable in view of the limited or nonexistent operating cashflows, insufficient to cover interest charges and capital repayments.

In the light of the obstacles innovative firms encounter in obtaining financial resources, the financing gaps, and the equity gap in particular, can be striking. Public measures to overcome the problem can be developed particularly during the seed and early stages (European Commission, 2005a), the stages most critical for firms' growth, when they have the greatest difficulties in obtaining external funds.

Public measures may involve among others: fiscal incentives, subsidies, the establishment of investment funds and financial instruments to assist risk capital investors (Landi and Rigon, 2006). In the seed stage in particular, when the entrepreneur's resources and those of his friends and relatives are the ideal source of financing, public measures might on the one hand encourage the use of such resources by granting tax concessions to those involved, and on the other make funds available at low interest or on a non-repayable basis through lenders acting as go-between for the public authority.[12]

In the start-up stage, the most delicate and risky, public measures are required to solve the small ticket problem through the establishment of special funds for the start-up of innovative firms, with public resources accounting for a significant proportion of those made available.

In the other two stages, and especially in the sustained growth stage, the need is not so much for public assistance as for an equilibrium in the use of external financial resources, with a suitable mix of self-financing, debt and equity capital.

Table 2.1 sets out the way in which innovative new firms behave and the financial solutions best suited to cover their needs, as well as the main measures adopted in public intervention schemes.

Table 2.1   Stages of innovation, forms of financing and public measures

Growth stage of the innovative firm	Level of financing required	Forms of external financing: type of contract	Intermediaries	Markets	Public measures
Seed	Low	Risk capital + Low-interest borrowing	Business angels Banks (go-between for public funds)		Tax relief Subsidies
Start-up	Medium–high	Risk capital + Low-interest borrowing	Business angels/venture capital Banks (go-between for public funds)		Subsidies to cover evaluation costs. Public resources for the establishment of funds for the start-up
Early growth	High	Risk capital + Borrowing	Venture capital + Banks		Public resources for the establishment of funds for firms in early growth
Sustained growth	High	Risk capital + Borrowing	Private equity/venture capital + Banks	Listing	Fiscal incentives to listing

Source: adapted from Landi (2005).

3
Equity Gap and Innovative SMEs

Elisabetta Gualandri

Introduction

The debate concerning the financing of innovative small and medium-sized enterprises (ISMEs) finds that these firms face an equity gap, in other words, a shortage of risk capital investment. The aim of this chapter is to define the concept of the equity gap within the broader concept of the financing gap.

The starting point is an investigation of the causes of this phenomenon, with specific reference to ISMEs in the start-up and early/sustained growth stages: studies on both the demand and the supply sides of the market for risk capital investment in this type of firm reveal that the equity gap is due to market failures, arising above all from information asymmetries.

The focus then switches to an analysis and assessment of the methods developed for measuring the equity gap and presents empirical evidence obtained from various contexts, with a particular focus on the United Kingdom. The problem of measuring the equity gap for ISMEs, as well as the reliability of the data obtained on its size and characteristics, is especially important, since policy-makers are currently directly involved in planning public intervention strategies and forms of public–private partnership intended to reduce the scale of the problem.

The clear market failures and the importance of ISMEs for economic growth underline the need for public measures and public–private part-nerships to bridge the equity gap. The possible role which measures of this kind can play is investigated in greater detail in chapter 8.

Financing gap and equity gap

A financing or funding gap occurs when, due to market failure, deserving companies do not receive the volume of financing they would obtain in an efficient market. The financial literature identifies various reasons for market failures: fiscal factors, information asymmetry problems and the consequences of agency and transaction costs. To these we must add the broader inability of some financial systems to support new businesses adequately and the financing of the most innovative projects.

The credit rationing caused by information asymmetries in particular is at the centre of a theoretical and empirical debate in which some conflicting conclusions have been reached.[1] Within the theoretical debate, the fundamental work demonstrating the existence of credit rationing is by Stigliz and Weiss (1981). De Meza and Webb (1987) come to the opposite conclusion, identifying cases in which markets have a credit surplus rather than a shortfall. Empirical proof of the existence of a funding deficit in the US is provided in particular by Kaplan and Zingales (1997; 2000). The role of relationship lending in overcoming the information asymmetries which make it difficult for new, small SMEs to access credit is investigated by Berger and Udell (1995).

It must be made clear that the term 'financing gap' merely identifies situations in which the demand for and supply of capital fail to come together, without making any distinction between the 'actual' and the 'perceived' gap; this can give us some idea of the difficulties involved in the various attempts to measure the equity gap, which are discussed in greater detail below. Obviously, simply stating that some SMEs do not succeed in obtaining capital does not in itself prove the existence of a financing gap and thus a market failure.[2] Even in an efficient market, some firms will still not receive financing, due to risk profiles higher than those acceptable to investors for the return expected.

The first proof of the existence of an equity gap, in the sense of a shortage of risk capital investment in the early stages of firms' lives, dates from the Macmillan Report,[3] published in the UK in the 1930s. Subsequent surveys of various contexts have revealed that this situation derives from shortcomings on both the demand and the supply sides of the risk capital market (European Commission, 2005a; OECD 2004; 2006a).

It also emerges that the degree of difficulty in obtaining risk capital and the characteristics of the equity gap (in terms of the type of enterprises and life cycle stages affected and the size of the amounts involved) are dependent on the level of development of the individual national financial system concerned. The crucial factors mainly involve the development of a private market for private equity, and the established presence of specialised intermediaries such as informal investors, in particular business angels, and venture capitalists. It is more or less true to say that equity gaps emerge for firms requiring financing in amounts higher than business angels are generally prepared to provide, but below the minimum thresholds acceptable to venture capitalists.

Another significant aspect is the need for efficient equity markets which supply private equity investors with satisfactory exit strategies for their investments in the SMEs segment.

Interest in the subject has been increasing, since it appears that an equity gap does exist and is symptomatic of obstacles to the birth and growth of firms typically financed by venture capital, with negative consequences for overall economic growth. In the US and Europe, there is proof of the dynamism of SMEs funded by venture capital investment, and that their contribution to innovation, economic growth and job creation is well above the national average. It also appears that university spin-offs are playing an increasingly important role in fuelling growth. Therefore, a lowering of the barriers to growth and improved access to risk capital finance for SMEs, with the involvement of venture capital investors, may bring important benefits in terms of innovation and economic growth overall.[4]

This study focuses on the equity gap for ISMEs in the start-up and early/sustained growth stages. While the birth and rapid development of new business ventures may be hindered by difficulty in accessing external financing in general (Berger and Udell, 1998), for ISMEs the financial constraints lie specifically in the lack of risk capital investment. Unlike other types of SMEs, the specific characteristics of innovative firms mean that during the initial stages of their life cycles, financing by means of risk capital is more appropriate than banking credit, in a reversal of the traditional hierarchy of sources known as the 'pecking order theory' (Myers and Majluf, 1984).

For innovative enterprises, the factors leading to market failure, such as information asymmetries and uncertainty, which penalise all SMEs in general, are further accentuated, making the use of bank financing channels unsuitable or unfeasible.[5] These obstacles derive specifically from the peculiar features of firms in this category, including[6] lack of a track-record; little or no capacity to generate cashflows to repay capital and interest in the early stages; the high risk level of innovative businesses; the high degree of information opacity; difficulty in risk assessment by banks; and a general lack of collateral.

Is there a case of equity gap for ISMEs?

Evidence from a variety of sources indicates that in the most developed countries there is in general no pervasive financing gap for SMEs. In the OECD states, the development of the financial markets and competition in the banking markets in particular have made the financing of SMEs attractive and banks have developed appropriate instruments and techniques. What we do find, in the case of Italy, are situations where SMEs tend to rely excessively on debt while access to equity finance is still difficult. The situation in developing and emerging markets, where there are significant difficulties in access to financial market, is profoundly different. However, even in the most developed countries, ISMEs may be seriously hampered by a financing gap, especially in the equity sector, because they have higher risk profiles than other SMEs (OECD, 2006a).

In the current discussion, it is not always immediately clear what qualifies an SME as 'innovative'. The OECD identifies ISMEs as a 'particular subset of SMEs that seek to exploit innovation for growth and competitive advantage. These enterprises are distinguished from other SMEs by the intent of the entrepreneur who runs it and the scope of growth' (2006a, p. 21). In addition, unlike traditional SMEs, innovative firms tend to use new technologies and/or innovative methods for the production of goods and the supply of services. This implies more difficulty than conventional firms experience in the rapid achievement of a positive cashflow. This sector consists to a large extent of high-tech firms.

Innovative firms have high risk levels (Hall, 2002): not only are these businesses in their early stages, but they are also types of business which often require investments with particularly uncertain outcomes and with fairly long time-scales. Innovative business requires a complex process, often with rapid swings in performance, where the lack of adequate financing for one stage in the life cycle may put the survival of the entire project at risk. In terms of the risk involved, the crucial steps in the life cycle of innovative firms are the seed and early stages, which lead from the development of the innovative idea to the production of prototypes, the start of production and finally the market launch. With regard to the forms of financing considered most suitable for the various stages of the life cycle of innovative firms (OECD 2004; European Commission, 2005a), the general assumption is that business angels will be involved in the seed and start-up stages, venture capitalists from start-up to early/sustained growth and private equity investors in the later stages. Public listing should and/or could be the final step in countries with exchanges specialised in listing and trading companies in the growth stages. It is this very fact that a range of different financing operations is envisaged for the different stages of their life cycle that makes the problem of financing ISMEs even more complicated.

The equity gap in ISMEs' start-up and early/sustained growth stages is caused by market failures resulting in the availability of an incomplete range of financial products and services in the specific segment of the financial system, which includes the types of investor best suited to provide financial support for these firms: venture capitalists and business angels.[7]

With regard in particular to the problem of information asymmetry which may lead to market failures, as discussed in chapter 2, we find:

1 objective difficulties faced by new and small enterprises in addressing sufficiently well-structured information to financiers;
2 few incentives for entrepreneurs to provide full information about a project's innovative contents;
3 difficulty on the part of potential financiers when it comes to assessing the project.

These problems occur alongside other forms of market failure. First among them is the 'small ticket problem' (Bank of England, 2001; Petrella, 2001), meaning the demand for small-scale financing operations, usually beneath the minimum threshold of interest for traditional venture capital investors given the information, due diligence, administration and business assessment costs involved. Problems may also arise when the time comes for the venture capitalist to liquidate his investment, since in many contexts there are no suitable financial markets on which firms of this type can be listed.

A comparison between the European and US financial systems reveals that in the former, the work of banks has traditionally been central, with relative under-development of suitable financial markets and specialist investors with the skill needed to assess innovative firms' investment projects and willingness to take on the risks involved in financing innovation. The European financial system thus tends to favour investments in firms with traditional, consolidated projects, to the detriment of ventures with more innovative projects which however offer less certain returns.[8]

On the demand side, it is also noticeable that entrepreneurs are reluctant both to provide the information needed to allow the evaluation of their business and to relinquish shares in or control of the embryonic/young firm. It emerges that there is often a genuine culture gap, making it difficult for entrepreneurs to conduct relations with potential investors and assess the various financial options available.

These aspects can be summarised in terms of two main equity gap scenarios: the 'finance gap' and 'knowledge gap' (Harding, 2002). In the finance gap, for some types of investments, potential investors consider that below a given threshold the costs of information are too high in relation to the expected returns, compared with large-scale projects with lower risk thresholds. This leads to a gradual increase in the mean values of investment operations. In the second case, the demand and supply sides in projects involving small amounts of funds suffer from an information asymmetry regarding the growth potential of some types of business, especially in the high-tech sector. This leads to the formation of investment portfolios favouring more mature, lower-risk sectors.

The availability of risk capital is the *sine qua non* for the birth and development of ISMEs and the generation of their beneficial economic effects. Given these problems, it is clear that there is a need for public action to bridge the equity gap on several levels. The development of methodologies for the assessment and measurement of the equity gap is an important step in facilitating such action.

Detecting and measuring the equity gap

Theoretical debate and empirical studies have been focusing for some time on verifying the existence of financing and equity gaps for SMEs. Studies have investigated the possible size characteristics of this phenomenon, considering that it may be larger for specific types of firms, for particular stages in their life cycles and for given countries or geographical areas, depending on the different stages of economic development.[9] Following the publication of the so-called Macmillan Report, in recent years in particular, studies have been performed in various national contexts to ascertain whether these gaps occur and monitor them in terms of the size of the investments involved and the types/sectors of firms and life cycle stages affected. Efforts have also been made to identify any geographical/regional dimension to the phenomenon. Since the evidence has been inconclusive for SMEs in general, attention has shifted to potential equity gaps occurring for ISMEs, mainly in the high-tech sector, especially during the early stages of their life cycle: seed, start-up and early/sustained growth. In spite of some caveats, these studies make an important contribution to the debate concerning the advisability and potential mechanisms of public measures to bridge or at least reduce the equity gap for ISMEs. They are capable of providing policy-makers with information of use for setting the procedures and contexts for incentive measures. It has proved more difficult to conduct similar surveys at the international level, and the results of such studies can be taken as no more than pointers to trends (OECD, 2006a).

The problem of measuring the equity gap is not easily overcome: since it is generated by market failures, the conditions that would be needed to allow supply and demand to come together in an efficient market must first be established. Moreover, it is difficult to prove the existence of financing gaps using statistical series, since they do not reflect unsatisfied demand (Bank of England, 2001). For this reason, many studies are based on interviews and/or questionnaires, in spite of the limitations and difficulties we examine below.

The studies performed so far give results which are often approximate and may vary with regard to a given context and also differ over time, partly in response to the economic cycle. However, even approximate assessment of the equity gap may assist policy-makers as they attempt to decide the type and breadth of actions and/or incentives to be introduced and the features of the target enterprises. Apart from providing a clearer identification of the problem, an improvement in these techniques may also provide the bases for assessing the efficiency and efficacy of the public measures introduced.

Three approaches can be identified in the main contributions to the debate.[10] They may be defined as the 'macro' quantitative approach, the 'micro' qualitative approach and the 'micro' quantitative approach.

The 'macro' quantitative approach

The first type of survey identifies the characteristics of the equity gap in a specific national context by monitoring the distribution of private equity investments by amount and by the firm's life cycle stage, and analysing the trend in risk capital investments in the start-up and expansion stages over time. This is followed by an international comparison, generally made by calculating the value of these investments as a percentage of GDP.[11]

Figure 3.1 illustrates the findings of research undertaken by the OECD for the period 2000–3. The results reveal different situations in the diverse countries, with regard to the total amounts of venture capital investment expressed as a percentage of GDP, and the distinction between the amounts invested in early stage and expansion financing. These findings are proof of the emergence of an equity gap with different characteristics in the various countries.

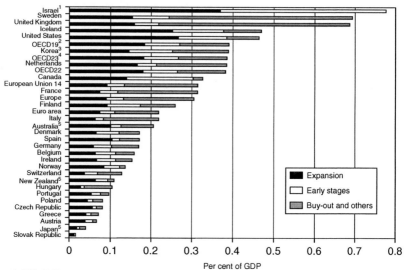

1. 2000–2002.
2. Europe, Canada and United States.
3. 1998–2001.
4. Europe, Czech Republic, Hungary, Poland, Slovak Republic, Canada, and United States.
5. 1998–2001.

Source: OECD, based on data from EVCA (Europe); NVCA (United States); CVCA (Canada); Asian Venture Capital Journal (The 2000 Guide to Venture Capital in Asia).

Figure 3.1   Venture capital investments by stages, in percent of GDP (averages 2000–3)

Source: Venture capital investments by stages (p. 70), *The SME Financing Gap* (Vol. I): *Theory and Evidence*, © OECD 2006.

The 'micro' qualitative approach

The second survey method, the most widely used at the national level, makes a qualitative analysis by means of interviews/questionnaires targeting experts mainly on the supply side, providing risk capital to SMEs: informal investors/business angels, venture capital and private equity firms, banks and government agencies.[12] This type of study tends to be adversely affected by the composition of the panel/sample, which has a fatally strong influence on replies, and by anecdotal convictions. It is also particularly difficult to monitor the business angels segment, and that of informal investors in general. With regard to the evidence of a demand-side equity gap, surveys have been performed by conducting interviews and organising panel discussions with entrepreneurs, but here there are even greater problems concerning the significance of the

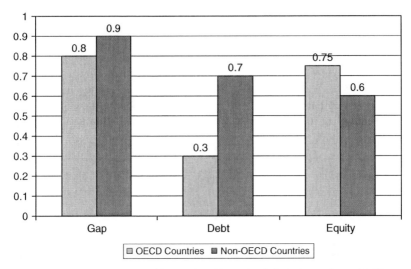

Note: In many cases of debt in OECD countries, this problem is limited to a sub set of SMEs, mostly start-ups and very young firms. Data is based on the responses of 20 OECD and 10 non-OECD economics.
Source: OECD SME and Enterpreneurship Financing Survey.

Figure 3.2   Is there a financing gap? Where is the gap?
Source: Is there a financing gap? Where is the gap? (p. 25), *The SME Financing Gap* (Vol. I): *Theory and Evidence*, © OECD 2006.

results, deriving from the panel composition criteria and the resulting degree of representativeness.

Surveys using interviews or questionnaires have also been conducted at the *international* level. In particular, the OECD has performed a questionnaire-based survey to find evidence of financing gaps in OECD and non-OECD countries (Figure 3.2). The analyses only allow the identification of trends: most significantly, they reveal the existence of an equity gap for ISMEs even in OECD countries, where no significant financing gaps were found for SMEs in general. In these studies, the difficulties described for national surveys are accentuated, together with the problem of the lack of comparable data and the different definitions of an SME used in the various contexts.[13]

As for qualitative analysis developed at the *national* level, the UK is a particularly interesting case because its capital markets are more developed than those of the other European states. The surveys performed reveal that most SMEs have few problems in accessing financing. But

Table 3.1   Assessing the finance gap

Question 1	Do you agree that there appears to be a continuing equity gap facing small and medium-sized enterprises seeking growth capital?
Question 2	If you agree that an equity gap persists, do you agree that it is most acute for firms seeking £250,000–£1 million?
Question 3	Are there particular issues facing high-tech firms in accessing equity finance?

Source: HM Treasury – Small Business Service (2003a), p. 59.

even in the UK, due to market failures, a minority of firms (especially the smallest and with the potential for rapid growth) have difficulty in raising funds to support the early stages in their life cycles: they are thus unable to exploit their growth potential, with negative effects for the country's economic growth.

The main studies performed until the late 1990s basically concentrated on SMEs in general. For high-tech SMEs, studied by the Bank of England survey (2001), proof of a financing gap is inconclusive: problems are identified for the start-up phase, but the study did not succeed in answering the crucial question of whether the causes lie on the demand or the supply side.

Several estimates of the equity gap have been published since the end of the 1990s. Based on interviews with those working in the sector, they are generally qualitative and focus on the supply side. The findings have been used as the basis of government policy (HM Treasury – Small Business Service, 2003a; 2003b). Table 3.1 lists the questions asked during a consultation with interested parties in 2003 by HM Treasury and the Small Business Service.

Various studies have identified equity gaps, estimated to lie between:

- £250,000 and £1.5 million, supply-side survey of 65 venture capital operators with small average investment amounts, business angels and business support agencies (Harding, 2002);
- £250,000 and £1 million, with differences between sectors, life style stages and rounds (consultation with interested parties, HM. Treasury – Small Business Service 2003a; 2003b). This threshold is also suggested by Mason and Harrison (2003), who use these findings to criticise the establishment of Regional Venture Capital Funds with maximum investment amount of £250,000. They reach this conclusion by analysing the supply-side methodologies followed and data

reported by the British Venture Capital Association (BVCA): in their opinion, amounts below £250,000 are provided effectively by business angels and small venture capital funds, not monitored by the BVCA.

Still focusing on individual national contexts, studies have been performed to calculate the size of the equity gap in Sweden and Finland. For Sweden, the gap is estimated to affect investment projects in the range of €100,000 to €500,000, with forecasts that this will rise over the coming years. Business angels are prepared to invest sums in this range, and are thus considered to be of fundamental importance in encouraging the growth of SMEs, and specific measures targeting them have been introduced (Itzel et al., 2004).

In 2004, a survey was conduced in Finland for TEKES (2005), the Finnish National Technology Agency, to ascertain whether fluctuations in the economic cycle affect the financing of high-tech enterprise start-ups. The method used involved in-depth interviews with a diverse group of 34 national and international players: managers, government agencies and experts involved in start-up operations. These interviews are backed by quantitative analysis of unpublished data. The study, which also used statistical data on the evolution of the venture capital sector, found evidence of an equity gap in Finland for enterprises in the first stages of their development (seed, start-up and early stage) requiring investments of between €200,000 and €1 million. This gap is traced to the economic downturn at the beginning of the twenty-first century, following the crisis in the high-tech sector, combined with a venture capital industry that is still immature (Maula et al., 2007).

One interesting survey conducted to discover whether the equity gap has a *regional* dimension compared the situations in the UK and Germany (Martin et al., 2005). The survey methodology was two-pronged: the first type of analysis concerned a cluster study based on the geographical location of venture capital operators, partly conducted with the aid of non-public data relating to the industries in the two countries. The second was a qualitative survey comprising interviews with venture capital operators. Considerable differences emerged between the two country cases, deriving from the different economic and financial contexts. The main difference is in the sectorial connotations of the equity gap: in Germany, the sector which seems most adversely affected by a shortfall in the availability of risk capital is low technology manufacturing, while in the UK the equity gap emerges in the information technology, life sciences and information sectors. This situation tends to reflect the fact that in Germany since 2000 a significant proportion of venture capital has been directed towards the high-tech sector, partly as a result of government intervention (see chapter 8).

The study reveals that, in spite of these differences, there is a geographical link between venture capital operators and the firms receiving investment. This is notwithstanding the fact that in the interviews, the operators maintained that regional considerations played no part in their decisions. The spatial proximity between the operators' headquarters and the investments made would not in itself prove the existence of regional equity gaps if the venture capital operators were evenly spread across the various regions. However, since the venture capital industry tends to be concentrated in just a few regions, the prospect of a regional equity gap does arise. In reality, the geographical location of venture capital operators may be seen as a response to regional differences in economic growth, and thus a difference in the demand for risk capital. Therefore, no conclusive proof of regional equity gaps emerges, because the study was not conducted from the demand side. From the policy-maker's point of view, it emerges that schemes intended to encourage venture capital investment in specific regions, in response to possible regional equity gaps, may yield poor results if there is no actual demand or in the absence of services providing backup to the venture capital industry, and also if there are no targeted actions from the demand side.

The 'micro' quantitative approach

The third procedure, the least used at present but the most interesting in methodology terms because of the information it may yield, concerns a quantitative approach, using empirical analyses of demand-side data-sets. Obviously, the value added of these studies depends on the type of data used, and ideally data requested for the specific purpose of monitoring the equity gap should be utilised.

The study by Harding and Cowling (2006) in the UK is based on both a qualitative analysis, using semi-structured interviews with experts in the sector, and an estimate of the demand-side equity gap using the data of the 2003 GEM (Global Entrepreneurship Monitor) survey. They find evidence of an equity gap of £150,000–250,000 at the lower end and £1.5–2 million at the upper end. A further gap for small amounts, between £10,000 and £30,000, is identified in the expansion stage for firms 18 and 24 months old, which need these funds to deal with regulatory and fiscal expenses.

One proxy for the latent demand for share capital has been obtained by estimating the proportion of small enterprises which have potential for accelerated growth in the UK, using an approach developed by the Small Business Administration in the US. In both contexts, the estimates indicate that between 5 per cent and 10 per cent of start-ups have a potential demand for equity. The definition of high growth used in the UK analysis includes companies which reach a turnover of at least £1 million and/or ten or more employees before the end of their fourth year (HM Treasury – Small Business Service, 2003b).

For Italy, the latent demand for risk capital was assessed for a sample of 167 innovative firms (see chapter 4). The adoption of an innovative evaluation model allowed the surplus demand for risk capital to be assessed as amounting to about €250,000 on average. These values do not provide an explicit estimate of the equity gap, but may confirm its existence, since the scale of the risk capital demand identified is in line with the thresholds stated in the main international studies.

Conclusions

The equity gap for ISMEs has been the focus of theoretical and empirical studies for some time, mainly with the aim of defining the most appropriate form of public intervention to help overcome the problem.

Although there is some degree of doubt concerning its exact extent, studies performed in various context tend to confirm that there is an equity gap affecting innovative firms in their start-up and early growth stages. These difficulties are due to market failures, on both the demand side and in the supply of risk capital funds, mainly arising from information asymmetries.

Our analysis of the different approaches developed for the assessment and measurement of the equity gap for ISMEs (examining the supply side and demand side, and quantitative and qualitative approaches) focuses on their limitations and level of significance.

However, interesting features arise from the 'macro' quantitative and 'micro' qualitative approaches. First, though not absolutely conclusive, there are findings which tend to link the equity gap to the type of financial system, and whether or not it includes a healthy number of private equity operators: venture capitalists and business angels. Second, the size of the equity gap in a given context appears to vary over time, probably due to differences in the survey procedures, the point in the economic cycle and the evolution of the financial industry. As the venture capital industry develops, the upper limit of the equity gap tends to rise, since as the market grows operators tend to move towards deals involving larger amounts.[14]

Fewer studies have concentrated on analysing the demand side, especially using the quantitative approach, due to difficulties in data collection and the definition of a suitable methodology.

For policy-making and other purposes, there is a clear need to improve the techniques for identifying and measuring the equity gap, and also defining its geographical and sectorial boundaries, especially with regard to the demand side and the quantitative approach. It is important to underline that quantitative analyses are able to evaluate the latent demand for risk capital, but cannot define precisley the exact size of the equity gap. The phenomenon can only be examined through interviews assessing how many enterprises have been unable to obtain equity investments after specific application to the market and/or investment firms. The strategy for the future must therefore be the adoption of methods capable of combining the two approaches, qualitative and quantitative, which are currently mainly applied separately.

With reference to the measurement problem, the model presented in chapter 4 can also be interpreted as an extension of the quantitative approaches developed on the demand side. This model allows the future demand for equity to be assessed more accurately than the methods currently in use.

The development of methodologies for the assessment and measurement of the equity gap is becoming more and more important for policy-makers in many countries, and within the EU as a whole, who are intending to proceed with the creation of intervention schemes to bridge the equity gap for ISMEs (see chapter 8). In some cases, the definition of these measures' context and type is guided to a certain extent by proxies for measurement of the equity gap itself, and the identification of regional, business and life cycle stage characteristics. Further developments in the methods of study will help to increase the efficacy of public intervention of this kind by focusing on suitable intervention schemes.

4
An Original Equity Requirement Estimation Model

Luciana Canovi and Valeria Venturelli

Introduction

In recent years, the question of whether the growth of Italian SMEs, and young, innovative firms in particular, is being restricted by a lack of equity capital, and if so to what extent, has attracted the attention of both researchers and practitioners. The main aim of this chapter is to identify and verify the causes that generate financial needs to be covered by equity, and to estimate the absolute and relative size of the investment required.

The chapter is divided into two main sections. The first examines the models adopted to compute the additional equity needed to finance the expected growth and the sample of SMEs to which the different models have been applied. Particular attention is paid to the sample selection criteria – crucial for a proper explanation of the results – and the structural characteristics which emerge from an analysis of the firms' financial statements. The second section surveys the key variables included in the models and evaluates the results stemming from their application. Finally, the main conclusions of the study are presented.

Equity requirement estimation models

A firm's growth, measured by the increase in its sales in a specific period, generates a growing need for financing, which will be covered partly by self-financing and current debts and partly by external sources, consisting of equity and loan capital (see Box 4.1). The models[1] developed in this study to estimate the need for additional equity differ in terms of the hypothesis adopted with regard to the dynamics of the additional financial requirement generated by the growth on one hand, and the role played by the different forms of coverage on the other.

The models can be classified in two groups. In the first, models 1 and 2 both assume that no significant changes in capital intensity, self-financing margin or current indebtedness as a proportion of sales are expected. They differ in relation to the hypothesis adopted concerning the role of financial indebtedness in covering additional financial needs. Model 1 assumes no change in the value of financial debt, that is to say financial debts will not increase during the reference period. In contrast, model 2 is based on the hypothesis that financial indebtedness may grow, subject to the constraint of maintaining a constant ratio between financial debt and equity.

The models in the second group, models 3 and 4, also consider the possibility of changes in capital intensity, self-financing margin and current indebtedness as a proportion of sales. Again, the models vary in terms of the assumption concerning the role of financial debt. While model 3 assumes constant financial debt, model 4 allows for variations in this parameter, as well as modifying the leverage ratio if necessary.

Box 4.1   An accounting definition of the variables used in the models

V = Revenues from sales and services

K = Capital intensity = total assets/revenues from sales and services, with total assets = total fixed assets + total current assets + total accrued income and prepaid expenses

D_f = Financial debts = bonds + convertible bonds + due to shareholders for loans + due to banks + due to other lenders + negotiable instruments + due to subsidiary companies beyond 12 months + due to associate companies beyond 12 months + due to parent companies beyond 12 months

D_c = Current debts/revenues from sales and services, with current debts = total debts – financial debts

A = self-financing margin = self-financing/revenues from sales and services, with self-financing = net revenue + total depreciation, amortization and writedowns – profits distributed

---

Model 1

Assuming that no significant changes in capital intensity, the margin of self-financing, current indebtedness as a proportion of sales or the level of financial debt are expected, the additional financial requirement generated by the growth in sales (FA) may be covered solely by self-financing (CA), by an increase in current indebtedness (CDC) and by growth in new equity (FE). Thus, the following equations apply:

$$FA = X \cdot V_{t-1} \cdot K \tag{1}$$

X = Expected rate of growth in sales

V_{t-1} = Sales for the previous period

K = Total assets/sales = Capital intensity

$$CDC = X \cdot V_{t-1} \cdot D_c \tag{2}$$

D_c = Current debts/sales

$$CA = X \cdot V_{t-1} \cdot A \tag{3}$$

A = Self-financing/sales

Applying model 1, the equity requirement (FE) is estimated as the amount outstanding after deduction from the additional financial requirement generated by the growth in sales (FA) of the amounts covered by the other forms of finance envisaged by the model (CDC and CA). Analytically:

$$FE = X \cdot V_{t-1} \cdot (K - D_c - A) \tag{4}$$

Model 2

Model 2 is developed on the assumption that the additional financial requirement may also be covered through an increase in financial indebtedness, subject to the constraint of maintaining a constant ratio between financial debt and equity.

Keeping the same hypothesis as in model 1, of a constant ratio of self-financing margin and current indebtedness to sales, equations (1), (2) and (3) still apply.

To measure the amount covered by new financial debts, two values have to be obtained. The first, CDF_1, derives from the fact that, since self-financing produces an increase in the firm's equity capital, financial debts can increase by an amount equal to self-financing multiplied by leverage, without any change in the latter. Analytically:

$$CDF_1 = \frac{D_f}{E} \cdot X \cdot V_{t-1} \cdot A \tag{5}$$

If the additional financing required exceeds the sources analysed so far (self-financing, current debts, first component of financial indebtedness), there is a shortfall, DIF, equal to:

$$DIF = X \cdot V_{t-1} \cdot \left[K - D_c - A \cdot \left(1 + \frac{D_f}{E} \right) \right]$$

However, the whole of this shortfall cannot be financed by means of equity, since in this case the leverage ratio would fall. The part covered by additional new debts – in compliance with the constant leverage constraint – provides the second component of the growth in financial indebtedness (CDF$_2$) and is equal to:

$$CDF_2 = X \cdot V_{t-1} \cdot \left[K - D_c - A \cdot \left(1 + \frac{D_f}{E} \right) \right] \cdot \frac{\frac{D_f}{E}}{1 + \frac{D_f}{E}} \tag{6}$$

The total coverage provided by financial indebtedness (CDF) is therefore the sum of (5) + (6). This can be reduced to:

$$CDF = \frac{X \cdot V_{t-1} \cdot \frac{D_f}{E} \cdot (K - D_c)}{1 + \frac{D_f}{E}} \tag{7}$$

Finally, the equity requirement at constant leverage, FE$_{LC}$, is obtained by subtracting all the forms of coverage examined so far from the additional financing requirement. More simply, the equity requirement at constant leverage is the same as the fraction $\frac{1}{1+D_f/E}$ of the financial shortfall:

$$FE_{LC} = X \cdot V_{t-1} \cdot \left[K - D_c - A \cdot \left(1 + \frac{D_f}{E} \right) \right] \cdot \frac{1}{1 + \frac{D_f}{E}} \tag{8}$$

Model 3

Removing the hypothesis of constant capital intensity, the additional financial requirement generated by the growth stems from two causes: on the one hand, from the variation in sales (the so-called sales effect) and on the other, from the variation in investments necessary to realize each unit of sale (the so-called capital intensity effect):

$$FA = X \cdot V_{t-1} \cdot K_{t-1} + V_t \cdot (K_t - K_{t-1}) \qquad (9)$$

where:

$X \cdot V_{t-1} \cdot K_{t-1}$ estimates the sales effect

$V_t \cdot (K_t - K_{t-1})$ assesses the variation in capital intensity

By deduction, the cover provided by current debt and self-financing is also affected by the 'sales effect' and by the variation in the different forms of coverage:

$$CDC = X \cdot V_{t-1} \cdot D_{c,t-1} + V_t \cdot (D_{c,t} - D_{c,t-1}) \qquad (10)$$

$$CA = X \cdot V_{t-1} \cdot A_{t-1} + V_t \cdot (A_t - A_{t-1}) \qquad (11)$$

Indicating with

$(K_t - K_{t-1}) \rightarrow$ variation in capital intensity $\rightarrow \alpha_t$

$(D_{c,t} - D_{c,t-1}) \rightarrow$ variation in the ratio of current debt on sales $\rightarrow \beta_t$

$(A_t - A_{t-1}) \rightarrow$ variation in self-financing margin $\rightarrow \mu_t$

the additional equity requirement, FE*, can be estimated by means of the following equation:

$$FE^* = X \cdot V_{t-1} \cdot K_{t-1} + V_t \cdot \alpha_t - X \cdot V_{t-1} \cdot D_{c,t-1} - V_t \cdot \beta_t$$
$$- X \cdot V_{t-1} \cdot A_{t-1} - V_t \cdot \mu_t$$

which can be reduced to:

$$FE^* = X \cdot V_{t-1} \cdot \left(K_{t-1} - D_{c,t-1} - A_{t-1}\right) + V_t \cdot (\alpha_t - \beta_t - \mu_t) \qquad (12)$$

Model 4

When estimating the equity requirement at variable leverage, FE^*_{LV}, where variations in capital intensity, self-financing margin and the ratio of current debt to sales are assumed, equations (9), (10) and (11) still apply.

The assumption of variable leverage (that is to say, the model allows for a variation in leverage from $D_{f,t-1}/E_{t-1}$ to $D_{f,t}/E_t$) implies that the first amount covered by new financial debts has to consider this variation. The first amount is equal to self-financing multiplied by leverage. Analytically:

$$\text{CDF}_1 = (X \cdot V_{t-1} \cdot A_{t-1} + V_t \cdot \mu_t) \cdot \frac{D_{f,t}}{E_t} \tag{13}$$

As in model 2, if the additional financing required exceeds the sources analysed so far (self-financing, current debts, first component of financial indebtedness), there is a shortfall, DIF, equal to FA – CDC – CA – CDF$_1$:

$$\text{DIF} = X \cdot V_{t-1} \cdot (K_{t-1} - D_{c,t-1} - A_{t-1}) + V_t \cdot (\alpha_t - \beta_t - \mu_t)$$
$$- (X \cdot V_{t-1} \cdot A_{t-1} + V_t \cdot \mu_t) \cdot \frac{D_{f,t}}{E_t}$$

Or in its reduced form:

$$\text{DIF} = X \cdot V_{t-1} \cdot \left[K_{t-1} - D_{c,t-1} - A_{t-1} \cdot \left(1 + \frac{D_{f,t}}{E_t} \right) \right]$$
$$+ V_t \cdot \left[\alpha_t - \beta_t - \mu_t \cdot \left(1 + \frac{D_{f,t}}{E_t} \right) \right]$$

As previously stated, the second component of the growth in financial indebtedness, CDF$_2$, is equal to $\frac{D_{f,t}/E_t}{1 + D_{f,t}/E_t}$ of the financial shortfall, DIF.

Adding CDF$_1$ and CDF$_2$ a partial CDF ($\overline{CDF}$) is obtained. Omitting the intermediate explanations:

$$\overline{\text{CDF}} = \frac{D_{f,t}}{E_t \left(1 + D_{f,t}/E_t \right)} \cdot \left[X \cdot V_{t-1} \cdot (K_{t-1} - D_{c,t-1}) + V_t \cdot (\alpha_t - \beta_t) \right]$$

$\overline{CDF}$ is not a measure of the entire coverage provided by financial debt. Since variable leverage is assumed, this hypothesis also requires modification of the *ex ante* stock of financial debt to fulfil the new financial leverage ratio. In other words, since a composition effect is introduced on the liability side, an additional component must be added to the ratio that defines the financial debt requirement. This element is equal to the variation in the weight of financial debt in the financial structure multiplied by the total sources of financing before the variation in leverage.

So, the total coverage provided by financial indebtedness (CDF) is equal to:

$$\text{CDF} = \frac{D_{f,t}}{E_t\left(1 + D_{f,t}/E_t\right)} \cdot \left[X \cdot V_{t-1} \cdot \left(K_{t-1} - D_{c,t-1}\right) + V_t \cdot \left(\alpha_t - \beta_t\right)\right]$$

$$+ \left(\frac{D_{f,t}}{1 + \frac{D_{f,t}}{E_t}} - \frac{D_{f,t-1}}{1 + \frac{D_{f,t-1}}{E_{t-1}}}\right) \cdot \left(D_{f,t-1} + E_{t-1}\right) \tag{14}$$

As previously seen, the part of the financial shortfall to be financed through equity capital is not only equal to the shortfall's fraction $\frac{1}{1+D_{f,t}/E_t}$; once more, the original stock of equity capital has to be modified to allow for variation in leverage. In this case it is equal to the variation in the weight of equity capital in the financial structure multiplied by the total sources of financing before the variation in leverage.

Summing up, the equity requirement at variable leverage is equal to:

$$\text{FE}^*_{LV} = \frac{1}{1 + D_{f,t}/E_t} \cdot \left[X \cdot V_{t-1} \cdot \left(K_{t-1} - D_{c,t-1}\right) + V_t \cdot \left(\alpha_t - \beta_t\right)\right]$$

$$- X \cdot V_{t-1} \cdot A_{t-1} - \mu_t \cdot V_t + \left(\frac{1}{1 + D_{f,t}/E_t} - \frac{1}{1 + D_{f,t-1}/E_{t-1}}\right)$$

$$\cdot \left(D_{f,t-1} + E_{t-1}\right)$$

Description of the sample

The sample studied is the result of an extraction from the AIDA Database, which contains economic and financial information about limited companies operating in Italy with sales in excess of €500,000. The extraction was restricted to companies having a registered office in Italy, operating in the manufacturing and service sectors, with a high technological innovation content.[2] The analysis was only conducted on micro and small share capital companies[3] in the growth stage,[4] incorporated starting from the year 2004, with financial statement data available for the period 2005–6.

Applying these selection criteria enabled us to identify a sample of 167 firms, 60 per cent of which belong to the micro categories. In terms of sectorial distribution, firms in the service sector are the majority (56.9 per cent), and within this sector, the category identified by code 72.20 (software consultancy and supply) predominates.

The sample of 167 firms was divided into four categories on the basis of size (micro or small) and sector (manufacturing or service). Class A groups

Table 4.1   Asset structure (%)

	Mean	Median	Standard dev.
No. = 167			
Current assets/fixed assets + current assets	85.7	90.7	14.8
Intangible fixed assets/fixed assets	40.1	27.0	35.8
Tangible fixed assets/fixed assets	53.2	62.5	36.1
Financial fixed assets/fixed assets	6.4	0.0	16.9

Source: processing of AIDA Database data.

41 micro manufacturing firms, class B 62 micro service companies, class C 31 small manufacturing firms and class D 33 small service firms.

Following standard practice, we trimmed outliers for each class identified in all key variables at the two standard deviations from the mean level.

Before applying the equity demand estimation models, we examined the structural characteristics of the financial statements of the 167 firms. We considered the composition of the investments and sources of finance and the structure of the profit and loss account. Unless otherwise specified, values are for 2006.

Among the assets, there is a strong prevalence of investments in current assets (Table 4.1). The mean value of the current assets/(current assets + fixed assets) ratio is very high (85.7 per cent), with a fairly low degree of variability.

When broken down by class (Table 4.2) these data show specific features which do not alter the overall picture. The relative weight of investments in current assets is slightly greater in micro than in small firms.

This finding would appear to reflect the coverage of financial needs by traditional means such as short-term bank borrowing and indebtedness to suppliers.

The composition of the fixed assets (Table 4.1) reveals that intangible fixed assets account for a considerable proportion of fixed assets overall (on average 40.1 per cent). The highest incidence of intangible fixed assets is found (Table 4.2) in small firms (C and D), especially in the service sector (D). This is to be expected given the decision to observe very new firms operating in highly innovative sectors. In firms of this kind, intangible assets typically constitute a large proportion of the invested capital. However, when assessing our findings it is important to remember that fixed assets account for only a relatively small proportion of

Table 4.2   Asset structure for the different categories of firms (mean value) (%)

	A	B	C	D
No.	41	62	31	33
Current assets/fixed assets + current assets	87.4	86.1	82.5	85.9
Intangible fixed assets/fixed assets	33.9	38.8	42.8	47.9
Tangible fixed assets/fixed assets	63.6	51.9	52.5	43.4
Financial fixed assets/fixed assets	2.5	8.7	4.7	8.6

Source: processing of AIDA Database data.

Table 4.3   Liability structure (%)

	Mean	Median	Standard dev.
No. $= 167$			
Debts/shareholders' funds + debts	84.1	88.8	14.8
Current debts/debts	95.0	100.0	13.2
Financial debts/debts	5.0	0.0	13.2
Due to banks/financial debts	15.2	0.0	34.7
Due to banks beyond 12 months/due to banks	17.0	0.0	37.0

Source: processing of AIDA Database data.

investments, and so the intangible component represents a considerable slice of only a fairly low figure. Financial assets also account for a very small proportion of fixed assets. On average, only 6.4 per cent of investments consist of shareholdings and financial receivables (Table 4.1). This indicator is higher than average in service sector firms, regardless of the firm's size (Table 4.2). The results are in line with the sample characteristics. The fact that there are no medium and large enterprises, which are normally large lenders to other firms or hold considerable shares in their capital, explains the marginal role of financial assets.

Debts account for the lion's share of liabilities (Table 4.3); on average debts represent 84.1 per cent of sources of financing, and the differences between the various classes are small. Debt dependency is highest among small manufacturing firms (Table 4.4). The financial statements of the 167 micro and small innovative firms thus confirm the general belief that Italian firms are heavily indebted.

An examination of the structure of firms' indebtedness provides very useful pointers to the direction of our subsequent analysis. The data show

Table 4.4 Liability structure for the different categories of firms (mean value) (%)

	A	B	C	D
No.	41	62	31	33
Debts/shareholders' funds + debts	83.7	82.9	87.0	84.0
Current debts/debts	94.7	95.3	95.4	94.5
Financial debts/debts	5.3	4.7	4.6	5.5
Due to banks/financial debts	14.3	14.7	13.6	18.9
Due to banks beyond 12 months/due to banks	15.9	16.2	13.5	23.0

Source: processing of AIDA Database data.

first and foremost the predominance of use of supplier credit and other forms of indebtedness directly related to day-to-day management. On average, 95 per cent of debts are current debts (Table 4.3). The median (100 per cent) is very similar to the mean, and the standard deviation is low (13.2 per cent). This supports the hypothesis that the current debts/total debts ratio provides a fairly close estimate of the scale of indebtedness. The key role of current debts in financing investments, which it should be remembered consist mainly of current operating assets, emerges in all classes, without any differences.

Conversely, financial debts account for only a small proportion of the total, and bank borrowing is absolutely marginal: on average, only 15.2 per cent of financial debts consist of debts to banks (Table 4.3). There is a high degree of variability in the average value, but a low level of dependency on bank lending emerges very clearly in all the classes examined, passing from the minimum value of 13.6 per cent for small manufacturing firms to the maximum value of 18.9 per cent for small service firms (Table 4.4). Finally, when the breakdown of bank debt by due date is examined (Table 4.3) it can be seen that only a very small proportion of loans are short-term; the average value of the short-term banks/banks ratio is 17 per cent, with a value above this occurring for small service sector firms only (23 per cent).

Our data highlight the fact that, unlike Italian firms in general, and SMEs in particular, the financial statements of the young, innovative companies studied here reveal that these companies make only marginal use of bank borrowing, especially the short-term financing most appropriate to the type of investments made. This tends to confirm the hypothesis that due to their structural characteristics – youth, membership of high-risk sectors – firms of this kind seem to find it difficult to

Table 4.5   Economic performance (%)

	Mean	Median	Standard dev.
No. = 167			
EBITDA/revenue from sales and services	10.0	7.6	10.7
EBIT/revenue from sales and services	7.7	5.5	10.2
Interest and financial charges/EBIT	18.8	7.9	53.6

Source: processing of AIDA Database data.

Table 4.6   Economic performance for the different categories of firms (mean value) (%)

	A	B	C	D
No.	41	62	31	33
EBITDA/revenue from sales and services	10.4	11.0	9.0	8.5
EBIT/revenue from sales and services	8.3	9.0	6.3	5.8
Interest and financial charges/EBIT	18.3	8.9	40.6	17.4

Source: processing of AIDA Database data.

build significant relationships with banks, especially with regard to borrowing to cover investments in current assets. The general belief that firms have not suffered from forms of credit rationing during the last few years is therefore not borne out by the financial statements of the firms observed, unless firms prefer indebtedness to other creditors, primarily their suppliers, to borrowing from banks (assuming that bank credit is available).

To assess economic performance, the incidence of gross operating margin and operating revenue on earnings was observed (Table 4.5). The ability to meet the cost of financial indebtedness was then evaluated by examining the financial charges/operating revenue ratio.

The EBITDA/sales ratio is low overall: the average (10 per cent) and median (7.6 per cent) values point to a low capacity for self-financing. In other words, earnings appear to be inadequate to cover investment needs, and thus external sources of finance are essential. The data broken down by category do not reveal much variation among classes (Table 4.6). The ratio tends to fall as firm size increases; moreover, the highest value (11 per cent) occurs in micro firms in the service sector. However, these differences are not significant.

The performance indicator obtained by comparing EBIT with sales (average 7.7 per cent) varies more from class to class. This is partly explained by the influence of amortisation and write-downs on the value of the ratio. These costs depend on the value of the assets to be amortised/written down, but are also significantly affected by the accounting procedures firms adopt, mainly for tax reasons. These procedures vary significantly from firm to firm and may produce more variable results in the EBIT/sales indicator. Here again small firms appear to suffer compared to micro firms (Table 4.6) since their profitability (6.3 and 5.8 per cent in the manufacturing and service sector respectively) is below average.

With reference to the compatibility between the costs of indebtedness and earnings margins (Table 4.5), the proportion of profit absorbed by financial charges is very low on average (18.8 per cent), but is extremely variable. The range is from the minimum value (Table 4.6) for micro firms in the service sector (8.9 per cent) to the highest value for small manufacturing firms (40.6 per cent). However, this last figure must be treated with caution since it is extremely volatile.[5] The analysis of the data overall supports the idea that the sample firms are able to support the costs of their financial structures. This is due to the low level of use of financial debt, especially in relation to banks.

Equity requirement for young innovative Italian micro and small firms

The application of the models allows identification of the causes which generate financial needs to be covered by equity, and estimation of the absolute and relative size of the financing required. The empirical analysis is divided into two steps. In the first we apply model 2 and then, after some methodological decisions, we present the result obtained from the application of model 4. If not otherwise stated, the values in the following tables refer to the situation at year-end 2006.

In general, the average rate of growth in sales of the firms in the sample is 151.4 per cent (Table 4.7). In spite of a high level of volatility, these firms enjoy very high average growth rates, which are used in the equity requirement estimation model. In particular, firms in the service sector grow more than their manufacturing counterparts; among the former, micro firms show higher patterns of growth than small enterprises.

The self-financing margin is 4.7 per cent and varies little across the different classes; nonetheless micro firms show the highest capacity for self-financing (Tables 4.7 and 4.8). Overall the self-financing margins are not particularly high, and thus the resources generated by the company's

Table 4.7 Model inputs

	Mean	Median	Standard dev.
No. = 167			
X – Rate of growth in sales (%)	151.4	79.4	203.9
A – Self-financing margin (%)	4.7	3.0	7.0
K – Capital intensity	0.68	0.64	30.2
D_c – Current debts/sales (%)	49.0	44.6	23.9
D_f/E – Financial debts/equity	0.57	0.00	213.2

Source: processing of AIDA Database data.

Table 4.8 Model inputs for the different categories of firms (mean value)

	A	B	C	D
Number	41	62	31	33
X – Rate of growth in sales (%)	94.2	196.4	99.5	186.8
A – Self-financing margin (%)	5.4	4.8	4.5	4.0
K – Capital intensity	0.72	0.64	0.76	0.61
D_c– Current debts/sales (%)	52.0	47.3	57.2	40.7
D_f/E – Financial debts/equity	0.4	0.8	0.5	0.4

Source: processing of AIDA Database data.

own operations cannot be the main means of providing the financing needed. It should also be borne in mind that the self-financing margin was calculated without taking into consideration any distribution of profits. Although not particularly important for firms of this kind, this should still be considered, because the distribution of profits would imply even lower self-financing margins than those recorded here.

The capital intensity value (0.68 on average) does not lead to the identification of any 'capital-intensive' firms; as expected, firms in the manufacturing sector show higher capital intensity than service sector enterprises. This implies that the additional financial requirement stems from the high average growth rates in sales, and this is particularly true for service firms, which have a higher rate of growth in sales and lower capital intensity compared to their manufacturing counterparts.

The role of current debt is particularly important when this value is measured by means of an indicator which links it to sales: on average, operating debt provides financial coverage for 49 per cent of sales. This

Table 4.9   Application of model 2 (average per firm)

	Mean	Median	Standard dev.
No. = 167			
CA/FA (%)	7.2	4.5	9.6
CDC/FA (%)	73.4	78.5	19.3
CDF/FA (%)	4.7	0.0	12.5
FE_{LC}/FA (%)	14.8	10.0	15.4
FE_{LC}/XV_{t-1} (%)	10.1	6.8	13.2
FE_{LC} (000€)	247.5	72.9	536.1

CA/FA – Self-financing/additional financing requirement; CDC/FA – Current debt/additional financing requirement; CDF/FA – Financial debt requirement/additional financing requirement; FE_{LC}/FA – Equity requirement/additional financing requirement; CDF/XV_{t-1} – Financial debt requirement/expected variation in sales; FE_{LC}/XV_{t-1} – Equity requirement/ expected variation in sales; FE_{LC} – Equity requirement at constant leverage

Source: processing of AIDA Database data.

source of financing, already highly significant for the sample on average and for all the classes identified, is especially significant for small enterprises in the manufacturing sector (57.2 per cent).

The last parameter considered, leverage, is fairly low (0.57). This is also reflected by the median value, which is equal to zero, although the range is wide, as the high standard deviation indicates. Although the financial leverage is fairly similar across the different classes, the highest indebtedness ratio (0.8) is found in micro enterprises in the service sector. Overall, the sample group seem not to make particularly aggressive use of leverage; therefore, the firms in the sample should not find it too difficult to maintain a constant degree of financial leverage, as envisaged by the models.

Assuming a constant indebtedness ratio, the additional need for financing generated by the growth in sales is covered (Table 4.9), on average, by self-financing (7.2 per cent), increasing current debts (73.4 per cent), new financial indebtedness (4.7 per cent) and for the remainder (14.8 per cent) by equity.

The results once again confirm the essential role of current debt and the secondary role played by internally generated funds. It should be underlined that the role of operating debt is often ignored, with a few exceptions,[6] in theoretical studies, because operating debt is a source of financing intrinsic to growth and is thus not picked up by analyses which focus on the relationship between equity and financial debt. The main

Table 4.10 Application of model 2 for the different categories of firms (average value per class)

	A	B	C	D
Number of firms	41	62	31	33
CA/FA (%)	7.9	7.6	5.9	6.7
CDC/FA (%)	73.9	72.3	78.1	70.3
CDF/FA (%)	4.4	4.7	4.4	5.2
FE_{LC}/FA (%)	13.8	15.4	11.5	17.8
FE_{LC}/XV_{t-1} (%)	10.1	9.1	9.7	12.5
FE_{LC} (€000s)	103.2	182.1	211.4	583.7

CA/FA – Self-financing/additional financing requirement; CDC/FA – Current debt/additional financing requirement; CDF/FA – Financial debt requirement/additional financing requirement; FE_{LC}/FA – Equity requirement/additional financing requirement; CDF/XV_{t-1} – Financial debt requirement/expected variation in sales; FE_{LC}/XV_{t-1} – Equity requirement/expected variation in sales; FE_{LC} – Equity requirement at constant leverage

Source: processing of AIDA Database data.

consequence is the undervaluation or sometimes the complete loss of the pivotal role performed by current debt in the coverage of financial needs.

The coverage provided by equity of the additional financial requirement generated by growth in sales, on average equal to 14.8 per cent, seems to be correlated with the economic sector (Table 4.10); the percentage of equity requirement is larger for the service than the manufacturing sector irrespective of size class, reaching the highest level for firms in class D.

When we look at the ratio between equity capital requirement and expected sales (on average 10.1 per cent), the highest percentage (Table 4.10) is in class D (12.5 per cent); confirming once more the role played by current debt, which is lower than average for firms in this class.

The fact that small firms in the service sector (class D) have the highest equity requirement is evident from several circumstances – first from the proportion of the total financial requirement covered by equity, then from the expected growth in sales and finally from the equity requirement expressed in monetary terms. In relation to the last, while the average value for the entire sample is €247.5 k, for the firms belonging to class D the average value is €583.7 k, a figure which conceals a high degree of variation.[7] Moreover, the equity requirement expressed in monetary terms seems to be correlated with business in the economic

Table 4.11   Application of model 4 (median value total and per class)

	Total	**A**	**B**	**C**	**D**
No.	167	41	62	31	33
CA/FA (%)	7.9	9.0	8.7	6.4	7.9
CDC/FA (%)	69.9	66.2	72.5	70.1	62.9
CDF/FA (%)	13.6	12.4	15.3	13.7	12.0
FE^*_{LV}/FA (%)	10.6	14.0	7.0	12.0	21.0
FE^*_{LV}/XV_{t-1} (%)	6.9	11.4	5.0	10.0	13.7
FE^*_{LV} (000 €)	149.3	123.5	105.8	301.7	613.6

CA/FA – Self-financing/additional financing requirement; CDC/FA – Current Debt/additional financing requirement; CDF/FA – Financial debt requirement/ additional financing requirement; FE^*_{LV}/FA – Equity requirement/additional financing requirement; CDF/XV_{t-1} – Financial debt requirement/expected variation in sales; FE^*_{LV}/XV_{t-1} – Equity requirement/expected variation in sales; FE^*_{LV} – Equity requirement at variable leverage

Source: processing of AIDA Database data.

sector (Table 4.10), and is higher for the service than the manufacturing sector irrespective of size class.

A further level of investigation was added to deepen the analysis through the application of model 4, which allows for variation in the relevant variables, in contrast with the previous model, where they were maintained constant. Some caveats must be stated. In particular, since these models are useful in particular for analyses centred on the individual enterprise, their extension to a large dataset requires the introduction of some hypothesises in relation to the relevant variables.

Model 2 implies that each firm maintains its intrinsic characteristics in terms of rate of growth in sales, capital intensity, self-financing margin, and so on; in model 4 we abandon these hypothesis and assume that the relevant variables for each firm can move. The results are crucially dependent on the assumptions introduced on the movement in the relevant variables. In our work, we have decided that the relevant variables move towards the average value for each class. In other words, we assume that the relevant variables for the next period (time t) are equal for each firm, to the average value for each class at time $t-1$. This implies that the values of the relevant variables in $t-1$ are those shown previously in Table 4.8.

Given the high degree of variability of the results, we focused the analysis on median values (Table 4.11), keeping in mind the caution needed when drawing firm conclusions from this kind of analysis.

The results obtained from the application of model 4 are generally in line with those provided by model 2. In particular, the marginal role of self-financing is yet again clear, as well as the pivotal role played by current debts. However, the median values for self-financing are higher for model 4, both for the overall sample and for each class. Conversely, in model 4 current debt accounts for a lower percentage of coverage of the additional financial requirement than in model 2. The combined effect of these findings implies a significant variation in the coverage provided by external financial resources (financial debt and equity capital); the contribution of both to coverage of overall financial needs is increased. This is the result of an increase in self-financing, which is not sufficient to compensate for the decrease in current debt. The growing role of external financial resources triggers a rise in the importance of financial debt and maintenance of the coverage provided by equity capital for the sample overall; moreover, the role of equity capital is boosted across all classes, with the exception of service sector micro enterprises.

Moving towards the average implies a higher level of equity in monetary terms compared to model 2. For the sample overall, the value of equity requirement in monetary terms doubles; the variations are even sharper for some classes, and the value actually triples for small enterprises in the service sector.

Conclusions

The main aim of this chapter is to develop an original model, in several versions, to measure firms' future demand for equity, with a particular focus on young firms in innovative sectors.

To test the models, a sample of 167 Italian micro and small share capital companies was selected. The extraction was limited to growing companies in the manufacturing and service sectors, with a high-tech innovation content. The sample shows, on aggregate, economic and financial characteristics in line with those of firms operating in traditional sectors: firms in the sample invest most of their resources in working capital and cover financial needs through current debts. As expected, self-financing margins are low and operating returns are well in excess of financial structure costs.

An observation of the values used as input for the estimation model leads to the conclusion first, that overall investments per unit of sales are low, second, that the role of self-financing in fuelling growth is absolutely marginal, and third, that it is essential for firms to be able to transfer a large proportion of their financing requirement to other non-financial enterprises.

Assuming a constant indebtedness ratio throughout the period surveyed (model 2), for the sample as a whole, the additional need for financing generated by the growth in sales is covered, on average, by self-financing (7.2 per cent), increasing current debts (73.4 per cent), new financial indebtedness (4.7 per cent) and for the remainder by new equity (14.8 per cent).

However, when the relevant variables move towards the average value of each class (model 4), the additional need for financing generated by the growth is covered, in terms of median values, by self-financing (7.9 per cent), increasing current debts (69.9 per cent), new financial indebtedness (13.6 per cent) and by new equity (10.6 per cent). Model 4 reveals a larger role for self-financing and financial variables, in particular in the form of financial debt, associated with a reduction in the coverage provided by current indebtedness.

Models 2 and 4 show that the additional equity requirement is clearly influenced by the coverage provided by current debt; the inclusion of this variable, not always considered in the literature, is essential if firms' financial problems are to be interpreted correctly.

Finally, the study measures the equity requirement in monetary terms. We find that the amount of equity needed, expressed in absolute terms, is on average tiny in both model 2 (€247,500) and model 4 (€149,300).

Today there is broad agreement among academics and practitioners that financing, particularly in terms of equity capital, is a crucial factor capable of limiting growth opportunities for the SMEs most involved in innovative projects. This clearly reveals the pivotal role played by venture capitalists as well as informal investors, such as business angels. However, situations may arise in which the equity requirement is too small to be economically viable for the venture capitalist (the so-called small ticket problem) but too large to be covered by informal investors, as outlined in chapter 3. Firms in this situation are faced with an equity gap, or a shortage of equity capital, especially during the initial phases of their life cycle. The results of our models, and in particular the tiny amount of the equity requirement discovered (although this cannot be taken as a specific estimate of the equity gap), could indirectly confirm the problem of a gap in the availability of risk capital.

5

The Intermediaries in the Risk Capital Industry

Alessandro G. Grasso

Introduction

Young plants and animals require specific environmental conditions or special forms of nourishment. It appears that young innovative firms are similar in having distinctive financing needs, which have to be covered by the right amount of the correct type of financial resources. Like infants, firms of this kind may have difficulty in communicating with their nurturers (problems of information asymmetry are particularly acute for this type of firm). To overcome these problems proportionally more attention has to be paid to sourcing the most suitable forms of finance.

Financing by means of risk capital is particularly important. Being able to call on specialists to provide investment intended to generate value greatly improves the results that can be achieved. Financial resources in this category – principally venture capital and private equity – support the birth of new business, allow the implementation of new strategies and corporate acquisitions, and sustain firms in crucial periods, such as generation handovers and other particularly difficult times in their life cycles.

This chapter takes a more detailed look at the risk capital industry, investigating the taxonomy of this area of the financial industry, the players involved and its distinctive features. The argument is relevant since, as chapter 6 shows, this sector is enjoying considerable success, reflected by the growing mass of funds invested. This success has attracted the attention of the academic world and more recently of policy-makers interested in creating conditions that favour the development of a dynamic, innovative entrepreneurial environment.

This chapter is divided into five sections. The first discusses a number of definitional problems, while the second describes the main types of operator active in the risk capital industry. The third section introduces the principal categories of operations, after which the next section focuses on the main kinds of risk involved in this activity. Finally, the investment process is examined in greater depth.

The definition: a critical issue

Any analysis of this source of financing requires a definition of what investment in risk capital entails. For our purpose, investment in risk capital defines the operations of professionals who purchase shares in the capital of firms which offer the prospects of growth, with the aim of achieving a capital gain when the shares are later sold. The underlying business principle is very simple: 'buy low and sell high' (NVCA, 2007, p. 15).

However, as we look more closely at this sector, we see that although the basic assumptions are the same, operations in this area may vary widely, due largely to the way in which risk capital investors' business practices have developed over time and in a variety of geographical contexts, adapting to the entrepreneurial system and the differing levels of development of the financial markets. The conventional literature describes this evolution by subdividing the various types of operations more or less in relation to the different life cycle stages of the investee firms. Normally, three main phases are identified: start-up, expansion and replacement investment.

While this segmentation is widely used for statistical purposes, the terms venture capital and private equity are also frequently used to define the operations of the various types of professional investors.

In the gradual standardisation of terminology at the international level, venture capital is coming to be seen as a subset of private equity. The definitions proposed by the two longest established investors' associations, the National Venture Capital Association (NVCA) and the European Private Equity & Venture Capital Association (EVCA), are more or less the same and inform us that private equity is an asset class which consists of equity investment in enterprises not listed on a stock market, while venture capital is, strictly speaking, a subset of private equity and refers to equity investments made for the launch, early development or expansion of a business.

Venture capital investment can be defined as the provision of share capital, or the underwriting of hybrid financing instruments, by specialist investors, in the medium-to-long term, in unlisted enterprises in the initial stages of their development cycles, which have high growth potential in terms of new products or services, new technologies or new market concepts. The investment is generally temporary and direct, and involves a minority holding, while the investor contributes financial and other know-how to the firm's development, enabling him to ensure that it increases its value and provides him with a capital gain on exit.

However, in spite of the standardisation of terminology witnessed of recent years, the meaning of these terms is not always absolutely clear, as the NVCA stress: 'there has been some recent confusion about the term private equity referring only to the buy-out/mezzanine portion of the private equity market' (2007, p. 57).

Achieving a clear definition of the meaning and context of this form of investment and the relative sector is no mere linguistic exercise: the lack of a common definition at the international level reflects uncertainty concerning the boundaries of this phenomenon which, together with the low level of disclosure provided by most of those in the industry, has restricted international statistical comparison for a long time and is making it a complex undertaking even today.

With regard to the problems of definition, according to some researchers a number of factors arise from the considerable increase in complexity of the various production sectors. On the one hand, firms' needs can no longer be identified in accordance with the traditional concepts which classify them on the basis of life cycle phase, while on the other, the application of rigid categorisation to the various types of investor is becoming less useful. According to Caselli and Gatti (2002), what really defines an investment operation as one of venture capital is not the life cycle of the investee company or the level of risk undertaken by the investor, but the nature of the risk itself. An operation involves venture capital when the investor assumes the entrepreneurial risk in addition to the financial and operating risks (Figure 5.1). This type of risk

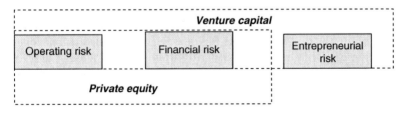

Figure 5.1 The different kinds of risk and the distinction between private equity and venture capital

is present when the investor's decision to invest in the business is dependent on a modification of the entrepreneurial formula of the company financed.

This factor is undeniably present when a new enterprise is founded, since by definition it must be based on a new entrepreneurial formula, but it also occurs in all expansion investments which allow existing companies to substantially redraw their competitive strategies, generating major changes in their operations. From this viewpoint, venture capital and private equity are two types of investment which succeed each other chronologically, depending on the firm's life cycle stage and the type of risk to which it is subject.

In this chapter, following the EVCA and NVCA definitions we use the term venture capital when looking at the activities of those investors who invest in firms in the phase of the life cycle starting from launch to expansion. Private equity is the provision of equity capital by financial investors over the medium or long term to non-quoted companies with high growth potential; as a consequence, venture capital is to be considered a subset of the general private equity activity.

Therefore, the venture capital investor is a financial intermediary capable of supporting and strengthening a company's growth and assisting it with strategic planning, management recruiting, operations planning or introductions to potential customers and suppliers (Gorman and Sahlman, 1989). In the light of these comments, it is clear that the demand for services linked to venture capital will probably come from new enterprises or existing firms which intend to speed up their growth process significantly.

Venture capital as a source of financing for the start-up and growth of enterprises is of major importance in an economy with a high proportion of SMEs, as in Europe, where companies in this category account for 99 per cent of the total and employ two-thirds of private sector workers. The European Commission (2006b) affirms that their success is inextricably linked with that of the EU.

The segment of private equity which concentrates on buy-out/mezzanine operations normally involves acquisitions of mature enterprises, with stable, clearly defined business plans, involving a lower degree of risk than operations in the venture capital segment. In operations of this kind, private equity operators generally use borrowed capital as a source of funds, and the term 'leveraged buy-out' is therefore used. This is a broad definition of the entire series of operations (both strictly corporate and strictly financial in nature) in which the aim is to acquire a company, or sometimes a corporate division, by exploiting the borrowing potential of the target company itself. The buy-out is carried through using borrowed capital provided by third parties as the main, and in some cases the only, source of financing. The relative loans are granted on the basis of the ability of the target company to meet the repayment commitments on the borrowed funds from its operating profits or the sale of non-strategic assets. Therefore, due to the large increase in indebtedness which they generate, for leveraged buy-outs to be successful, the efficiency of the target companies must be improved through organisational and managerial restructuring policies, cost-cutting exercises and the reinforcement of core business areas and the sale of those considered surplus to requirements, in order to stabilise cashflow trends.

However, the scale and number of such operations in recent years has drawn attention to the possible consequences of the resulting high levels of indebtedness, which place a large amount of stress on the organisational structure and risk causing a misalignment between the short-to-medium-term objectives of the private equity investors and the long-term aims of the target company. The apparently pitiless way in which they restructure the companies they acquire and their huge profits have created the image of private equity investors as greedy exploiters, relentlessly seeking profits just as 'locusts look for food'. One sign of this was the British General Workers' Union (GMB) protest at the Super Return conference in Frankfurt, which rapidly gave rise to a wide-ranging discussion of the role of the private equity industry (EVCA, 2007a).

The operators

After our examination of the definition of risk capital investment, it is important to make the high degree of complexity of operations of this kind clear once more. Such investment does not only involve acquisition of a holding in the company's equity or semi-equity, but may also include additional services of varying breadth and depth: strategic and managerial consulting, personnel recruitment, financial know-how and legal, fiscal and accounting advice, as well as assistance derived from the investor's network of acquaintances and relationships.

In view of the scope of these activities, it is useful to understand who the players who undertake risk capital investments are and how they operate, providing a variety of scenarios which will help to define the main characteristics of those involved.

In the international context, the subjects who engage in risk capital investment make up a composite universe; they differ from each other in the legal forms used, the aims pursued and the way in which the funds are raised. The differences between the investors found in the different economic contexts have a variety of origins, including the difference in the type of promoter organisation involved, and fiscal, organisational and legislative factors (Gompers and Lerner, 2006).

The first distinction is between institutional and other investors. Institutional investors engage continuously in risk capital investment; as we shall see, they are intermediaries established for this specific purpose, or financial operators which implement a systematic diversification of their asset portfolio. Non-institutional investors engage in operations of this kind on an occasional basis. If the definition is used, business angels, often classed as informal investors, may be further subdivided into the institutional and non-institutional categories, depending on the degree of continuity of their involvement in this investment area.

Another internationally used classification distinguishes between captive and independent investors, depending on the mechanisms used to raise funds for investment (Sahlman, 1990). Captive operators are direct offshoots of other financial or industrial institutions and obtain their capital from the parent company: they therefore do not use the capital market as a source of financial resources and their operating independence is limited. Most players in this category are financial institutions, such as merchant banks and corporate investors. Conversely, independent risk capital investment firms offer their services to a large number of investors; they therefore require results proving their ability to achieve good returns to persuade the potential investors to supply the capital they need. Recently, in response to the interest attracted by this form of investment, there has been an increase in the number of semi-captive firms, which use resources derived from the group to which they belong and from the capital market.

There is a further distinction between public and private investment organisations. For private operators, the aim is either to achieve an economic return or to acquire a technology in synergy with their own core business. Public investment organisations, on the other hand, use private equity and venture capital investments as a tool to support depressed geographical areas and disadvantaged industrial sectors, and to support the economy and employment in more general terms. This is demonstrated by the fact that, as we shall see in chapter 8, the role of public investment organisations is very closely correlated to the degree of development of the private sector, since its aim is to cover the areas of business where the latter is not active.

A more detailed classification can be drawn up on the basis of legal/organisational structure and operating characteristics (Table 5.1).

Table 5.1 The operators in the risk capital industry

Type of operator	Principal type of investment
a) Business angels	Initial start-up stages
b) Incubators	Initial start-up stages
c) Corporate venture capitalists	Venture capital
d) Closed end funds	Private equity and venture capital
e) Investment firms	Private equity and venture capital
f) Merchant banks	Private equity

Below we briefly examine these operators' main characteristics, focusing on the investors involved in the early stages of the enterprise's life cycle. Generally speaking, it is useful to remember that business angels and incubators usually engage in risk capital investment operations involving the first stages of the enterprise's life cycle: the seed, start-up and early stages. The other operators usually intervene during later phases. Nonetheless, exceptions can be recorded. As far as public investment organisation is concerned, they may be structured as closed-end funds or genuine venture capitalists. They often take the form of public–private partnerships.

Business angels

In the US and UK, where business angels are an established part of the financial scene, they are generally described as subjects with financial resources, managerial skills and a wide range of acquaintances, which they make available for the development of a business. This category is often referred to as the 'informal venture capital segment'. Since many operators in this sector wish to remain anonymous and not provide information about their investment activities, the lack of objective data makes it impossible to produce statistics representative of the entire sector and, as the European Commission (2003c) reminds us, we must be very cautious when drawing conclusions. This is because the market in which business angels operate is extremely heterogeneous: while some subjects make investments in a range of €500,000–1 million, there are also networks of business angels investing up to €4–5 million. Some of these operators may find themselves competing with venture capital firms. Syndicated operations by business angels are becoming more and more common, especially in the UK and Canada, where the US development model is being adopted (European Commission, 2003c).

Various studies inform us that business angels can play a very important role in reducing the problems of information asymmetry which may discourage traditional financiers, banks and even venture capitalists themselves.[1] By making early stage investments, they can help to facilitate access to other types of financial resources and thus assist in closing the equity gap. Their role is not merely that of suppliers of capital: they provide firms with formal and informal advice and mentoring, which is often an even more important contribution to their development than the capital itself: in this stage, the enterprises' financial needs may still be small, but their need for know-how is immense.

In the US, the role played by business angels in the seed and early stage operations is important: in 2005 they participated in about 50,000 projects, with an average investment of $5 million (Committee on Small Business House of Representatives, 2006). Unfortunately, the lack of reliable data on business angels' interventions do not permit us to evaluate the role played by informal investors in Europe.

More and more countries are introducing tax incentives to encourage potential business angels to purchase shares in SMEs. For example, the British government allows investors to deduct part of their investments from their income tax liability and to obtain tax exemptions on their capital gains. In the US, significant tax breaks on income tax, and especially on capital gains, have fostered the consolidation of the business angel system, with the benefits described above.

Incubators

This category of investors is more diversified than that of business angels, although they too provide support for the launch and development of new business ventures. The sector's complexity becomes apparent when we consider the classification of the possible different types of incubators in terms of structure, services offered and objectives. A distinction can be made between independent, private (profit-oriented) incubators, public (non-profit) incubators and incubators originating from the university system.

The founders of profit-oriented incubators may be individual entrepreneurs, private industrial groups or financial institutions, which assess the investment on the basis of profit only. The activities of corporate incubators are often in synergy with those of the companies which founded them. The companies admitted are selected on the basis of criteria which depend to a large extent on the purposes for which the incubators were created. They contribute to the success of start-ups in a variety of ways, one of which may be placing their own specialist staff in the various firms. They have close links with the risk capital market and adopt equity business models, investing in the firm's share capital or charging for the services supplied.

Non-profit incubators make premises and various services available to innovative firms at cost price, or in some cases free of charge. Their function is usually to develop new business initiatives and create new employment opportunities in particularly disadvantaged areas, where local government institutions hope to generate progress by this means.[2]

Lastly, university incubators are founded with the aim of encouraging interaction between university research and the world of business. The main intention is to bring research out of the university by encouraging the use of its results as the basis for the formation of companies, and promoting the application of research findings in industry. University incubators are generally non-profit and are located on campuses. They may be part of the university organisation itself, or run by university consortia. Unlike the other models, they have strong links with the world of research and often focus on specific areas in which the university that created them excels, such as nanotechnology, biotechnology, life sciences, and so on.

While the number of private incubators has decreased over time, the number of university incubators has gradually risen.

Over the years there has been a profound evolution in the role played by incubators, their organisations and the services offered, and there are currently sometimes considerable differences between the functions they provide: premises and shared resources, specialist services and networked knowledge.

Incubators differ from both business angels and venture capitalists in the completeness of the accessory services supplied (from assistance in drafting the business plan to the sharing of technological resources, assistance with accounting services, legal and tax consulting, assistance in implementation of the marketing plan, and so on), since they serve ventures still in the seed capital stage or, in the most extreme cases, projects which are still more business ideas than enterprises as such.

Corporate venture capitalists

They are captive operators, generally the specialist divisions of large industrial corporations. They are therefore highly specialised in the various high-tech sectors such as life sciences, biotechnology, information technology and telecommunications. Their operations may take many different forms, involving the acquisition of minority or majority holdings, almost always through an increase in the capital of the investee company. This particular investor's final objective is not the generation of a capital gain, but rather the acquisition of the financial venture by the parent company.

Closed-end funds

Closed-end funds are financial intermediaries which raise funds for professional joint investment purposes through the sale of shares. These funds are a vehicle both for the collective investment of savings and for the raising of huge financial resources from institutional investors and corporations. The fact that they are closed-end makes this type of instrument particularly suitable for the medium-to-long-term investments typical of private equity and venture capital operations.

Funds of this kind, traditionally the most common category of investor, often enter into limited partnerships, which we discuss below. Their management strategies depend on the regulatory framework in each country: in some states, they are obliged to diversify their investment portfolio, while in others their managers have complete freedom of action. Some closed-end funds are prepared to invest in any stage of the enterprise's life cycle, while others are more specialised, focusing their activities on individual industrial sectors, enterprise life cycle stages or geographical areas.

Apart from their closed-end nature, instruments of this type have other features which make them particularly adaptable and effective for risk capital investment activities:

- *The separation between the fund and the company which manages it*; the fund invests third-party capital. This allows the management team to act independently and select what it considers to be the best investment opportunities, and reduces the decision-making time involved in the preparation and finalisation of investments. Within the fund's organisational structures, the managers' priority objective is the optimisation of the risk/return combination. As we shall see, this is facilitated by incentives (carried interest) which give an entrepreneurial aspect to the fund managers' role.
- *The fund's pre-set life*: The life cycle of the closed-end fund, which will be wound up when the shares are liquidated, enables investors to see the real outcome of the operations in the form of the return generated, within a pre-defined time scale.

Investment firms

They engage in merchant banking activities, but are not directly derived from banks; rather, they are independent operators which work as companies and obtain the funds needed for their operations from institutional investors.

Although apparently similar to closed-end funds, investment firms differ from them above all from a formal point of view, since the assets they manage are the capital of the company itself. Each investor is therefore also a shareholder in the investment firm.

From an operational point of view, they are able to undertake the same operations as a merchant bank, but the focus is different because their main activity is the acquisition of lasting holdings in the capital of new enterprises, in both the initial and later stages of their development.

Merchant banks

Merchant banks are captive organisations, part of the banking system, which supply various financial services. These include share acquisitions, financial consulting, assistance in extraordinary financial operations (mergers, acquisitions and restructuring) and assistance during the initial public offering (IPO). The distinctive features of merchant banks in the risk capital market are linked to the fact that there are no limits on operations in terms of time and quantity. Moreover, they can obtain a return in terms of both capital gain and fees for the advisory services they provided.

It is therefore clear that risk capital investment is not merchant banks' core business, but merely one of their areas of activity.

The proportion of the venture capital market occupied by each of the types of operator described above is different in each country. In the US and the UK, the majority of venture capitalists are structured as single companies that manage several funds simultaneously, each legally distinct from the other, in a limited partnership. As mentioned, the success of this organisational structure is essentially due to the fiscal advantages that can be obtained. In continental Europe, the prevalent structure is the closed-end fund, similar in many respects to the limited partnership found in the US and UK (EVCA, 1999).

Types of operation

Risk capital operations undertaken at different stages in the development of a company vary in financial scale, prospects and underlying assumptions, and are the outcome of the combination of two key features of this type of investment business: the availability of capital and know-how. As mentioned above, apart from the standard distinction based on legal/organisational form, there is a further segmentation of the risk capital market which distinguishes between types of operation on the basis of the target enterprise's life cycle stage.

Operations, and the relative risks accepted by the investor, are subdivided into:

- start-up financing;
- expansion financing;
- change (or replacement) financing.

As the firm's maturity increases and it moves on from one stage to the next, the capital needed to carry out the operation and the know-how required change, and the level of risk involved also varies.

Start-up financing

This category includes all operations intended to support the birth of a new enterprise, in both the seed and the very early launch stages. Vesper (1993) produced a model which identifies a number of essential steps to be performed during the creation of a firm: those involved must take the opportunity, perfect the idea, protect against copying, establish the team, obtain financing, start up the business and launch the product. Application of this model to the venture capital context enables us to define the specific characteristics of investments of this kind: in the start-up stage, they constitute more a contribution to defining the business plan than a financial operation as such.

A widely accepted classification breaks down start-up operations by development sub-stage:

- The term *seed financing* is used when the investor is involved as early as the trial stages, when the entrepreneur has an idea or an invention rather than a product. The technical worth of the product or service is not proven and often the investor is working with someone who is not yet an entrepreneur in the sense of acquiring the necessary skills. Generally, the strategy and business plan have not been drawn up and the operator requires managerial, technical and scientific know-how.
- The subsequent *start-up stage* is when production begins, even though the commercial worth of the product/service has still not been

absolutely established. Compared to the previous phase, trials have now been completed and the product has been developed and verified. The bases for founding a business are thus present.

- Finally, *first stage financing* supports the speed-up of the growth in production.

From this we can see that, in the initial stages, the new enterprise requires both financial resources and technical know-how; this explains why these stages are dominated by business angels, incubators and corporate venture capitalists.

Expansion financing

This risk capital investment area includes investments intended to increase the rate of development and expansion of enterprises which have successfully concluded the crucial start-up stage. These investments have a lower level of risk than those in the initial start-up stages, since the investee companies have an organisational structure and a portfolio of products/services which have been presented on the market with some degree of success, as well as established relationships with both suppliers and customers. Due to these factors, prior assessment of investments made in this stage is less problematic.

Generally, three types of operations are included in this category:

- *Second stage financing.* Once the commercial worth of the product/service has been verified, the investor provides funds to increase the production capacity and sales. The aim is to speed up the enterprise's growth. In this stage, the firm is starting to generate cashflows, but new funds have to be raised to support the additional investments needed to achieve optimal growth.
- *Third stage financing.* The company is now in a position where it has to consolidate its growth by defending its position against competitors and developing new plans and strategies. These may include the launch of new products, expansion and diversification of production or distribution operations, or the acquisition of competitor firms.
- *Fourth stage financing.* The investor puts his funds into a mature company with consolidated positions. These investments are often over even shorter time scales but are of a larger size, made before the company takes major steps such as stock market listing or a merger. In investments of this kind, the financial aspect is of much greater importance than the investor's management input.

Change (or replacement) financing

The third category of risk capital investment is intended to finance the processes by which the firm consolidates the competitive positions it has acquired, and often coincides with changes of varying importance in the company's ownership structure. Investments in this category are more independent than the others we have seen of the stage the company has reached in its development. Here again, the literature identities various sub-categories:

- *Replacement capital* is the term used when the investor buys into the firm to replace minority shareholders wishing to dispose of their holdings, whose departure does not signify a major change in the company's strategy.
- A *buy-out* involves a radical change in the company's ownership.
- *Turnaround financing* is undertaken when the company is in serious financial difficulty, which can only be solved through radical action on the part of the owners and/or managers. Here the project is one of financial, and more often operational, restructuring of the target company. Therefore, as well as capital, the investor contributes professional know-how, which assumes considerable importance. Turnaround operations thus often take the form of management buy-ins, in which the investor provides financial resources and puts in place a new management, given further incentives through participation in the business risk.

Types of risk undertaken

As we have seen, the risks undertaken by a risk capital investor are high, although they are theoretically lower in the case of development, growth consolidation, mezzanine and buy-out operations. In the case of venture capital operations, on the other hand, investments are intended to develop new business ideas, and new products or technologies not yet, or not fully, proven. The abilities of the entrepreneur, who is often young, are thus crucial to the success of the project. Moreover, in most cases, and in the early stage in particular, the enterprise has few or no assets which can provide the financier with collateral, although anyone operating in this sector is not interested in collateral as the basis for an investment.

As well as the strictly financial risks involved in the provision of risk or debt capital (which are thus not specific to venture capital, since they are the same in other forms of investment), unlike other investments, venture capital projects also involve:

- A *product risk*, deriving from the nature of the business; this is particularly high in the early stage, because the venture capitalist makes his investment at a time when the technical soundness of the business itself still has to be verified.
- A *market risk*, related to the size and structure of the demand for the business being financed and the company's position in relation to any competitors; here again, the early stage is particularly problematic as the business's commercial soundness is still uncertain.
- A *managerial risk*, deriving on the one hand from uncertainty regarding the entrepreneur's ability to bring his business into being successfully, and on the other from the fact that his contribution to achieving this is essential. Once again, this risk is particularly high in the early stage, because the entrepreneur is the holder of the idea underlying the project and the technical means for bringing it about.

These risks, present during the initial stages of the company's life cycle, explain why seed and early stage investments can be so unattractive (as they require large amounts of know-how and professional skill) and why such high returns are possible, although in most cases they are not achieved.

Figure 5.2 illustrates the entire investment cycle. It shows that the cashflow reaches its lowest ebb in the central stage of the seed phase of the start-up, when investments have to be made to start the business (R&D and creation of the organisational, production and sales structures) and earnings are still minimal.

The studies[3] reveals that there is a grey area, the so-called equity gap, in which business angels and incubators are no longer able to support the investee's growing financial needs, but institutional investors (closed-end funds, investment firms and merchant banks) are not yet involved. Due to the particular profile of the investment, with high levels of uncertainty and information asymmetries, which require specific technical skills and know-how, and also the dimensions of the operation (still too small to provide satisfactory returns in relation to the level of risk involved and the agency costs incurred), investors in these last-named categories normally prefer not to invest in firms in this phase of their growth cycle.

The uncertainty and information asymmetries are even greater in the case of innovative SMEs (ISMEs), making it even more difficult for

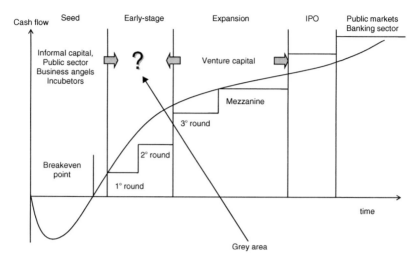

Figure 5.2 The entire investment cycle – the existence of the equity gap
Source: European Commission (2005a, p. 8).

them to access funds. Earnings cannot be quantified with any degree of certainty and are extremely variable, while returns are low, especially during the early stage. Moreover, the evaluation of firms in this stage is particularly problematic: a large proportion of their assets are intangible and difficult to evaluate in monetary terms before they have generated positive commercial returns. Financing ISMEs is therefore considered riskier, due to the difficulty in overcoming the problems of information asymmetries. This has led to the proliferation of government initiatives to attempt to fill the equity gap facing innovative firms, as described in chapter 8.

The investment process in private equity and venture capital

An operator making an investment in risk capital[4] implements a strategic plan with a beginning, duration and end. The fact that these investors work to a limited time horizon means that when the potential investment is assessed, it is essential to define its possible performance and to forecast all possible future scenarios in order to evaluate the compatibility between the expected return and the riskiness of the target investment. The meaning of the term 'strategy' is the subject of much discussion in the literature; here, by strategy we are referring to a system of specific

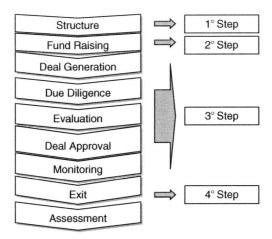

Figure 5.3 The operating cycle of a risk capital investor

objectives intended to guide medium-to-long-term development decisions. This concept must not be confused with management planning.
The difference lies in the fact that the strategy sets the system of aims
to be achieved, while planning decides the actions and tools needed to
attain them. Thus, the strategy is agreed first, and planning and action
then follow. The appropriate term for a risk capital investment is thus
strategy, since the investor is undertaking an operation with a limited
time scale.

Many studies[5] have investigated the fund-raising, deal finalisation,
monitoring and exit stages of investments of this kind. In-depth analysis
of investors' operations has allowed us to draw up a figure illustrating the
operating cycle of a risk capital investor (Figure 5.3).

For the purposes of this chapter, the operating cycle of a risk capital
investor can be summarised in the following steps:

1 organisational structure;
2 fund-raising aspects;
3 phases related to the investment process as such: origination, evaluation, acquisition of the holding, management and monitoring of the
   investment;
4 decisions related to the exit strategy.

From the organisational point of view, the *structure* adopted by many
independent or semi-captive investors at the international level is the

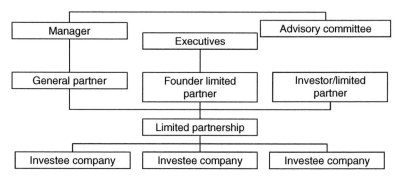

Figure 5.4   The structure of the limited partnership

limited partnership (European Commission, 2006a), which is a contract between two clearly identified parties: the limited partners and the general partners (Figure 5.4). The institutional investors, who supply the capital, are the limited partners, while the professional private equity managers or venture capitalists act as general partners and are responsible for management of the funds received. The limited partnership has a pre-set duration (normally ten years), during which the general partners select the deals, structure the operations, perform monitoring so that action can be taken if the investees' performance falls below expectations and study the best ways out in the interest of the limited partners. In exchange, they receive a management fee to cover the routine overheads, and above all a share of the return generated by the investment (carried interest). This type of remuneration structure limits the problems of moral hazard between the limited and general partners. It must also be said that, since they are independent investors, the general partners will be interested in raising new funds by establishing new limited partnerships, and will only be successful if they can show a track record in line with the risk/return profile required by investors.

In addition to limited partnerships, there are other forms of organisation in general use, such as venture and development capital investment trusts (VDCITs) and venture capital trusts (VCTs) found in the UK. Trusts are listed closed-end funds. VCTs are a particular kind of private equity fund, where the profits distributed to investors enjoy lower rates of taxation in exchange for constraints on the type of investments chosen. They have been developed with two clear aims: to encourage investment in the venture capital of young companies; and to attract non-professional investors towards this sector of asset management.

Fund-raising is of fundamental importance for the subsequent implementation of the investment strategy. The fund-raising strategy must therefore be carefully planned, profiling the category of investors who may be interested in the project and deciding the best approach to adopt. The main fund-raising channel is the network of relationships between the project's promoters and the potential investors. The fund-raising strategy will vary depending on whether or not the operation is the first time those involved have worked in this area. The operator normally starts to raise new funds when the vehicle used is almost ready for full investment and the track-record of the operations performed is available for examination. It is important to note that when an investor, such as the limited partner, undertakes to pay in a given amount of capital, this amount is the theoretical maximum investment. Generally, the venture capitalist will request the sums needed to finance the investments approved in such a way as to minimise the funds granted and not invested in order to maximise the internal rate of return. These transfers from investors to venture capitalists are called draw-downs.

Gompers and Lerner (2006) underline various factors influencing fund-raising policy, such as changes in regulations which may affect specific categories of investors (for example, pension funds), possible changes to tax law, the performance of the global economy and the operator's reputation.

For 2006, according to EVCA, in Europe pension funds were the largest contributor to the funds raised, followed by fund of funds, banks and insurance companies, as outlined in chapter 6. In the US, the situation is quite different, with an important role played by private individuals investors and academic institutions.

Sources of venture capital and private equity funds also differ across countries; for example, banks are particularly important in Germany and Japan, corporations in Israel and pension funds in the UK (Mayer et al., 2004). In fact, in Germany, banks are by far the most important source of finance for the venture capital industry, and pension funds are conspicuously absent. By contrast, in the UK pension funds, other institutional investors and individual investors provide funds to as many companies as banks. Contrary to popular opinion, government (typically local authority) funding plays a more important role in the UK than it does in Germany and is negligible in the other countries. Funds for the Israeli venture capital industry come from a wide variety of sources, with industrial corporations (typically from the US) being the single most popular source. In Japan, non-banking financial institutions (for example, securities firms, credit card or leasing companies and mortgage institutions) are the single most important category of finance, followed by banks and insurance companies. Venture capital funds in Germany tend on average to use fewer sources of funds than venture capitalists in other countries; by contrast, funds in Israel, Japan and the UK tend to use a large number of sources of finance; in particular, about a third of the UK funds report using at least four different sources.

To understand the complexity of the risk capital *investment process*, it is worth quoting a statement made by Doriot in 1940: 'Always consider investing in a grade A man with a grade B idea. Never invest in a grade B man with a grade A idea' (cited in Bygrave and Timmons, 1992, p. 12). When choosing his investments, if he is to make choices which are sufficiently rational from a financial point of view in a context with a high degree of information uncertainty, the investor needs the interaction of a number of objective factors (the strict application of selection methods) and subjective ones (experience and intuition). The use of a strict assessment method is vital for the best use of one of the resources in short supply for the venture capitalist: the time needed to manage the investment. The tendency is thus to implement strict pre-selection, with the aim of reducing the number of possible projects considered and optimising the time involved in each. According to NVCA (2007), for every 100 business plans that come to a venture capital firm for funding, usually only ten or so get a serious look, and only one ends up being funded.

The process by which the target company or enterprise project is assessed can be divided into two stages (Caselli and Gatti, 2002):

a) *Pre-investment phase*, involving assessment of the presence and importance of a number of critical factors which may decide whether or not the investor is interested. This initial screening stage depends to a large extent on the strategic orientation of the risk capital investor: non-profit, profit or strategically oriented.

b) *Selection process*: this is the central stage of the assessment process, setting the values which will form the focus of the negotiations between the operator and the investee project. In this stage, all the audits necessary for the final assessment of the investment are performed, with evaluation of its current status and above all its future potential. This audit process is known as the due diligence investigation, and is carried out in order to verify the truthfulness and formal correctness of the information on the basis of which the company is evaluated. This complex activity is vital in that it protects the capital invested if it should subsequently emerge that the data used for the assessment,

supplied by the company or the entrepreneur, were intentionally mis-
leading, triggering errors in the investor's estimate. Depending on the
aspects surveyed, the due diligence investigation can be subdivided
into:

- *Market due diligence*, which allows the investor to understand
  fully the potential and risks of the specific market in which
  the company operates and its positioning within the market.
  The market due diligence is developed in order to compare the
  results with the future plans presented in the business plan of the
  entrepreneur.
- *Environmental due diligence*, which considers the legislation and
  environmental regulations to identify the impact of changes on
  the company business.
- *Financial due diligence*, performed to evaluate the economic/financial
  aspects of the company's plans and define the necessary financing.
- *Legal due diligence*, which focuses on the problems of a legal nature
  that may influence the evaluation of the company or business.
- *Tax due diligence*, which analyses the fiscal aspects related to the
  company, in order to find potential liabilities and pitfalls.

Once the due diligence phase has been concluded, the main objective
of the final evaluation is to set the price, and thus the composition of
the capital employed.

The exact composition of the funds which operators use to make their
investments varies over time in response to changes in market conditions and financial innovation; it also varies depending on the size and
nature of the deal. The funds venture capitalists use for operations involving small firms, usually in the early stages of their life cycle, consist of
equity, shareholder loans and sometimes senior amortising debt. The
level of indebtedness is usually close to zero. In deals involving medium-
sized enterprises, borrowed capital accounts for a larger proportion of the
funds used, either as the main or a secondary component, as in the case
of mezzanine debt. Deals relating to mature (mainly large) companies
have a higher degree of financial leverage, with a complex debt capital
structure.

It must be remembered that a risk capital investor, and especially a
venture capitalist, does not merely finance a business project; he provides
the entrepreneur with a genuine partner. In this sense, private equity is
not just an asset class: it actually has a dual nature, as asset class and
active investor. In chapter 6 we discuss private equity from the point of
view of the returns it is able to yield and offer to investors.

The type of support in the choice of strategic plans and operating management depends on the nature of both the venture capitalist and the investment. The distinction is usually made between hands-on investors, whose non-financial contributions to the firm are of considerable importance for its growth, and the hands-off variety, who simply supply share capital and monitor the performance of their investment (Sweeting and Wong, 1997).

Risk capital investment can be considered as a hybrid system: a variant of *relationship-based financing* (Gompers and Lerner, 1998), which depends on the efficient operation of the *arm's length financial system* (Black and Gilson, 1998). Investment in risk capital, and especially venture capital, has to overcome a variety of problems. Start-ups, which have not yet built up a reputation on the markets in which they work, or in the capital markets, are faced with the problems of the agency costs arising from the information asymmetries between borrowers and lenders. Relationship-based financing is able to mitigate these factors by encouraging the screening, monitoring and control of the venture-backed firms (Gompers, 1995).

Venture capital investors have four main tools at their disposal for efficient regulation of their relationship with the firm in which they have invested:

- Through *stage financing* (Gompers, 1995; Sahlman, 1988): the capital is provided in a number of consecutive rounds, often each conditional on the achievement of targets set in advance. In this context, the firm's prospects are assessed on a regular basis. The shorter the gap between financing rounds, the more often the venture capitalist monitors the progress the company has made, providing him with a larger amount of information. In effect, the role of staged capital infusion is similar to that of debt in leveraged buy-out operations: 'keeping the owner/manager on a tight leash and reducing potential losses from bad decision' (Gompers and Lerner, 2006, p. 161).
- The use of *special instruments* such as convertible preferred shares offers a means of solving the trade-off between providing sufficient incentive for the entrepreneur and allowing the investor to monitor the firm (Gompers, 1997).
- *Board representation* allows involvement in defining the main lines of the company's strategy, while using restrictive covenants places restrictions on the firm's freedom of action (Kaplan and Stromberg, 2003).
- Last but not least, the use of *specific contract clauses*, approved at the point of investment, relating to possible disinvestment options,

reduces the degree of uncertainty about the way out, crucial for the success of the investment (Szego, 2002).

The common denominator in all of these investments is that the investor (venture capitalist or operator in private equity) is not a passive investor, but has an active and vested interest in guiding, leading and growing the companies they have invested in. The aim is to create value through the expertise gained from past investments in other firms.

In the context of private equity, evaluation is never merely a theoretical or abstract term; it always takes the form of a real, effective price, which will form the basis for the transaction.

The price of the deal depends less on valuation methods involving general parameters than on a calculation based on data which are as near as possible to reality and can be tested, leaving it to the market and the negotiations to identify the correct parameter. Therefore, the aim of the evaluation process of the target firm is not so much to estimate its value as to supply a price. This process is therefore also influenced by the negotiations between the parties and the relative bargaining power of each. Consequently, although the literature provides a variety of evaluation methods, at an international level the calculation method most widely used in the private equity and venture capital market is the multiples method, due to the simplicity, immediacy and easily identifiable nature of the parameters considered (Gervasoni and Sattin, 2000).

The *exit stage* is the final step in the investment process. At the end of the holding period considered appropriate, the investment must be disposed of in order to bring the risk capital operation to completion.

The institutional risk capital investor is a temporary partner whose interest is in achieving a capital gain by selling the holding once the objectives have been achieved. Disinvestment is thus the crucial operation by which the investor disposes of all or part of his holding.

The problems the investor may face are identifying the best time to disinvest and choosing the channel for disposing of his investment.

The moment when the investor disposes of his holding in the firm's equity is almost never decided in advance; it will depend on the company's growth pattern. If the investment is successful, the venture capitalist disinvests when the firm has reached the planned level of development and its value has increased accordingly. If the project is a failure, for example because the new product or technology has not been successfully established on the market, the investor pulls out when he is convinced that the company's financial problems are insurmountable.

The disinvestment channel may be chosen when the initial deal is finalised or selected later: depending on the weight given to the disinvestment strategy when the investment decision is taken, the literature makes a distinction between the path sketcher and opportunist approaches (Wall, 1998). The path sketcher investor plans his exit in advance, and during the lifetime of the investment concentrates his efforts on achieving the pre-set aim; the opportunist investor, on the other hand, does not plan a way out when deciding whether to make the investment, confident that he will be able to obtain the best possible conditions when the time comes to disinvest.

There are several exit models:

- *Trade sale* (merger and acquisition) through private agreement with varying methods: sale of the holding to new shareholders, industrial or financial; merger with other companies; sale of the holding to the majority shareholder or management.
- *Quotation*, after a public offering.
- *Write-off.* This is not an exit strategy as such, but rather the worst-case scenario, in which the value of the holding is written off if the investment ends in bankruptcy.

Choosing the right models and times is fundamental, moreover the decision is affected by a variety of factors. There are external factors, such as the conditions on the financial markets, and internal ones, such as the size of the holding to be disposed of. The situation changes a great deal depending on whether a majority or minority holding is to be sold; a trade sale is generally preferred in the former case, and stock market listing by means of an initial public offering in the latter.

Apart from the external and internal variables, in most cases listing on a stock market is the favoured way out, but careful consideration must be given to its advantages and disadvantages. The main benefits derive from:

- demand from a wide spread of buyers, allowing equity holdings to be disposed of gradually, taking advantage of any increases in the share price;
- the possibility of obtaining higher prices when market conditions permit; positive return for the corporate image.

The main disadvantages are:

- the cost factor, this is considerably more expensive than the alternative disinvestment mechanisms;

- lock-up clauses, which may prevent liquidation of the entire holding;
- the impossibility of using this option in the case of firms which are not of interest to the market, for example due to their small size.

If listing is the selected way out, the choice of market as described in chapter 7 is extremely important. Choosing the stock market on which a company intends to have its shares listed is crucial, especially with regard to the effects of this decision on corporate strategy overall. Apart from effects directly linked to the firm's financial management, membership of a financial market also has consequences for the company's image and credibility in relation to customers, suppliers and potential partners.

Normally, mergers and acquisitions represent the most common type of successful exit for risk capital investments and serve as an alternative to an initial public offering exit. However, it must be underlined that this form of exit is particularly complex, especially because the agreement of both the management and the other shareholders is required. The management may block operations of this kind if the buyer is an industrial partner, fearing possible substitutions. This way out is normally quicker, has none of the costs involved in stock market listing and is the only possible option in the case of many enterprises, and, finally, the buyer may be strategically interested in the company offered for sale and thus willing to offer a higher price.

Once the holding has been sold, the risk capital investor will be able to distribute the revenues from the sale to the limited partners.

6
Size and Evolution of the Risk Capital Industry

Alessandro G. Grasso

Introduction

Operation in the risk capital industry is a very complex undertaking. This complexity derives both from the different main objectives which may be pursued through investments of this kind and the wide variety of organisational/institutional forms involved. Further uncertainty arises from the lack of a standardised definition; this is a hindrance to the publication of data in forms allowing fully reliable comparisons to be made. Nonetheless, this chapter intends to provide a quantitative picture of the private equity and venture capital industry, highlighting the most recent developments in the sector and outlining the main differences still affecting some of the main countries in the European area.

Our survey starts from a comparison between the US and Europe, the two macro areas of reference in which this industry is most highly developed, before moving on to examine in depth the trends in the main European countries: the UK, France, Germany, Sweden, Italy, Spain and the Netherlands, chosen because they accounted for 95 per cent of the total investments in private equity in Europe during 2006.

The drivers of evolution

According to data supplied by the EVCA (2007a), at year-end 2006, private equity operators world-wide were managing funds of an amazing $1.3 trillion, almost 100 times more than 15 years ago. This growth rate and the increasing attention focused on the sector by the academic world, policy-makers and, more recently, the media, may lead us to forget that private equity is in fact a very recent phenomenon.

This growth in the funds raised and capital invested has been accompanied by a growth in quality terms, involving both the types of operators and the operations carried out, as the industry continues to extend its geographical and operating boundaries.

Generally, the growth drivers of this sector of the financial industry can be studied from both the demand and the supply sides. From the demand side, faced with the gradual reduction of the role of banks, which has occurred in many economies, and especially in Europe, enterprises have been searching for the right amounts of the appropriate types of capital to support and grow their business ideas, especially in the most innovative sectors. In addition, the presence of specialist equity investment firms, viewed as a positive sign by traditional lenders, has often been useful in providing more favourable conditions for access to credit. Simultaneously, for the first time in history the delicate generational handover has occurred in a large number of enterprises concurrently, creating an opening for professionals specialising in the management of this crucial transition.

On the supply side, investors have been looking for new investment opportunities enabling them to increase the return on their portfolios. As we shall discuss in detail in chapter 7, the growth of the financial markets and the creation of new markets and specific segments focusing on firms with high growth potential has expanded the range of possible disinvestment strategies, making it easier for the risk capital investment sector to achieve large capital gains. The rising number of market operators of this kind and the ongoing consolidation of their performances has attracted ever-increasing attention from investors. Paradoxically, this high degree of attention may become the main cause of a future deceleration in this sector, because 'the financial performance of the industry ultimately drives its success' but 'when there is too much money chasing too few good deals, those good deals tend to be bid up in price early on, making it difficult for venture capital general partners to reward their investors with suitable returns' (EVCA, 2007a, p. 22).

Although investment in risk capital has historical origins (the operations undertaken by British merchants in the fifteenth century, or the later role of the India companies in the development of international trade are only the most obvious examples), there is general agreement that the real venture capital and private equity market was born in the US with the pioneering activities undertaken from the 1940s by L. Rockefeller and J. Whitney. At that time, the investment process was almost entirely in the hands of families and private investors who used their own resources, since the practice of raising funds from the public and institutional investors had not yet been established (Wilson, 1985). The foundation of the American Research and Development Corporation (ARD) in 1946 was the first major step towards the creation of a financial sector operating on the principles of private equity and venture capital. Specifically, the ARD pioneered the practical experimentation of a number of features of venture capital as we understand it today: it raised funds from the public, invested in high-tech enterprises and provided managerial assistance to firms.

In practice, such activities were limited in scale until 1958, when the US Congress passed the Small Business Investment Act. Together with other measures discussed in detail in chapter 8, this Act authorised the establishment of Small Business Investment Companies (SBICs), private firms which could access financing and collateral to allow them to invest in unlisted small enterprises. Subsequently, reductions in the rate of taxation of capital gains, and especially the repeal in 1979 of the Employee Retirement Income Security Act (ERISA), which forbade pension funds from investing in venture capital or other high-risk asset classes, encouraged strong growth in the flows of funds towards this type of intermediary. With the passage of time and the coming to maturity of the sector, this growth has increased dramatically, in spite of periods of contraction of economic growth and alternating trends in share prices on the official markets.

Turning our attention to Europe, the birth and development of the private equity market can be traced to the UK. It is a widely believed that, apart from sporadic individual events such as the establishment in 1945 of the Industrial and Commercial Finance Corporation (ICFC), known today as 3i – Investors in Industry – one of Europe's biggest institutional investors, until the 1980s the European private equity sector was about a quarter of a century behind its US counterpart in terms of its development (Cary, 1999). The birth of a real European venture capital and private equity industry can be traced to the 1980s, with a number of formal measures, (Gervasoni and Sattin, 2000). Among them, in December 1980 the Council of Europe, recognising the strategic importance of the development of new technologies and the difficulties European small entrepreneurs were having in accessing the risk capital market, decided to create its Venture Capital Liaison Office, with the task of establishing contacts between potential investors and investees. Subsequently, in August 1983, the EU was involved in the formation of the European Private Equity and Venture Capital Association (EVCA). Partly thanks to these organisations, since the 1990s the European market has enjoyed rapid growth, even though, as we shall see, there have been periods of sharp deceleration.

Elsewhere, with the exceptions of Canada, Israel and Japan, the risk capital investment sector has developed with a time-lag of several decades, although the gap has been narrowing. Wright et al. (2005) provide an interesting survey of the research which has attempted to explain the drivers underlying the growth of private equity and venture capital in different geographical contexts.

Black and Gilson (1998) show that the larger number of operators involved in this sector in economic systems which have more highly developed stock markets may be explained by the greater ease with which exit strategies can be created. Jeng and Wells (2000) and Megginson (2004), on the other hand, support the reasoning of Black and Gilson, but consider that the growth of market capitalisation is not vital for the appearance of venture capital and private equity operators; in their view, policy measures can have more impact by modifying the regulatory framework. Jeng and Wells also make an important distinction between factors that encourage the spread of early stage rather than later stage venture capital, noting that the process of stock market listing (IPOs) is only crucial for later stage investment. In this area, Bottazzi and Da Rin (2002) reveal that the presence of venture capital intermediaries does not necessarily lead to an increase in the number of stock market flotations. Nye and Wasserman (1999) studied the growth of the venture capital sector in India and Israel, and concluded that different degrees of political interest, quality of infrastructures and cultural factors may create differences in the development of venture capital markets. Kenney et al. (2002) reached similar conclusions from their examination of the Asian markets. They also suggest that the risk capital investment industry may generate different types of operators, with specific objectives, depending on the economic context.

The importance of risk capital investment at the international level during the last few years is due to the role of a variety of factors. On the one hand, a large number of developing countries are pursuing radical reforms in an attempt to attract the attention of investors seeking new business areas as the number of investment opportunities in the traditional market contracts (Gompers and Lerner, 1998); on the other, opportunities are arising for transnational investment (Aylward, 1998) by foreign operators in economic contexts where there is little domestic capital available, helping to stimulate the financial and economic growth of these contexts (Maula and Mäkelä, 2003). Recently, the sovereign funds have also been turning their attention to this area, especially the

Chinese government, which purchased a 10 per cent stake in one of the world's largest private equity fund management firms, Blackstone Group Investment, at the time of its stock market flotation.

Alongside the increase in the amount of capital raised, the regulators have also been showing increasing interest in the risk capital investment sector. For example, in 2006, for the first time, the Financial Services Authority (2006) turned its attention to the private equity market by surveying its recent developments: the growing level of institutionalisation of the investor base, a strong role for the managers of the investee companies, development of a secondary market in the sector, standardisation of the private equity model, more competition and an increase in the number of corporate delistings.

Europe vs. the US: a closer look

Although the trend in Europe and the US, the two most highly developed geographical areas (Figure 6.1), has been one of growth overall, there have been times when the market has contracted. The favourable trend in the financial markets, which have thus offered a possible way out for this type of investment, has been one influence on operators' investment decisions.

As Figure 6.1 shows, historically the amount of funds raised for private equity operations has been higher in the US than the European market, although the gap between the two is gradually closing. Until 2000 the US market grew rapidly, peaking at almost 2 per cent of GDP. This value, never subsequently equalled, was followed by a drastic decline, triggered by the bursting of the dot.com bubble on the stock markets, which in 2002 brought the situation in the US in line with that in Europe. The US market then started to grow again rapidly, reflecting the sector's flexibility and maturity. In Europe, at the same time, after two years of relative tranquillity, the annual commitment as a proportion of GDP increased drastically, almost making up the historic deficit compared to the US.

This outstanding performance of the European market can be traced to the many large industrial groups' need for restructuring and privatisation, the problems related to the generational transition as the founders of many firms bowed out and the opportunities for the launch of new, high-tech business ventures. These conditions provided a growing number of opportunities for investment in start-up, expansion, replacement and buy-out operations, while simultaneously attracting huge amounts of capital, partly from foreign investors, especially from the US, in search of more attractive investments. It is worth mentioning that 28.8 per cent

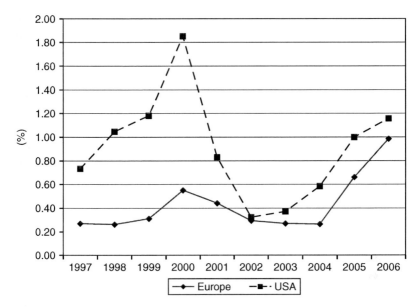

Figure 6.1   Europe vs. US – funds raised on GDP (%)
Source: elaborations on EVCA (2007a) and NVCA (2007). For GDP: Eurostat and US Bureau of Economis Analysis.

of the funds raised on the European market in 2006 came from US investors (EVCA, 2007a).

Considering the expected allocation of the funds raised in 2006, both the US and the European markets confirm the trend noted since 2001, in which buy-out operations continue to be the main investment strategy (Figure 6.2). In Europe, the amount of capital committed for venture capital investments surged to €17.5 billion, but in spite of this, three-quarters of the funds raised were utilised for buy-out operations. On the US market, the funds raised for venture capital operations amounted to $29.9 billion, and here again the attractiveness of buy-outs was confirmed, accounting for 80.4 per cent of the capital committed.

Focusing on venture capital operations alone, and considering the 2002–6 trend, there is a clear prevalence of expansion operations on both the US and the European markets (Figure 6.3). Bearing in mind the definitions supplied by the two largest associations in the industry, different segmentations emerge in the venture capital sector as a whole; to allow more immediate comparison, we subdivided venture capital into two discrete areas. To avoid terminological confusion, the two areas are called

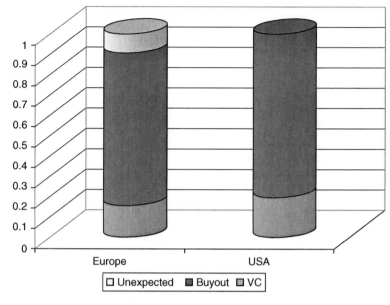

Figure 6.2   Europe vs. US – expected allocation of funds raised in 2006 (%)
Source: based on EVCA (2007a) and NVCA (2007).

Stage A and Stage B. Stage A includes all investments made in firms in the initial, seed and start-up stages of their life cycles, and Stage B, all operations relating to the subsequent expansion stage.[1] Considering Stage B alone, for the US market the average threshold is around 80.4 per cent for the period. The European market also shows a clear prevalence of Stage B operations, although for 2006 an increase in the amount invested in seed and start-up financing operations can be noted. Seed operations in particular grew considerably, with an increase from €97 million in 2005 to €1.7 billion in 2006, while start-up investments in Europe doubled, rising from €2.3 billion in 2005 to €5.7 billion in 2006.

A picture of the European private equity industry

Moving on to a more detailed analysis of the European market, we looked in depth at the seven most important countries (United Kingdom, France, Sweden, Germany, Spain, the Netherlands and Italy), which account for about 95 per cent of total European investments in private equity in 2006 (Table 6.1).[2]

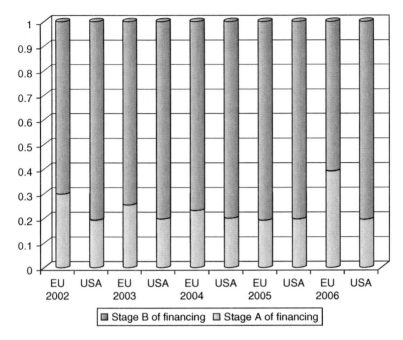

Figure 6.3 Europe vs. US – investment composition by stage, 2002–6
Source: elaborations on EVCA (2007a) and NVCA (2007).

Table 6.1 The private equity market in 2006

	Funds raised (€m)	Amount invested (€m)	Funds raised on GDP (%)	Amount invested in GDP (%)
United Kingdom	74,993	40,897	3.92	2.14
France	10,617	10,100	0.59	0.56
Sweden	9,397	4,259	3.00	1.36
Germany	2,819	3,518	0.12	0.15
Italy	2,275	3,415	0.15	0.23
Spain	2,884	2,815	0.29	0.29
Netherlands	2,609	2,393	0.49	0.45
Total	105,594	67,397	1.13	0.72
Total (excl. UK)	30,601	26,500	0.41	0.36

Source: elaborations on EVCA (2007a).

Some interesting data emerge from the comparison between volumes invested and funds raised, evaluated in absolute terms and as a fraction of GDP (Table 6.1).

The figures for commitments and investments in relation to GDP highlight the difference between the UK and continental Europe. The UK historically is the European country which has achieved and consolidated the highest degree of development in its risk capital market. Its large lead in this area is explained by cultural reasons and by the fact that the sector has been established for longer in the UK than elsewhere in Europe. This aspect has significant repercussions on strategic factors, such as the amount of experience built up by operators and how well informed investors tend to be with regard to risk capital investments. The UK's role clearly emerges if the average figure for the total sample of the seven countries is compared with the figure excluding the UK. Sweden is also well ahead of the other European states, as the sector is growing strongly in this country.

In addition, Table 6.1 enables us to point out the discrepancy between the amount of funds raised and invested. This difference allows us to identify a clear time lag between fund-raising and investment opportunities probably underlying the market shortage of operations that meet the risk/return profiles required by operators.

In terms of fund-raising strategies, considering only the funds raised in 2006 and not including the capital deriving from realised capital gains, the major role played by financial institutions as investors is clear (Table 6.2). The most important category of investor may vary depending on context; in Italy, the banking system has the lion's share, since 70.7 per cent of private equity firms are captives, while in the UK the key role is played by the pension funds, which supply capital to independent operators. Funds of funds are found in all the contexts considered, while academic institutions, major players in the UK, have only recently begun to consider this investment area in the rest of Europe. Bearing in mind the considerable influence of the UK market on the total figure, the European statistic indicates that government agencies play an important role, in particular in Germany and Spain.

Turning our attention to the ability of the economic context to attract capital, reinforcing the statement made initially, 2006 confirms Europe's importance as an investment area (Table 6.3). When the situation is examined at the country-by-country level, two scenarios emerge. On the one hand, we have Sweden and the UK, where a major proportion of the capital committed is used for investment abroad; on the other, in the other sample countries more than two-thirds of the funds raised

Table 6.2 Private equity – source of funds by type of investor in 2006 (%)

	United Kingdom	France	Sweden	Germany	Italy	Spain	Netherlands	Total	Total (no UK)
Pension funds	33.4	9.6	23.7	5.8	5.2	10.6	16.8	27.9	13.8
Fund of funds	18.2	17.9	13.3	20.9	27.8	24.1	25.3	18.3	18.8
Banks	11.7	18.8	10.6	14.7	48.1	31.5	30.8	14.2	20.5
Insurance companies	10.3	18.8	0.3	13.6	1.9	1.6	8.8	10.0	9.0
Private individuals	6.7	18.5	10.7	19.6	10.8	16.8	7.2	8.9	14.5
Government agencies	10.1	4.5	0.6	11.4	1.1	9.2	4.3	8.4	4.1
Academic institutions	5.1	0.0	0.1	2.0	1.5	0.1	0.0	3.8	0.3
Corporate investors	4.3	3.0	0.2	1.0	0.0	4.8	5.2	3.7	2.1
Capital markets	0.1	6.8	3.2	8.6	0.3	0.9	1.0	1.3	4.3
Not available	0.0	2.1	37.3	2.4	3.2	0.4	0.4	3.5	12.4

Source: based on EVCA (2007a).

Table 6.3   Private equity – geographical distribution of investments in 2006

	Domestic (€m)	Domestic (%)	Other countries (€m)	Other countries (%)	Total investment (€m)
United Kingdom	22,248	54.4	18,649	45.6	40,897
France	8,370	82.9	1,730	17.1	10,100
Sweden	2,809	66.0	1,450	34.0	4,259
Germany	3,174	90.2	344	9.8	3,518
Italy	3,373	98.8	42	1.2	3,415
Spain	2,529	89.8	286	10.2	2,815
Netherlands	2,048	85.6	345	14.4	2,393
Total	44,550	66.1	22,847	33.9	67,397
Total (excl. UK)	22,302	84.2	4,197	15.8	26,500

Source: based on EVCA (2007a).

Table 6.4   Private equity – initial and follow-on investments in 2006

	Initial investment (€m)	Initial investment (%)	Follow-on investment (€m)	Follow-on investment (%)	Total investment in year (€m)
United Kingdom	36,334	88.8	4,564	11.2	40,898
France	8,682	86.0	1,419	14.0	10,101
Sweden	3,561	83.6	698	16.4	4,259
Germany	3,196	90.8	322	9.2	3,518
Italy	1,503	44.0	1,912	56.0	3,415
Spain	2,623	93.2	192	6.8	2,815
Netherlands	1,859	77.7	534	22.3	2,393
Total	57,757	85.7	9,640	14.3	67,397
Total (excl. UK)	21,424	80.8	5,076	19.2	26,500

Source: based on EVCA (2007a).

are invested within national borders, with a peak for the Italian market, where this figure reaches 99 per cent.

When a distinction is made between initial and follow-on investments (Table 6.4), it can be seen that on average 86 per cent of the investments made are in firms in which the investor did not previously have a holding. This is particularly true in Germany, the UK and Spain, while in

Italy a surprisingly high proportion of funds are used for follow-on operations, with about 56 per cent of capital allocated for the continuation of operations already underway.

Turning to the subdivision by sector of investment (Table 6.5), according to the EVCA definitions, when the data are split between high-tech and non-high-tech firms, the majority of operations are seen to involve non-high-tech companies. This fits in with various expectations. First, as we shall see, the main type of operation is the buy-out, and at present most of these still tend to involve companies in traditional sectors. Second, it is difficult for statistics to provide confirmation of a progressive shift in investors' attention towards innovation, which is gradually although slowly gaining momentum, at least in some regions of Europe. When the type of investment is considered in relation to GDP, as previously seen in Table 6.1, the figures for both the UK and Sweden differ significantly from the average.

Interesting findings emerge from an observation of the data on the types of operators involved (Table 6.6). The role of the public sector is very small in terms of amount invested and the number of investments made. Only in Spain does the figure invested in 2006 exceed €100 million. In the other countries in the sample, it is only in Sweden that the capital invested exceeds €50 million, while in the UK and the Netherlands the EVCA reports no involvement on the part of public operators at all. In the case of Italy, 53 per cent of the early stage investments made in 2006 were by public operators, especially at the regional level (AIFI, 2007). The investment firms established by the regional governments, therefore, seem to be the main source of financing for innovative firms in the seed and start-up stages. It must, however, be pointed out that we are talking about 53 per cent of not very much; the total amount of early stage investments made by public operators in 2006 was just €28 million. When we cross the figures for the number of operations and the amount invested, Germany is the only country in which the average amount invested by public and private operators is the same, at €4 million. In the other countries considered, even when public investors are involved, the small size of the operations they undertake clearly emerges. This is in line with the findings of the literature on the public role in supporting the initial stages of a firm's life cycle (see chapter 8).

With regard to the breakdown of investments by type, in 2006, for the aggregate of the European countries considered here, there was an overwhelming preference for buy-out operations of the kind already described; operations of this kind absorbed about 69 per cent of the €67.3 billion invested (Table 6.7).

Table 6.5 Private equity – sectorial distribution of investment in 2006

	High-tech (€m)	High-tech (%)	Non-high-tech (€m)	Non-high-tech (%)	High-tech/GDP (%)	Non-high-tech/GDP (%)
United Kingdom	8,384	20.5	32,514	79.5	0.44	1.70
France	1,349	13.4	8,751	86.6	0.08	0.49
Sweden	736	17.3	3,523	82.7	0.23	1.12
Germany	469	13.3	3,049	86.7	0.02	0.13
Italy	247	7.2	3,169	92.8	0.02	0.21
Spain	297	10.6	2,518	89.4	0.03	0.26
Netherlands	716	29.9	1,677	70.1	0.13	0.31
Total	12,196	18.1	55,201	81.9	0.13	0.59
Total (excl. UK)	3,813	14.4	22,687	85.6	0.05	0.31

Source: based on EVCA (2007a).

Table 6.6 Private equity – public vs. private sector operators in 2006

	Private sector (%)	Public sector (%)	Total investment (€m)	Private sector on GDP (%)	Public sector on GDP (%)	Private average amount invested (€m)	Public average amount invested (€m)
United Kingdom	100.0	0.0	40,897	2.14	0.0000	20	0
France	99.9	0.1	10,100	0.56	0.0008	8	0
Sweden	98.8	1.2	4,259	1.34	0.0165	8	1
Germany	98.7	1.3	3,518	0.15	0.0019	4	4
Italy	99.2	0.8	3,415	0.23	0.0019	16	1
Spain	95.1	4.9	2,815	0.27	0.0140	6	1
Netherlands	100.0	0.0	2,393	0.45	0.0000	8	0
Total	99.6	0.4	67,397	0.72	0.0029	12	1
Total (excl. UK)	99.0	1.0	26,500	0.35	0.0037	7	1

Source: based on EVCA (2007a).

Table 6.7 Private equity – stage distribution by percentage of amount invested in 2006

	Seed (%)	Start-up (%)	Expansion (%)	Total venture capital (%)	Replacement (%)	Buy-out (%)	Total later investment* (%)	Total amount invested (€m)
United Kingdom	3.8	10.2	12.7	26.7	6.1	67.2	73.3	40,897
France	0.0	5.3	13.6	18.9	1.2	79.9	81.1	10,100
Sweden	0.3	3.8	12.2	16.3	5.7	78.0	83.7	4,259
Germany	0.9	6.6	19.2	26.7	2.8	70.5	73.3	3,518
Italy	0.1	0.7	28.3	29.1	4.8	66.0	70.9	3,415
Spain	1.1	8.3	23.4	32.8	11.2	55.9	67.2	2,815
Netherlands	0.6	2.1	17.7	20.4	2.4	77.2	79.6	2,393
Total	2.4	8.0	14.5	25.0	5.2	69.8	75.0	67,397
Total (excl. UK)	0.4	4.7	17.4	22.4	3.8	73.8	77.5	26,500

*Later investment: Replacement + buy-out.
Source: based on EVCA (2007a).

Table 6.8   Private equity – stage distribution by number of investments in 2006

	Seed	Start-up	Expansion	Replacement	Buy-out	Total
United Kingdom	136	567	734	110	491	2,038
France	0	335	611	66	362	1,374
Sweden	43	198	194	19	92	546
Germany	68	269	525	16	91	969
Italy	13	44	94	25	67	243
Spain	110	137	316	19	51	633
Netherlands	7	58	148	14	85	312
Total	377	1,608	2,622	269	1,239	6,115
Total (excl. UK)	241	1,041	1,888	159	748	4,077

Source: based on EVCA (2007a).

While a significant proportion of investments were in expansion financing operations (14.5 per cent), in 2006 other types of venture capital operations accounted for extremely small quotas, with an average of 8 per cent at the aggregate level for start-up financing and 2.4 per cent for seed financing. When the influence of the UK is excluded, the weight of investments in the early stages is even lower.

Apart from the UK, the countries among those considered which have the largest proportion of venture capital investments are Germany, Spain and Italy. When these venture capital investments are subdivided into the three main segments, the differences among the situations in these countries clearly emerge. In Italy there is a sharp prevalence of expansion operations, while in Spain and Germany investments are more evenly distributed over the first two stages.

When we consider the number of investments made by type (Table 6.8), as it would be reasonable to expect, there are fewer buy-out than expansion and start-up financing operations, since these investments require more capital. It is worth highlighting the situation in Spain and Germany, where more than 10 per cent of operations provide seed financing, confirming the comments made on the growth of the private equity segment specialising in new business ventures in these two countries. The situation in France is partly different, with no seed operations and about 30 per cent of all operations involving start-up financing.

Confirming the points just made, Table 6.9 provides the figures for the average investment size for each type of investment. The distribution of investments is the same for all the countries considered. As the firm proceeds through its life cycle, the amount invested increases. This is in line

Table 6.9 Private equity – average amount invested per stage in 2006

	Seed (€m)	Start-up (€m)	Expansion (€m)	Replacement (€m)	Buy-out (€m)	Total average (€m)
United Kingdom	11.43	7.36	7.08	22.68	55.97	20.07
France	0.00	1.60	2.25	1.78	22.31	7.35
Sweden	0.33	0.83	2.67	12.74	36.10	7.80
Germany	0.46	0.87	1.29	6.11	27.25	3.63
Italy	0.30	0.56	10.27	6.61	33.66	14.05
Spain	0.29	1.71	2.08	16.64	30.88	4.45
Netherlands	2.18	0.85	2.86	4.11	21.74	7.67
Total	4.38	3.37	3.37	12.98	37.96	11.02
Total (excl. UK)	0.40	1.19	1.19	6.26	26.14	6.50

Source: based on EVCA (2007a).

with the fairly conservative risk profile typical of the European private equity industry down to the present day and with the findings in the literature, which reports that the size of operations increases as the target company matures. It is thus logical that buy-out operations absorb the most capital. With reference to venture capital, it is worth noting that in the UK and the Netherlands, the average amount invested in the seed capital stage is greater than that for start-up operations. Another figure of interest, related to the seed stage, is that in the UK €1.55 billion was invested in 136 operations, with €11.43 million invested on average.

Finally, turning our attention to the disinvestment channels used in 2006, it emerges that within the sample as a whole the most widely used channel is trade sale, followed by sale to financial institutions and divestment by repayment of preference share/loans (Figure 6.4).[3] Disinvestment by means of stock exchange listing was the option pursued in several cases, and the volumes involved in this channel were larger than in 2005 (EVCA, 2007a). Write-offs account for less than 5 per cent of disinvestments. The disinvestment channel depends not only on the operator's preferences, but also on the current macroeconomic conditions.

When our analysis is extended to consider country-specific factors, we find that in Italy the financial institutions play a leading role; this is to be expected for a market where investments are in more mature firms, which attract the attention of financial operators. In the UK, on the other

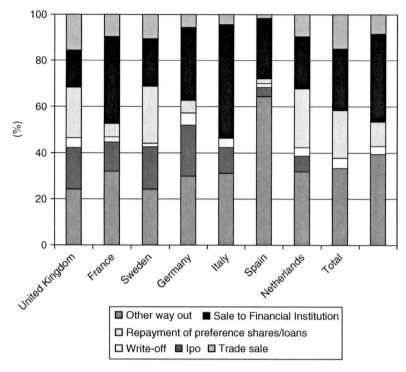

Figure 6.4 Private equity – way-out mechanisms distribution in 2006 (%)
Source: based on EVCA (2007a).

hand, most disinvestment is by means of the listing process, reflecting
the higher level of efficiency achieved by this country's stock markets.

Risk capital investment as an asset class

The record of the funds raised in Europe and the US reflects investors'
faith in the private equity industry's ability to prosper in the medium-
to-long term and generate worthwhile returns.

It should be remembered that the yield of the market for institutional
investment in risk capital over any given period of time is affected by a
number of factors, in particular:

• the size of the market, the number of operators it involves and its
  consequent level of competitiveness, which affects the prices of the
  target firms;

Table 6.10 Europe vs. US – performance of private equity investments (%)

	One year	Three years	Five years	Ten years
Total venture capital Europe	17.2	5.0	−2.0	4.1
Total venture capital US	7.0	9.1	−1.2	20.5
Total buy-out Europe	29.6	15.3	8.3	14.3
Total buy-out US	21.6	15.6	9.1	8.8
Total European private equity	36.0	13.0	5.0	11.0
Total US private equity	16.5	13.0	6.0	11.0

Source: based on EVCA (2007a) and NVCA (2007).

- operators' success in creating value in the venture-backed firm, which depends on their level of professional expertise and on the characteristics of the target firm itself;
- the efficiency of the disinvestment channels and their economic performance; this is key to the availability of a range of good disinvestment opportunities and the opportunity to exploit positive trends in the market and company evaluations to obtain higher prices.

Table 6.10 shows the returns achieved by private equity operators, divided between venture capitalists and buy-outs, for the US and Europe. It is clear that the trends in performance tend to be the same in both the US and the European markets. In the long term, the performance of private equity investments is good, yielding about 11 per cent per annum, net of all the commissions paid to the operators. This positive return is maintained throughout the period considered, and in 2006 the European market showed a return of 36 per cent over one year, outperforming the US market, which achieved 16.5 per cent. This justifies the figure on European fund-raising, which reflects the high level of interest of US operators in this market.

With regard to the segmentation of performance by type of operation, according to classical financial theory, with application of the risk/return principle, seed and start-up operations should be more profitable in the light of their higher risk profile. However, the real figure may be sharply different since, as we have seen, in spite of operators' efforts to limit the degree of uncertainty concerning future events, the final return on the operation is strongly dependent on contingent factors.

If we look at the European market in the short and long term, it is clear that buy-out operations offer the best returns for investments. Over a ten-year time horizon, buy-outs generated returns of 14.3 per cent, while the average return on venture capital was 4.1 per cent. In the short term, the yield provided by venture capital investments is decidedly better, at 17.2 per cent, but it is still below the return provided by buy-out operations at 29.6 per cent.

The situation of the US market is different with regard to medium-to-long-term returns. As classical theory indicates, in this market the net return achieved by venture capital investors over a ten-year period is higher, at 20.5 per cent per annum, than the return on buy-out operations, which is 8.8 per cent. However, if the time scale is shortened, the trend becomes the same as in the European markets. In 2006, buy-out operations generated returns of 21.6 per cent, while the yield on venture capital operations was stationary at an average of 7 per cent.

Another factor that can effect the return on investment in the European and US markets is the average amount invested in venture capital operations. This is particularly evident when targeting technology firms: €900,000 in Europe, €6.1 million in the US. This figure is even more striking when referred to seed and start-up financing operations: for this kind of firm, in Europe it is €500,000 and €800,000 respectively, while in the US it rises to €1.8 million and €4 million (EVCA, 2007a). The differences in terms of average amount invested can have various effects, including limiting the potential growth of the investee enterprises, and thus limiting the return on the investment (European Commission, 2006a).

From the asset management point of view, investments in risk capital are classified within the alternative investments category. Among others, this category includes hedge funds, real estate funds and private equity funds. It is not uncommon for private equity and hedge fund operators to be placed on the same plane. Without going into detail, we can state that hedge funds, like private equity firms, are often active investors in the risk capital of the enterprises in which they hold shares. On the one hand, this active involvement distinguishes them from traditional institutional investors, while on the other, it is due to this role in corporate governance that the distinction between hedge funds and private equity funds may be fuzzy (European Commission, 2006c). The active involvement may assume various forms: from putting public pressure on the management to obtain changes in business strategy, to membership of the board of directors and the imposition of new managers. One indirect effect of this active participation is that it creates the need for regulation of the financial markets to control it (European Central Bank, 2007). However, unlike private equity investors, hedge funds often have an excessive orientation towards short-term objectives. This may also be true of private equity in some cases, but its investments normally have medium-to-long-term time horizons.

Once the main distinction between the most important segments of the alternative investment category has been made clear, viewing the risk capital investment market as an asset class highlights several key features:

- It is an extremely heterogeneous market, with a wide difference in returns between the various operators.
- Performances cannot be assessed immediately. The investment portfolio consists of financial assets which often cannot be valued with any certainty since they are not traded on the financial markets. Moreover, the earnings of private equity investors, and especially venture capitalists, follow a trend known as the J-curve phenomenon: during the initial years of operations returns are negative, since the annual operating costs have to be met and no disinvestments are made. This phenomenon means that the early loss of value of an investment in a venture capital fund does not necessarily give an indication of the profitability of the investment over time. For the same reason, comparing the profitability of a two-year-old fund to one that has been operating for, say, seven or eight years would not be meaningful (Dantas and Raade, 2006).
- The lack of information transparency, the varying opinions as to what actually constitute private equity and venture capital operations, and the high level of discontinuity in the results depending on the time horizon considered all render comparisons between statistical studies problematic.

As seen, we are thus faced with an economic sector in which no immediate, definitive conclusions can be drawn.

There is no denying the amount of interest in this sector, reflected by the high flows of capital into it on several occasions, attracted by the high returns achieved in a many cases. In the US buy-out market, for example, three periods can be identified: between 1986 and 1998 the private equity industry raised about $16–18 billion a year; the subsequent decline was followed by a second period from 1995 to 2000, during which the inflow of capital again accelerated, reaching a new record of $80 billion in 2000; finally, after another decline between 2001 and 2003, investors' interest returned, with $150 billion collected in 2006 (Chew, 2007).

In spite of the considerable inflow of capital, various studies have revealed uncertainty concerning the sector's profitability; Conroy and

Harris (2007) state that the average net rate of return for investors in private equity operations has not been as attractive as many people suppose. The risks are often underestimated and returns overestimated, largely due to the methods used to estimate and report the value of investments. Moreover, the situation varies depending on the geographical context. On average, the return on venture capital investments in Europe is very low. According to the data analysed by Dantas and Raade (2006) as of 2003 the average annual return on investments made at five and ten years was +2.3 per cent and +8.3 per cent. The performance of investments in early stage firms was particularly disappointing, with an annual return after five years of −1.8 per cent and after ten years of +1.3 per cent. In the case of expansion investments, the annual returns rise to +4.6 per cent and +10.7 per cent respectively in the same time frame. These data clearly reveal uncertainty with regard to the ability of venture capital investments to compete with alternative assets, such as hedge funds or real estate funds, on the basis of the return in proportion to the risk undertaken. In the US market, we find a venture capital industry with significantly higher annual returns: +22.8 per cent and +25.4 per cent respectively, on the same five- and ten-year time horizons. In the case of early stage investments, returns are even higher, with +54.9 per cent and +37 per cent, while the returns on expansion investments are less outstanding, although still significantly higher than those achieved in Europe – +19.4 per cent and +20.4 per cent.

One of the basic causes of this disparity is the fragmentation of the European market, which restricts its efficiency. Since the opportunities for cross-border investments are still very limited, many firms are not sufficiently specialised and do not develop the expertise required to make investments in specific sectors, especially those with a high degree of innovation. As a result, the European market is less efficient and its returns are unattractive compared to those available in the US (European Commission, 2006c).

As already mentioned, profitability levels in the risk capital investment industry vary widely. Kaplan and Schoar (2005) compared the median return on investments made and liquidated between 1980 and 2001, and obtained figures of +13 per cent for buy-out and +11 per cent for venture capital operations, with average returns of +18 per cent and +17 per cent. The comparison reveals that while some funds have achieved very high returns, the earnings provided by others have been extremely low.

There is also the problem of defining the risk/return profile of risk capital investments due to a number of factors, including the measurement of returns, the fact that these are not liquid investments and the representativeness of prices.

It is difficult to calculate the return on investments during the investment instruments' life, because the prices of operations not yet concluded are recorded at the purchase cost, or not reported at all. In addition, these are investments in instruments such as limited partnerships or closed-end funds, which are not liquid because there is no obligation to list them, and the assets in which the fund invests are often themselves not listed, and so any stated prices are not truly representative. Conroy and Harrys (2007) state that a significant part of the value assigned to a fund arises from the 'remaining value to paid-in', estimated by the general partner, which at the end of 2004, in the European market, was 40 per cent of the value expected by the investors.

Cumming and Walz (2004) show that the differences in return among all the types of risk capital investments derive to a large extent from the corporate governance mechanisms adopted; in the contexts with the highest degree of legality, performances are better (Cumming et al., 2007).

Conclusions

Differences remain on the quantitative level between the US and European markets with regard to the amounts of funds raised, with the US market leading the way, although the gap is gradually narrowing. However, from the qualitative point of view, the industry's development seems to be powered by quite similar drivers on both sides of the Atlantic, with a prevalence of buy-out operations and the concentration of venture capital operations in the expansion financing segment.

This similarity between the two areas can be explained if we consider the primary role played by the British private equity market in Europe. Like their US counterparts, British operators give particular importance to objectives linked to economic efficiency, achieved by exploiting the economies of scale generated by the huge amounts of assets managed, and they therefore concentrate on investment operations of a higher average size. The situations in the other European countries vary.

Apart from the UK, the countries with the largest proportion of venture capital investments are Germany, Spain and Italy. However, the new area of genuine venture capital investment seems to consist only of Germany and Spain, where the focus on the development of high-tech firms is attracting operators' interest. In Italy, on the other hand, there is a clear prevalence of expansion financing operations.

In countries such as France, Sweden and the Netherlands, investors showed a decided preference for replacement and buy-out operations during 2006.

One of the explanations lies in the high returns associated with buy-out operations and later investment projects in general. The excessive focus on buy-out operations may have put the brakes on the development of the venture capital segment. It is, however, undeniable that the growth of the venture capital market has been affected by factors related to both the demand and supply of risk capital. In this area, various studies of the US market reveal that it is probably demand, rather than the availability of capital, that restricts the growth of the industry (Gompers and Lerner, 1998).

This same conclusion emerges from our earlier survey, which identifies a clear lag between fund-raising and investment. This discrepancy confirms the market shortage of investment opportunities that meet the risk/return profiles required by operators.

Paradoxically, this surplus capital might in itself be the cause of another problem. One of the most important challenges with which the sector has to deal is the crowding of the market due to the availability of huge amounts of money at low cost. Competition between funds is growing fast, and this is partly a healthy development, but price competition may become excessive due to the fact that all the capital is being offered to the same limited number of firms. An excess of supply can have an inflationary effect, making it more difficult to generate value after the acquisition.

Another factor which may restrict the industry's growth is the availability of high skill levels among operators. Bottazzi and Da Rin (2002) find that in Europe venture capital is not systematically associated with particularly dynamic companies, whether we look at sales growth, new employment or stock market performance. As Bottazzi and Da Rin underline, their study does not allow definitive conclusions to be drawn, but the supply of skilled human capital emerges as one of the potential problems. There is no doubt that the venture capitalist has to operate in an extremely complex context: a start-up relies on the talent and skills of its founder, who knows more about its technical aspects than anybody else. This makes it particularly difficult to assess performances and, as stated in chapter 5, the investor is required to provide technical skills above and beyond financial expertise as such.

Another problematic factor is the perception that the market, in the widest sense, has of these operators. Calling risk capital investors locusts may be unjustified, but the problem of their relations with the market and its stakeholders in general is a growing one. If private equity wishes to survive in the long term, it must establish an acceptable relationship with all stakeholders. Unlike alternative operators, such as hedge funds, private equity investors constitute an asset class whose results depend on their ability to create value for the firm in the broadest sense.

7
The Role of Equity Markets

Fabio Braga and Massimo Demasi

Introduction

The relationship between financial markets and small and medium-sized enterprises (SMEs) is complex and involves a wealth of issues. At the company level, going public is one of the most important decisions a firm may take. Listing on the public market has a profound impact on a company's life because it extends financing sources, drives deep organisational changes and exposes management's actions to the scrutiny of the market. At the macroeconomic level, efficient equity markets, making an important contribution to general financial development, should foster the competitiveness of an economy and its long-term growth.

Despite being an important source of capital, the distance between SMEs and financial markets may be massive. The complexity and the cost of going and being public may prevent small firms from reaping the benefit of equity markets' pools of liquidity. Although debt capital markets also play an important role, we focus on equity markets as they are a primary source of external capital for non-financial firms. Moreover, being listed on the equity market is often a necessary condition in order to issue other classes of securities. At the end of 2007, more than 43,000 companies were listed on stock markets around the globe with a market value of almost $61 trillion. During 2007, there were more than 2,900 newly listed companies. The total value of capital raised by new and currently listed companies was around $900 billion.

In this chapter, we discuss some of the issues that characterise the role of equity markets in the financing of SMEs. The topic is vast and we were faced with the decision to choose just a few issues. The selection is certainly biased by our tastes and the practitioner view taken. A major decision was to focus on small and medium-sized enterprises rather than on innovative ones. The main reason is that in the second half of the 1990s, stock exchanges developed equity markets dedicated to innovative, technology and high growth firms. These 'new markets' were characterised by very low entry requirements but high transparency standards (Goergen et al., 2003). The early success of new markets was remarkable, but the burst of the 'dot.com bubble' proved fatal to them. In hindsight, the assessment of these markets should not be too harsh. With new markets, European stock exchanges experienced a proactive role in organising and managing markets for less established firms, responding to the need of equity finance by innovative, usually small firms. The positive effects of the development of these markets were their contribution in the development of new financial intermediaries and the establishment of some successful companies. The strong initial public offering (IPO) activity on these markets is linked to the growth of the venture capital industry in some countries.[1] Many large companies currently listed on main markets were at that time start-ups that could not have raised any capital in the absence of new markets.

The relatively recent emergence of alternative markets dedicated to SMEs is a contribution in the same direction: the role of stock exchanges in promoting entrepreneurship and growth. The focus of alternative markets is on small, often young companies that need equity to finance growth. Alternative markets do not focus on innovative sectors like new markets, but target small businesses that would find it too costly and complex to be listed on main markets. The establishment of alternative markets is, according to our view, a very significant contribution to financial development. Small firms may suffer from a lack of alternatives and availability of financing sources which hamper their development. The aim is, to some degree, akin to the one that inspired the development of new markets and is the central focus of this book: how to bridge the equity gap.

The chapter is organised as follows: in the next section, we provide a rationale for the role of equity markets in terms of benefits accruing to firms and investors. Then, we discuss the structure of the main European markets and segments dedicated to SMEs. Some time is required in order to fully assess the relative success of these markets, and hence current evidence may be only preliminary. In the following section we analyse the IPO process and what differentiates the listing of small and medium-sized enterprises from that of large companies by looking at the Italian market. Once public, in order to take advantage of the benefits of being public, liquidity becomes an important attribute for shares of SMEs. The next section compares the relative liquidity of shares of SMEs with those of large companies and across different European markets. Finally, we summarise our argument and conclude.

Financial markets and the financing of SMEs

A developed financial system minimises asymmetric information problems, pools savings optimally and allocates capital to the most productive use. Financial development matters for growth. The financial system does not merely respond to economic development, but is an essential contributor to it. A large body of theoretical and empirical research now confirms that higher initial levels of financial development are followed by higher growth rates.[2]

Some studies highlight that the impact of financial development on growth is not homogeneous and certain classes of firms and industries seem to benefit most. Interesting research by Rajan and Zingales (1998) suggests that financial development influences growth mainly by raising the growth rate of new firms rather than the average size of existing ones: small firms, which are usually most in need of external finance, seem to benefit most from financial development. Carlin and Mayer (2003) highlight that, in financially underdeveloped economies, collateral, like tangible fixed assets, assumes a disproportionate importance for external financing. Industries that rely heavily on outside equity financing end up employing a lower than optimal share of intangible assets, including research and development (R&D) or human capital. Small and innovative firms seem to benefit most from financial development.

The financing patterns of SMEs are peculiar and hint at the presence of greater financing constraints than those borne by large companies. The degree of asymmetrical information is usually more intense for small and medium-sized enterprises than for large ones. Information on small enterprises, especially when they are not publicly traded, is often limited and less timely. Moreover, by being usually younger, small businesses have less reputation capital. Finally, the lack of adequate collateral, the reduced bargaining power with financiers and the presence of fixed costs in financing activity further contribute to making external finance more expensive. This would suggest the presence of a strong pecking order of financing sources for small enterprises and, as a consequence, a greater reliance on internally generated funds.

The presence of financing constraints is a matter of empirical evidence. A recent study by the European Central Bank on the corporate finance in the euro area offers some interesting, stylised facts (ECB, 2007).

Despite evidence of the presence of financing constraints being somewhat mixed, size appears to matter considerably in explaining different patterns in financing choices and balance sheet structure. Euro area small and medium businesses have higher cash holdings than larger firms and a higher debt to cash flow ratio. Larger cash buffers are usually aimed at making investment activity less dependent on external financing, a variable frequently associated with the presence of financing constraints. Moreover, SMEs rely on loans more than large companies do. When the small size is coupled with product or process innovation, asymmetrical information problems are even deeper; and this makes financing constraints more severe. Innovative firms have much of their assets in intangibles and undertake risky projects, making traditional debt financing unsuitable. Debt holders bear the downside risk, but do not share the upside benefit of successful innovation. For these firms equity is more appropriate than debt as a source of finance, but the costs of acceding to equity markets may be too high. This rationale justifies, for example, the creation of new markets in the 1990s. The complexity and intrinsic riskiness of the business of many companies listed on new markets made bank loans an unsuitable source of finance. Moreover some of these companies, given the absence of a track-record, would have found it very difficult, if not impossible, to be listed on main markets. The creation of new markets allowed innovative companies to find an adequate venue in which to raise capital.

Banks and markets are the primary institutions of the financial system. They provide essential, complementary but not perfectly substitutable services.[3] A primary role of the stock market is to facilitate external equity financing. At the IPO stage, firms are able to finance growth by raising a large amount of fresh capital. As we shall see, small and medium enterprises do raise, in relative terms, more new equity than large firms do. Afterwards, being public allows them to tap the equity gap by seasoned offerings or by issuing different classes of securities. A liquid and efficient stock market provides a favourable environment for the development of specialised intermediaries like venture capitalists, which is especially important in the early stage financing of small firms. Aside from easing the financing gap, the stock market also fills the information gap. The development of information intermediaries (auditors, media, rating agencies and analysts) makes the price mechanism a valuable signal to monitor and steer management decisions. By making a firm's capital tradable and hence liquid, the stock market allows better risk management techniques to be employed, with a positive effect on the cost of equity. Going public has a profound impact on corporate governance.

A listed company is required to comply with high standards in terms of governance and transparency, which help to mitigate agency problems. Once public, a company usually expands its brand knowledge and enhances its credibility with clients, suppliers and commercial partners. The development of equity markets dedicated to SMEs has large benefits not only for firms but also for investors. Empirical research suggests that small capitalisation companies tend to perform differently from large cap stocks. Small and medium companies represent a distinctive asset class and investors benefit from size diversification. The presence of a 'size factor' has been investigated in financial economics literature. Petrella (2005) asks whether euro area small caps are a distinctive asset class. The analysis is conducted over the four largest euro area stock markets – France, Germany, Italy and Spain – in the period 1999–2002. The study employs a mean variance spanning test in order to establish the existence and to determine the magnitude of benefits deriving from size diversification. Petrella establishes that the shift in the efficient frontier due to the inclusion of euro area small caps is statistically significant. The extent of benefits from size diversification accrues, however, with different degrees as the length of the investment horizon changes, given that the lower liquidity of small caps implies higher transaction costs.

The importance of size for strategic asset allocation is mirrored by the emergence in the mutual fund industry of some countries of funds specialised in mid- and small capitalisation stocks. In the UK 60 funds, specialised in domestic small caps, were managing around €11 billion at the end of 2007 and weighed over 1.7 per cent on the total industry's assets under management. Well behind are, conversely, the mutual fund industry in Italy and Germany, where the weight of specialised funds is less than 0.2 per cent in both countries. On this account and in order to favour the mutual fund industry, many stock exchanges created a set of indices that could provide benchmarks specifically dedicated to small caps.

The development of segments and markets for SMEs in Europe

Stock exchanges organise and manage markets in order to facilitate the listing of companies and to attract liquidity by guaranteeing fair, orderly and efficient trading on the secondary market. In recent years, stock exchanges have concentrated their efforts in encouraging the listing of small and medium companies.

This commitment is clearly motivated by the fact that SMEs are a major component of value created in Europe. As Table 7.1 shows, the

Table 7.1   Breakdown of value added by enterprise size class (%)

Number of employees	Small and medium			Large >250
	1–19	20–49	50–249	
Belgium	27.1	12.5	18.3	42.1
France	27.4	11.3	15.6	45.8
Germany	27.1	9.5	18.5	45.0
Italy	43.2	11.7	16.0	29.1
Netherlands	26.4	12.6	21.3	39.6
Spain	37.9	13.9	16.8	31.5
Sweden	27.4	10.3	17.9	44.4
UK	25.1	8.8	16.8	49.3

Data refer to value added as of 2005 except for UK, 2004

Source: elaborations on Eurostat data.

contribution to total value added stemming from non-financial small and medium enterprises is, across large European countries, always more than 50 per cent. Even after excluding companies with fewer than 20 employees (which have little propensity to list on a public market), small companies account for 25–30 per cent of total value added across Europe. A large degree of variability is present nonetheless. Small and medium enterprises account for more than two-thirds of total value added in Italy (71 per cent) and Spain (69 per cent). Very small companies (those with fewer than 20 employees) account for 43 per cent of total value added in Italy, 18 per cent higher than that of the UK. Less significant, but still relevant, are SMEs in Germany (55 per cent) and the UK (51 per cent).

Stock exchanges have several options in order to favour the listing of small and medium enterprises. A difficult equilibrium has to be found between the strictness of listing and ongoing requirements and the cost these requirements impose on companies. High requirements certainly increase the appeal of mid- and small companies for investors, but also drive compliance costs up, possibly leaving many companies far from the equity market. From the point of view of a stock exchange, this trade-off resulted in two main options: the definition of segments inside the main market and the set-up of alternative markets. Moreover, in order to facilitate the investment by institutional investors, stock exchanges provide benchmark indices for almost all segments and markets dedicated to mid- and small caps.

This section analyses segments created inside main markets and alternative markets for mid- and small caps. We look at markets managed by Bolsas y Mercados Españoles (BME), Borsa Italiana (BIt), Deutsche Börse (DB), Nyse Euronext (when considering only European business, we will simply refer to Euronext),[4] the London Stock Exchange (LSE), Nasdaq OMX (when considering only European business, we will refer to OMX)[5] and the Swiss Exchange (SWX).

A complete description of the micro-structure of each market is beyond the scope of this section. We concentrate on differences in listing requirements and market models between mid- and small caps and large caps. With respect to market models[6] in particular, we discuss the choice between order-driven and quote-driven markets and between auction and continuous trading forms (a general introduction to these concepts is given in Appendix 7.1).

Segmentation of main markets

By defining segments for mid- and small caps inside main markets, stock exchanges aim to:

- give companies that want to come to the fore to find an adequate context, with higher listing and ongoing requirements in terms of corporate governance, liquidity and transparency; and
- separate small and medium-sized companies from large caps, facilitating the identification of a specific asset class.

Segments dedicated to mid- and small caps inside main markets (Table 7.2) have been created by Borsa Italiana (STAR and Standard segments), Euronext (compartment B and C), OMX (small and mid-cap segments and, only for Danish Market, MidCap-plus and SmallCap-plus) and SWX (Local Caps segment).

Market segmentation may respond to different purposes. In Euronext and OMX the goal is to create transnational markets, where mid- and small caps distinguish themselves from large caps only in terms of size. STAR and Plus segments are instead characterised by higher requirements aimed at strengthening investors' confidence and maximising listing value. SWX is the only stock exchange that offers small companies with a local presence and with a limited range of shareholders (typically family-owned enterprises) the opportunity to list in a segment of the main market that is characterised by lower requirements; as we shall see, this is an option that is generally offered by alternative markets dedicated to small caps.

In particular, Euronext and OMX created a single official list: Eurolist (which includes Paris, Amsterdam, Brussels and Lisbon markets) for Euronext, and Nordic list (which includes Copenhagen, Helsinki,

Table 7.2 Specific requirements for main markets' segments dedicated to mid- and small caps

Markets	Segments	Market capitalisation	Specific requirements		
			Corporate governance	Transparency	Liquidity
Blt	STAR	<€1 bn	• composition of the board of directors (minimum number of non-executive and independent directors) • creation and working of internal committees • remuneration of directors: creation of a remuneration committee and remuneration linked to company results • internal control committee (composed by non-executive directors only, the majority of which independent) • limits to internal dealing in the period preceding the board's meeting	• publication of quarterly reports within 45 days of the end of each quarter* • transmission to Blt of the quarterly, half-yearly and annual accounts in the format specified by Blt • publication of financial accounts and price-sensitive information on the company website in Italian and English • appointment of a specialist which has to publish at least two research reports a year and organise meetings between company management and professional investors	• higher minimum free float: 35 per cent** for newly listed companies (the general requirement is 25 per cent) and 20 per cent to remain STAR • appointment of a specialist (undertaking to support Liquidity)
Euronext	Standard Compart. B Compart. C	<€1 bn Between €150 m and €1 bn <€150 ml			
OMX	Mid-cap Small cap	Between €150 m and €1 bn <€150 m			

MidCap-plus	Between €150 m and €1 bn	• quarterly reports • publication of corporate announcements in English • IR presentation at least twice a year • definition of a minimum content of the company's website	• minimum daily turnover: DKK 755,000 (€101,322) • average bid-ask spread ≤ 2 per cent • order coverage (availability of orders on the book) ≥ 90 per cent
SmallCap-plus	<€150 ml	• quarterly reports • IR presentation at least once a year • definition of a minimum content of the company's website	• minimum daily turnover: DKK 150,000 (€20,130) • average bid-ask spread ≤ 4 per cent • order coverage (availability of orders on the book) ≥ 90 per cent
SWX	SWX local caps	Lower amount of capital resources: CHF 2.5 m (instead of CHF 25 m)	• lower free float: 20 per cent and a free float market cap of at least CHF 5 m (instead of 25 per cent and CHF 25 m)

* Following the implementation of the Transparency Directive, all companies listed on a regulated market have the duty to publish an interim management report; according to Italian regulations the interim report must be published within 45 days of the end of the quarter (1st and 3rd quarters). Given the new regulatory framework, Borsa Italiana is analysing possible amendments to the quarterly reports requirement.

** For companies already listed, the minimum free float to access Star segment is 35 per cent if the company is listed for less than one year and 20 per cent otherwise.

Source: Exchanges' market rules and websites. Exchange rate: European Central Bank (as of 29 February 2008).

Stockholm and Reykjavik) and Baltic list (Riga, Vilnius and Tallin) for OMX. STAR and Plus segments focus instead on higher corporate governance (only for STAR), transparency and liquidity requirements.

Corporate governance is the set of policies and laws by which a corporation is controlled and directed. Corporate governance requirements for STAR companies stem from the adoption of the Corporate Governance Code, a document created by a committee representing the Italian business and financial community. Most of the Code recommendations are now compulsory for STAR companies. For non-STAR companies the adoption of standards is based on the 'comply or explain' principle.

Transparency is frequently a sought attribute for mid- and small cap companies. Higher transparency is achieved by strengthening the flow and comparability of information among companies. Price-sensitive press releases and annual and periodic standardised reports must follow similar timing, format and content. Also very important is direct contact between the company's management and the financial community. The company is required to strengthen the relationship with the market by appointing an investor relator and by organising regular meetings between analysts and management. The presence of many press conferences and road-shows in a few days makes it difficult for analysts to cover mid- and small caps too. In order to support institutional investors' interest in SMEs, some exchanges organise regular meetings between companies and the financial community. Another important topic is the analysts' coverage. To increase the number of analysts following SMEs, Borsa Italiana included among specialists' duties the publication of at least two research reports a year, as well organising meetings between company management and investors. For the same reason, Euronext created the role of mid- and small caps experts: intermediaries with teams specialising in research and sales on mid- and small caps that produce regular reports. Euronext supports the activity of mid- and small caps experts through promotional activity and by creating a label assigned to experts.

To ensure adequate diffusion of the company's shares and to foster liquidity, stock exchanges can impose a minimum free float requirement (both at the listing and ongoing). For potentially illiquid shares, the exchange may also require the presence of an intermediary that supports liquidity by continuously displaying bid and ask satisfying maximum spread and minimum quantity parameters. These intermediaries take different names in different exchanges: liquidity providers (Euronext and OMX), specialists (Borsa Italiana), designated sponsors (Deutsche Börse) and market makers (London Stock Exchange). For simplicity, we call them liquidity providers. The liquidity support allows traders to find a counter-party and get an estimate of company value (particularly important for thinly traded stocks). Specialists that operate on the STAR segment have the peculiar characteristic of also providing corporate broking services, such as research reports and the organisation of meetings with professional investors.

Market models, which set out the way in which trading activity is organised, are not directly linked, at least in general, to company size, but are structured on the basis of the share's liquidity. Liquidity, which is the ease with which a security may be converted into cash, is a multifaceted quality and there are many attributes that help qualify whether a security is liquid or not. This is reflected in different measures employed by stock exchanges across Europe, including the average daily turnover and frequency of trades (Borsa Italiana), the number of trades (Euronext), the market impact (Deutsche Börse) or being a constituent of an index (LSE). Usually market capitalisation is very well correlated with trading activity, and thin stocks are generally those issued by small companies.

Small caps listed on main markets are traded in order-driven systems. The only exception (Table 7.3) are small caps listed on the LSE that are not included in the FTSE all share index. These shares are traded on a hybrid system, SETSqx, where quote- and order-driven market models coexist. In particular, trades can be executed either with a market maker, if present, or on the order book, during four auctions a day. In order to avoid excessive price volatility and to concentrate liquidity, the trading of thin stocks in most of the markets is carried by auctions only. Stock exchanges usually set different timings of opening and closing auctions of thin stocks as compared to those of more liquid ones. Their simultaneous occurrence may reduce small cap stocks' liquidity, given the usual larger interest traders have in blue chips. Different trading hours are hence useful to allow traders to concentrate on small caps auctions. In main markets managed by Borsa Italiana, Deutsche Börse and Euronext, the appointment of a liquidity provider, which undertakes to respect minimum requirements related to liquidity support, allows continuous trading to take place for thin shares. Euronext established the role of 'auction liquidity provider', giving in this way the possibility of appointing a liquidity provider to companies that do not desire to be traded continuously.

Alternative markets for mid- and small caps

European stock exchanges created many markets with the purpose of facilitating the flotation of small caps; this resulted in alternative markets

Table 7.3   Main markets' segments market model

	Order-driven vs. quote-driven	Trading forms	Liquidity provider
BME	Order-driven (floor trading also available)	Auction and continuous trading Less liquid shares are traded only by auction without continuous trading	No
BIt	Order-driven	Auction and continuous trading. Standard segment divided into two classes: • class 1 with same trading phases than large caps and STAR but different trading hours; • class 2 (less liquid shares) with only auction and without continuous trading	• Compulsory for STAR segment • Discretionary for other segments
DB	Order-driven (floor trading also available)	Auction and continuous trading Less liquid shares are traded by auction without continuous trading	Discretionary
Euronext	Order-driven	Auction and continuous trading Less liquid shares are traded only by auction without continuous trading	Discretionary
LSE	Order-driven: SETS (FTSE All Shares) Hybrid (order- and quote-driven): SETSqx (main market equities not traded on SETS)	SETS: auction and continuous trading SETSqx: auction and quote-driven (market makers)	SETS: discretionary SETSqx: discretionary
OMX	Order-driven	Auction and continuous trading	Discretionary
SWX	Order-driven	Auction and continuous trading	No*

*Swiss Exchange is planning the migration of equity market to the new trading platform Quotematch, introducing the possibility to have market makers.
Source: Exchanges' market rules and websites.

characterised by less stringent listing and ongoing requirements. These markets are either Regulated Markets, like the Italian Mercato Expandi, or Multilateral Trading Facilities (MTFs), like the Alternative Investment Market (AIM).

AIM was launched by the LSE in 1995 and partly inherited the experience made on the Unlisted Securities Market. Borsa Italiana introduced Mercato Expandi in 2003 as a result of fundamental restructuring of Mercato Ristretto and Mercato Alternativo dei Capitali (MAC) in 2007. Most of the other alternative markets were established between 2005 and 2006. Euronext launched Alternext, first in Paris and then in Brussels and Amsterdam (in 1996 Euronext also launched the Marché Libre in Paris and in 2004 the Free Market in Brussels). OMX set up First North, replacing the pre-existing Sweden Nya Marknaden in the Nordic countries, and then First North Baltic in the Baltic states. Finally, Deutsche Börse launched Entry Standard, a segment of Open Market.

The last European alternative market established is the Spanish MAB. In March 2008, the domestic regulator approved the new segment dedicated to mid- and small caps into MAB, a market established in 2006 for trading SICAVs.

With the exception of Mercato Expandi, the markets listed in Table 7.4 have the legal status of MTFs. All markets are characterised by low entry requirements in terms of minimum capitalisation, free float and track-record. Moreover, EU directives impose more stringent requirements for companies listed on regulated markets.

The AIM so far has been most successful in attracting domestic as well as foreign small companies. Companies listed on the AIM do not have to make a public offer (with the exception of investment companies) or have a minimum free float. The main requirements are the appointment of a nominated advisor and a broker, the publication of an admission document available to the public and, for new businesses only, a one-year lock-in period for related parties and applicable employees.[7] As a consequence of not being a regulated market, the obligation to issue a prospectus scrutinised by the regulator applies only to public offerings.[8] Although the publication of the prospectus is not mandatory, the admission document replicates much of information required for the prospectus. The role of the nominated advisor is crucial, because it is responsible for assessing the suitability of AIM entrants and for advising and guiding the company on its responsibilities under AIM rules. Specific rules are provided to regulate the activity of nominated advisors and their obligations to the Exchange. With respect to transparency duties, information requirements for AIM companies are limited compared to

Markets	Legal status	Main listing requirements				Sponsor/ Listing partner
		Minimum capital	Track record	Profitability	Free float	
BME – MAB	MTF	No	2 years	No	€2 m	Asesores registrados
Blt – Expandi	Regulated Market	€1 m	2 years	Result from recurrent activities > 0 EBITDA > 0 $\left\|\frac{net\ financial\ position}{EBITDA}\right\| < 4$	10% and €750,000	Listing partner (only during the admission period)
Blt – MAC	MTF	No	1 year	No	No minimum free float minimum diffusion is guaranteed by: • institutional placement dedicated to institutional investors, or • one institutional investor among shareholders, or • 20 professional investors from among the shareholders	Sponsor (at least 3 years from listing)
DB – Entry Standard (Open Market)	MTF	No	1 year	No	No	Listing partner
Euronext – Alternext	MTF	No	2 years	No	For a public offer: €2.5 m For a private placement: no minimum free float For admission of company from another market at least €2.5 m	Listing sponsor (at least 2 years from listing)
Euronext – Marché Libre	MTF	No	2 years	No	No	Sponsor
OMX – First North	MTF	No	No	No	• 10% and a sufficient number of shareholders, or • appointment of a liquidity provider	Certified advisor
LSE – AIM	MTF	No	No	No	No	Nominated advisor

Source: Exchanges' market rules and websites.

the main market and are mainly related to price-sensitive information, unaudited six-monthly reports, audited annual statement, corporate transactions as reverse takeovers and minimum content of information provided on the company website

A similar framework has been created on other MTFs, although small differences exist in terms of minimum track-record and minimum free float. In all cases, requirements are less stringent than those of main markets. The Entry Standard imposes listing and ongoing rules similar to AIM, with the exception of the track record.

The admission to Alternext can be achieved through a public offer of at least €2.5 million or by a private placement. The listing by a private placement requires a capital increase of at least €5 million and the presence among shareholders of qualified investors during the two years prior to the admission. Based on the listing procedure chosen, there are different listing requirements. For a public offer, the publication of a prospectus is compulsory and Euronext requires a minimum free float. For private placements, the company has a duty only to publish the offering circular and there is no minimum free float requirement. A minimum track-record is always required. The Marché Libre and the Free Market have the fewest requirements among markets organised by Euronext. The admission and the first trading day are the responsibility of the sponsor, which must be a Euronext trading member.

Admission to First North requires a minimum free float of 10 per cent and the presence of an adequate number of shareholders. It is possible to waive the minimum free float if a liquidity provider is appointed. Of particular interest is the fact that OMX can ask companies with a market cap of more than €150 million and more than 50 per cent of the capital held by foreign investors to publish announcements or press releases in English.

The market that differs most from the other alternative markets is the Mercato Expandi. Expandi has higher requirements than other markets dedicated to mid- and small caps (minimum limits in terms of capitalisation, liquidity and track record), although still lower than those required for the Italian main market. A necessary condition to be listed on Expandi is compliance with certain profitability and financial requirements, a provision not even required for companies listing on the main market. Unlike what is required for the main market, companies listing on Expandi do not have to publish a business plan. The different legal status of Expandi and higher listing requirements as compared to other alternative markets called for the launch in 2007 of the MAC, a MTF dedicated to mid- and small caps with lighter listing and on-going requirements and a deep involvement of banks and accountants in the listing process. MAC is a market dedicated to professional investors. On the MAC there is no duty to publish a prospectus or have a minimum free float. Similar to the STAR segment, specialists operating on the MAC must publish at least two research reports a year on the issuer and organise a meeting between company management and professional investors at least once a year.

Given the small size of companies traded in, markets dedicated to mid- and small caps (or in many cases to small and micro caps) may suffer from lower liquidity compared to main markets. This has called for distinctive market models compared to those organised for main markets. As described in Table 7.5, some exchanges opt for quote-driven systems (or hybrid systems) to assure the constant display of bids and asks. The Italian MAC opted for a market model where the whole order book liquidity is concentrated in a single weekly auction. During the auction, the specialist operates as liquidity provider entering orders on the book. During the rest of the week, there is an off-auction period in which the specialist operates as market maker entering quotes on the information system, concluding trades outside the book and reporting them to the stock exchange. Given the professional nature of the market, Borsa Italiana set a minimum trading lot of €50,000.

Alternext created a hybrid market model, where shares can be traded both on and off the order book with a market maker. On the book, continuous trading is possible only for more liquid stocks. Less liquid stocks are traded only by auction. During the pre-auction period, market makers undertake a duty to enter bid and ask quotes within a maximum spread for shares they choose. The AIM created two separate market models: SEAQ, a pure quote-driven system for companies with at least two market makers, and a hybrid system, SETSqx (the same trading system where less liquid shares of the main market are traded). Almost all stock exchanges that only employ order-driven systems allow companies to appoint a liquidity provider. In particular, for MAB companies the presence of a liquidity provider is compulsory; for the Expandi companies, the appointment of a specialist is the condition to be traded continuously; and for the Entry Standard companies, the appointment of a specialist is the condition to be traded continuously only for less liquid shares. The only market not providing for the appointment of liquidity providers is the Marché Libre, even if the Belgian Free Market allows the sponsor to become the liquidity provider.

With just a few years of data available (Table 7.6) the assessment of the relative success of alternative markets is only tentative. Certainly,

Table 7.5   Market models for alternative markets

Markets	Order-driven vs. quote-driven	Trading forms	Liquidity provider
BME – MAB	Order-driven (floor trading also available)	Only auction For most liquid stocks continuous trading should also be possible	Liquidity provider
BIt – Expandi	Order-driven	• auction and continuous trading for companies with a specialist undertaking to support liquidity • only auction for companies without a specialist	Specialist (discretionary)
BIt – MAC	Hybrid (order and quote-driven)	• Friday one auction • from Monday to Thursday: a specialist enters quotes and trades are executed off order book	Specialist
DB – Entry Standard (Open Market)	Order-driven (floor trading also available)	Auction and continuous trading Less liquid shares are traded only by auction	Designated sponsor (discretionary)
Euronext – Alternext	Hybrid (order and quote-driven)	Order-driven: • auction and continuous trading for liquid stocks • only auction for less liquid stocks Quote-driven: duty to quote bid/ask during time in which the order book is open	Liquidity provider and market maker (both discretionary)
Euronext – Marché Libre	Order-driven	Auction only	No
LSE – AIM	• Order-driven: SETS (FTSE AIM UK 50 constituents and reserves) • Hybrid (order- and quote-driven): SETSqx (stocks not traded on SETS with fewer than two market makers) • Quote-driven: SEAQ (stocks not traded on SETS and with at least two market makers)	SETS: auction and continuous trading SETSqx: auction and quote-driven system SEAQ: quote-driven	Market makers discretionary for SETS and SETSqx and compulsory for SEAQ
OMX – First North	Order-driven	Auction and continuous trading	Discretionary

Source: Exchanges' market rules and websites.

Table 7.6 The size of European alternative markets

	Listed companies (end of 2007)	Market capitalisation (€bn, end of 2007)	2005–7 IPOs	raised Capital (€bn)
Borsa Italiana	301	733,614	68	11,801
– Expandi	35	10,742	23	971
– % on total	10.4	1.4	33.8	8.2
– MAC	3	99	3	99
– % on total	1.0	0.0	4.4	0.2
Deutsche Börse	761	1,439,955	174	17,523
– Entry Standard	112	n/a	89	996
– % on total	14.7	n/a	51.1	5.7
Euronext	1,043	2,888,313	220	45,975
– Alternext	113	5,738	106	989
– % on total	9.8	0.2	48.2	2.2
LSE	2,586	2,763 981	1,093	97,011
– AIM	1,347	132,829	856	29,166
– % on total	34.2	4.6	78.3	30.1
OMX	951	849,923	171	8,134
– First North	126	5,623	64	1,182
– % on total	13.2	0.7	37.4	14.5

Source: elaborations on data by Borsa Italiana, FESE, LSE, PWC and WFE data.

the importance of alternative markets dedicated to small and medium enterprises has grown appreciably in terms of the number of new listings and capital raised. Since 2005, 1,141 firms have been listed by IPO on alternative markets. The AIM alone hosts 856 IPOs. Even once we exclude AIM (which is at a more developed stage), the number of IPOs on all other markets is remarkable at 285. Thanks to the fast growth rate of new listings in the last three years, alternative markets now account for a relevant share in the total number of listed companies. At the end of 2007, companies listed on AIM accounted for more than 34.2 per cent of the total number of domestic listed companies on the LSE. This is equal to 14.7 per cent for Entry Standard, 13.2 per cent for First North, 11.4 per cent for Expandi and MAC, and 9.8 per cent for Alternext. The share of the total market capitalisation, albeit smaller than that of the number of listed companies, is growing briskly. Companies listed on AIM account for 4.6 per cent of total domestic market capitalisation. Expandi and MAC account for a combined market capitalisation of over 1.4 per cent on Borsa Italiana.[9] In all other markets, this is still well below 1 per cent. It is reasonable to expect that the weight of market capitalisation of alternative markets is likely to remain limited. The vigorous flow of new listings and capital raised has, nevertheless, contributed to increasing their size. Capital raised in 2005–7 by companies listed on alternative markets was €33.3 billion. Again, London AIM accounts for the bulk of the total capital raised, with €29.2 billion. IPOs on First North raised almost €1.2 billion, while those on Expandi and MAC raised €1.1 billion. Newly listed companies on Alternext and Entry Standard raised slightly less than €1 billion.

Going public by Italian small and medium-sized enterprises

In this section, we compare small and medium-sized enterprises with large ones by looking through the lens of the IPO process. In an initial public offering, a private company offers investors its shares, which are then listed and traded for the first time on a stock exchange. Even though IPOs have been a lively topic in financial economics for some decades now, empirical and theoretical literature has continued to flourish. The privatisation of large companies in some European countries and the surge in listings of technology, start-up companies in the US and Europe in the late 1990s further contributed to establishing IPOs as a major economic issue. We do not pretend to offer an exhaustive and in-depth study of IPOs or to discuss the effects that going public has on a firm's financing and investment decisions. Rather, we present some stylistic facts that highlight the distinguishing features of going public by small and medium companies.[10]

Looking at what happens when a company goes public for the first time is particularly instructive because much information is revealed during the IPO process. At this stage, the firm faces crucial decisions: how much capital to raise, how to estimate and price its value and the post-IPO governance and ownership structure. The assessment of the pros and cons is even more crucial for a small company since, as we shall show, it usually incurs high costs and faces great uncertainty.

The analysis here concerns the Italian market only: we focus on Italian firms listed on Borsa Italiana by the mean of an IPO in the period 2002–7. This period covers both the 'cold' phase following the bursting of the dot.com bubble, from 2002 to 2004, as well as the strong recovery of new listings which started in 2005. The last three years have witnessed a resurgence in listing activity that, at least in terms of capital raised, is comparable to the new listings wave that took place at the end of the late 1990s. Since 2002, 86 companies have been listed on Borsa Italiana by an IPO, raising almost €16 billion. We omitted from the sample financial businesses, investment and privatised enterprises and companies that, albeit conducting a public offer on Borsa Italiana, were already listed on other stock exchanges. This resulted in a sample of 64 IPOs. The definition of a small or medium company contains some discretionary elements. It is important to stress that the meaning of a small and medium company in the stock market is, to some extent, different from the definition employed for non-publicly listed companies. The European Commission (Eurostat, 2007) classifies a company as small or medium if it is independent of a large enterprise, has fewer than 250 employees and generates an annual turnover of less than €50 million. Generally speaking, small firms listed on equity markets are usually larger in terms of employees and turnover than those that match the corresponding EU definition. Companies with fewer than 20 employees are rarely listed and the costs of going public may barely match the benefits. Rather than contrasting firms on the basis of the market or the segment they belong to, we divided the sample by size only. Various methodologies are available, for example fixing specific thresholds in terms of market capitalisation, or on the basis of the sample distribution (like quartiles or quintiles). We selected the threshold approach and defined small companies as those with market capitalisation of less than €100 million on the first day of trading; medium-sized companies are defined as having a market capitalisation of €100–500 million; and large companies are those with market capitalisation of more than €500 million.

A comment on the thresholds employed in this section is appropriate. Market participants and investors usually employ a different segmentation, and a small company is usually defined as having a market cap of less than €1 billion. The segmentation of main markets according to this threshold is common practice and it reflects the investors' point of view rather than the firm's. Our analysis of liquidity follows this kind of segmentation. Here we look at the IPO process from the firm's point of view.

Table 7.7 presents descriptive statistics. The sample covers 64 IPOs, spanning companies as small as €26 million market capitalisation to companies with more than €5 billion. The total offering value of these IPOs is almost €11 billion. As we can see, medium-sized companies represent the bulk of the sample, comprising slightly less than 47 per cent. Small and large companies are more equally represented – 30 per cent

Table 7.7   Descriptive statistics – Italian IPOs breakdown by market capitalisation (2002–7)

		Small <€100 m	Medium €100–500 m	Large >€500 m	Total sample
Number of IPOs		19	30	15	64
% on total sample		30	47	23	100
Company's age at the IPO (years)	average	25	37	67	41
Market cap (first day of trading) – €m	average	58.4	271.3	1,282.0	445.0
Capital raised – €m	average	19.4	100.5	493.1	168.4
Industry breakdown* – number of firms					
Oil and gas		–	–	1	1
Basic materials		1	2	1	4
Industrials		6	12	6	24
Consumer goods		6	7	4	17
Health care		2	–	1	3
Consumer services		1	4	1	6
Telecommunications		–	–	–	–
Utilities		–	2	–	2
Financials (only real estate)		–	1	1	2
Technology		3	2	–	5

* The industry breakdown follows the Industry Classification Benchmark (ICB).
Source: elaborations on Borsa Italiana – R&D data.

and 23 per cent respectively. As expected, small firms are considerably younger than large ones at the IPO. The average market capitalisation of small companies is slightly less than €60 million. Medium-sized companies have an average market capitalisation of around €270 million, while large companies have almost €1.3 billion. On average, small companies raised €19 million, while large ones raised almost €500 million. The breakdown by industry (according to the Industry Classification Benchmark) shows that IPOs by industrial and consumer goods companies make up nearly two-thirds of the whole sample, in part reflecting the underlying industrial structure of the Italian economy. The health care and technology sectors are relatively more common among small companies, while in this segment there are fewer IPOs in the consumer services sector. Oil and gas companies are, as expected, represented only in the large segment. As already mentioned, the IPO is a complex and in some ways a lengthy process. In this section we focus on three features.

First, we look at the structure of the offer and the costs of going public. Second, we examine the pricing of the IPO. And third, we present data on the presence of institutional investors in firms' ownership before and after the IPO.

The structure of the offer

The most frequently cited reason for going public is to raise capital, both at the IPO as well as afterwards once, thanks to the liquidity of its shares, the firm is better able to tap new financing needs by seasoned offerings.[11] Table 7.8 shows how the destination of the proceeds raised at the IPO changes according to size. We can see that small companies issue, on average, 75 per cent of the total capital raised by primary, new shares, rather than selling secondary shares owned by pre-IPO shareholders. The amount of capital raised by primary shares sharply declines with size, being least for large firms (28 per cent). This evidence is quite robust across countries and time. Paleari et al. (2007) show similar results when comparing main markets with alternative markets dedicated to SMEs: on average European firms listed on alternative markets issue more than 80 per cent of the offering value through new shares, while this share is only 60 per cent for companies listed on main markets. Whether the new capital is used to sustain organic growth or external acquisitions, or to reduce the leverage in debt, is a less straightforward question to answer. Early empirical evidence from the Italian stock market (Pagano et al., 1998) highlighted that newly listed companies employed new capital to reduce leverage or to invest in other financial assets and companies, rather than to make new investments. A more recent study by Franzosi and Pellizzoni (2005) based on 127 IPOs by independent (excluding equity carve-outs) Italian SMEs during 1995–2002 shows that newly listed companies increase, on average, the growth rate of investments and the number of acquisitions after the IPO.

For any given amount of capital raised, the firm must decide whether to address the offer to the public through a public offer, or to a selected number of investors by a private placement. In a private placement, the company usually offers its shares to professional investors, such as banks, mutual and pension funds or other institutional investors. The firm, as advised by the sponsoring bank, must weigh the costs and benefits of each option. Usually a public offer is more expensive than a private placement, largely because of the higher selling costs incurred when addressing a large number of small investors. Table 7.8 shows that the most frequent offering option for both small and large companies is to combine a public offer with a private placement. Small companies,

Table 7.8   Offering characteristics – Italian IPOs breakdown by market capitalisation (2002–7) (%)

	Small <€100 m	Medium €100–500 m	Large >€500 m
Offer type			
– by public offer only	0	0	0
– by private placement only	32	7	0
– by public offer and private placement	68	93	100
Post-IPO free float	36.1	40.5	38.4
Capital raised by			
– primary shares	74.6	55.9	27.6
– secondary shares	25.4	44.1	72.4
Amount subscribed by			
– public	20.5	20.3	23.1
– domestic institutional investors	64.4	38.2	19.0
– foreign institutional investors	15.1	41.5	57.9
Total direct costs (as a % of capital raised)	8.7	6.2	4.4

Source: elaborations on Borsa Italiana – R&D data.

however, frequently decide to list by private placement only: almost one third of small companies list in this way. This alternative is chosen in 7 per cent of medium companies but is never preferred by large companies. Certainly, as the size of the capital to be raised increases, the public offer becomes a compelling option; a private placement would imply that a narrow base of institutional investors commits a large amount of capital in a poorly liquid security. It is well known that many of the direct costs associated with IPOs are more or less fixed and this produces a strongly declining cost curve as the offering value increases.

In Figure 7.1 we plot direct costs, expressed as a percentage of capital raised, as a function of the offering value. We can see the decline in total costs as the value, and hence the firm's size, increases. Direct costs are comprised of underwriting, management and selling fees as well as legal and marketing costs. Although not reported here, other significant expenses are management's time and costs related to the company's reorganisation. The size of the offer is not the only determinant of costs, but is certainly an important one. Other things being equal, large companies incur costs that are relatively about half those faced by small companies. For small companies these costs are, on average, 8.7 per cent of total capital raised, while for large companies they are as low as 4.4 per cent.

The decision regarding the mix of private placement and public offer has important consequences in terms of the composition of the post-IPO

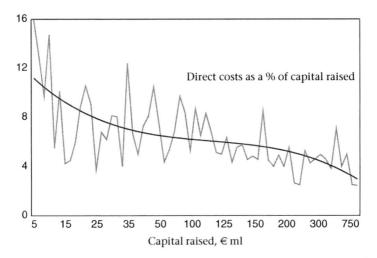

Figure 7.1 Direct IPO costs by offering size – Italian IPOs (2002–7)
Source: elaborations on Borsa Italiana – R&D data.

shareholder base. Recent studies highlight that the structure of the offer reflects the different preferences of the controlling shareholder compared with a more concentrated or dispersed shareholder base, or whether the IPO is an exit option or a way to raise capital while still retaining control. Despite the frequent use of private placements by small firms, the composition of the allocated shares is not very different across sizes. In small companies, the public subscribes 21 per cent of the offer while in large companies the figure is over 23 per cent. Notable, and not immediately related to the type of the offer, is the lower share subscribed by foreign institutional investors in small firms (and to some extent medium-sized firms also). Foreign investors subscribe only 17 per cent of the offer for small companies and almost 60 per cent for large companies. This may be because either they seek fewer shares or because fewer shares are allocated to them. A very tentative explanation supports both reasons once we assume, as we should, that domestic institutional investors have superior information about the true value of small domestic companies. Uncertainty about the true value of small companies is usually greater than about large ones. Local proximity partly helps to reduce information asymmetry and foreign investors may be at disadvantage as compared with domestic institutions, which can benefit from a network of better informed agents. This would imply, *ceteris paribus*, that foreign institutional investors demand fewer shares. Moreover, as we shall see, the way shares are allocated in the book-building procedure may advantage domestic investors who, by disclosing their superior information, receive a more favourable allocation of shares. This is confirmed by the higher over-subscription rate of foreign investors over domestic ones observed among small companies IPOs than large ones.

Setting the IPO price

Setting the offer price is probably the most important point of the IPO process and much of the economic literature is devoted to how firms are valued and priced. There are many ways to set the price: by single or discriminatory price auction, by fixed price or by book-building. Moreover, the price may be set before the start of the offer or only once indications of interest come in. In many countries, including Italy, the most common way to determine the offer price is the book-building procedure and to fix the price after the end of the public offer. Book-building consists in the collection of indications of interest from institutional investors (the public is a price-taker) by the lead investment bank that coordinates the offer. Such indications usually consist in quantities and prices[12] at which each investor is willing to subscribe. These indications are then used by the investment bank to create a demand curve (Cornelli and Goldreich, 2001; 2003) and hence to determine the final offer price. Usually the bids are collected inside a generally non-binding price range. Book-building emerged as a successful means to set the offer price. It is a fairly precise pricing mechanism, while still leaving discretion to the underwriter. Many different classes of proxies have been employed to value uncertainty. One, albeit noisy, measure is provided by the book-building range. Everything else being equal, the higher the uncertainty about the true value of the company, the wider the range and the more the investment bank relies on the market to set the price. Usually this uncertainty is higher for small or innovative firms than for large and traditional ones. As we can see from Table 7.9 the book-building range is around 22 per cent for the whole sample. Contrary to what might be expected, the book-building range is somewhat narrower for smaller than for medium and large companies. The large variation in the data, however, makes the difference in the average of book-building ranges between small and large companies statistically insignificant.

Under-pricing is one of the best-known and most investigated patterns in the IPO literature.[13] Under-pricing consists in setting the offer price below its market value, which results in large returns on the first day of trading. What is remarkable is that, although to different

Table 7.9 IPO pricing – Italian IPOs break down by market capitalisation (2002–7) (%)

		Small <€100 m	Medium €100–500 m	Large >€500 m
Book-building range	average	20.6	21.7	24.7
	median	19.4	22.2	21.7
Under-pricing	average	8.5	5.0	3.5
	median	4.5	4.3	3.4

Source: elaborations on Borsa Italiana – R&D data.

degrees, it is a very robust fact across time, countries and institutional frameworks. Many theories have been put forward to account for this phenomenon,[14] from asymmetrical information models to institutional or behavioural explanations. A description of the underpinnings of each theory requires more space than is available here. One explanation, consistent with the subject dealt with above concerning the allocation of shares to institutional investors, links the degree of valuation uncertainty to under-pricing. An information revelation theory, first developed by Benveniste and Spindt (1989), assumes that investors are at an informational advantage compared to both the underwriter and the issuing firm. The underwriter, in order to provide an incentive to well-informed investors to reveal valuable information about the true value of the firm, has to under-price the issue. More under-pricing should be seen as a reward for the degree of information asymmetry: the greater the information gap, the higher the value of information and hence the degree of under-pricing. Table 7.9 shows that under-pricing varies with size, with small firms experiencing more under-pricing than large ones. In our sample, small firms have, on average, under-pricing equal to 8.5 per cent, 5 per cent higher than that observed for large ones. The stronger under-pricing of small companies is well documented elsewhere. Similar evidence across European and US markets may be found in Paleari et al. (2007), who illustrate that the degree of under-pricing declines, albeit not in a linear fashion, with size. In order to offer a benchmark to the degree of under-pricing found in our sample, in Goergen et al. (2003) companies listed on Italian Nuovo Mercato between 1999 and 2000 had an average under-pricing of 19 per cent, and those listed on all Euro.NM between 1996 and 2000 were under-priced by around 31 per cent.

Table 7.10   The role of professional investors – Italian IPOs breakdown by market capitalisation (2002–7) (%)

	Small <€100 m	Medium €100–500 m	Large >€500 m
Presence of professional investors before IPO (frequency distribution)			
VC/Private Equity	21.1	30.0	20.0
Banks	15.8	23.3	6.7
Institutional investors	5.3	10.0	–

Ownership change at the IPO						
	Before IPO	Post IPO	Before IPO	Post IPO	Before IPO	Post IPO
VC/Private Equity	34.0	16.2	10.3	2.9	48.6	9.6
Banks	22.2	9.0	6.8	4.3	3.0	2.2
Institutional investors	9.7	6.1	16.9	3.1	–	–

Source: elaborations on Borsa Italiana – R&D data.

The role of professional investors

We turn, finally, to the presence of institutional investors in the capital of enterprises at the IPO. Venture capitalists and other specialised institutional investors play a crucial role in the financing of small and innovative firms.[15] Their primary role is to select and support promising entrepreneurs. The stock market is a natural exit route for these financiers, by which they obtain a return for the capital and other services, like management and industry expertise, they provide to the firm. The complementary and reinforcing relationship between the stock market and the venture capital industry is well known and documented (Black and Gilson, 1998; Becker and Hellman, 2005). In the absence of the stock market, the venture capitalist would have no other choice than to sell out on the private market, perhaps at a lower price as a consequence of the low liquidity of its stake. This would make venture capital a less profitable activity and narrow the financing menu of SMEs. As already pointed out, the development of new markets in the late 1990s has helped to boost the European venture capital industry. The capital raised at the IPO by the venture capitalist provides fresh funds to finance a new stream of equity investments.

In Table 7.10 we summarise the presence of professional institutional investors, including banks, as shareholders before the IPO. Overall in 25 per cent of IPOs at least one venture capitalist or private equity fund was present, and in almost 40 per cent of the IPOs at least one professional investor was present. We do not find a significantly different presence of venture capitalists and private equity investors in small enterprises compared to large companies. On average 21 per cent of IPOs by small companies are backed by at least one venture capitalist or private equity investor. Medium-sized companies show a somewhat higher frequency, with 30 per cent of IPOs venture-backed. As we know, the private equity industry can be divided into two segments: venture capitalists that engage in early stage financing of small and growing firms, and buy-out funds that are more focused on the restructuring of established medium and large private companies (European Central Bank, 2007). Given that we are unable to single out the two segments, it is not surprising to observe the presence of venture capitalists or private equity funds in both small and large companies. More remarkable is the difference in the presence of other professional investors. Banks and other institutional investors are substantially more present in small and medium enterprises compared to large firms, evidence that may call for further research. Finally, data on post-IPO ownership confirm that these institutional investors do not exit completely from the company at the IPO but, for signalling reasons, retain a substantial ownership after the listing.[16]

Liquidity in secondary markets: a European comparison

In the previous section we concentrated on the IPO process from the point of view of an enterprise going public. In this section, we take the investors' point of view. The fundamental role of the market is to provide liquidity to investors (Handa and Schwartz, 1996). Secondary market liquidity is nonetheless crucial for enterprises too: the ability to buy and sell stocks with a low price impact reduces the liquidity risk and hence the cost of capital.

Many factors influence share liquidity. In this section we report liquidity measures for different sizes and different markets or segments. Various studies confirm that across markets medium and small companies are less liquid (Munck and Mortensen, 2003). Stock exchanges articulated their offer on the basis of the different needs of enterprises and investors. As underlined in the previous sections, companies' commitment to the market and the market model set by the stock exchange contribute to establishing the success of a market in terms of share liquidity. By taking the investor's point of view, we define mid- and small caps differently from the way employed in the previous section. Companies are divided into four classes based on their market capitalisation: micro caps (€<100 million), small caps (€100–300 million), mid-caps (€300–1,000 million) and large caps (>€1,000 million). We first compare how liquidity changes across markets and segments along equal size classes. Second, we assess the extent to which exchanges succeeded in attenuating the liquidity gaps between their small and large caps.

The comparison between liquidity classes is based on a sample of 4,891 companies. The period of analysis is the whole of 2006 and shares are divided into classes based on 2006 year-end market capitalisation. The sample is made up of shares traded on BME, Borsa Italiana (MTA and Expandi), Deutsche Börse (Official and Regulated Market and Entry Standard), Euronext (Eurolist and Alternext), LSE (Main Market and AIM), OMX (Nordic list and First North Stockholm) and SWX. We exclude from the sample foreign companies, investment companies and companies whose trading at the end of the year was indefinitely suspended. Two measures are employed to assess shares liquidity: median turnover and median turnover velocity (the ratio of annual turnover and market capitalisation).[17] Median turnover is calculated as the median of the daily median turnover of each share included in the class. Moreover, we only take into account the order book trade (with the exception of LSE and OMX, where the database also includes negotiated deals). Median turnover velocity is computed as the median of the annual turnover velocity of each share included in the class. The use of the median, as compared to the average, allows us to evaluate liquidity even in the presence of outliers. Finally, the liquidity of each class is presented as the turnover of the most representative stock on the most representative trading day and as the annual turnover velocity of the most representative stock.

Prior to focusing on liquidity comparison, it is important to stress differences in terms of the presence of micro and small caps in the analysed markets. This has a high impact on sample composition. In particular, Table 7.11 shows a lower incidence in both absolute and relative terms of these companies in the Italian and Spanish markets. Micro caps and small caps represent more than 70 per cent of the listed companies on the markets managed by Deutsche Börse and LSE, about 60 per cent on Euronext and SWX, about 40 per cent on Borsa Italiana but only 20 per cent on BME.

To compare the liquidity of companies with similar market capitalisation, turnover is a better measure. As Table 7.11 shows, the STAR segment of Borsa Italiana, the Plus segment of OMX and BME are the most liquid trading environments for micro caps. By contrast, trading activity is

Capitalisation classes

	<€100 m			€100–300 m			€300–1,000 m			>€1,000 m		
	No of firms	Turnover (€)	Turn. vel. (%)	No of firms	Turnover (€)	Turn. vel. (%)	No of firms	Turnover (€)	Turn. vel. (%)	No of firms	Turnover (€)	Turn. vel. (%)
Blt	64	51,496	75%	54	182,279	48%	72	608,110	58%	88	6,133,502	97%
STAR	18	84,354	81%	21	233,834	73%	34	891,587	78%	2	942,127	39%
Standard	31	47,807	88%	28	134,615	42%	36	439,127	39%	4	1,992,815	70%
Expandi	15	21,015	28%	5	80,313	18%	2	501,565	73%	2	1,777,618	15%
BME	9	65,010	30%	17	278,270	88%	31	583,780	58%	70	8,304,690	93%
Deutsche Börse	409	2,410	11%	97	63,990	25%	78	531,275	40%	110	9,531,158	115%
Reg & Off Mkt	361	320	6%	92	65,820	25%	78	531,275	40%	110	9,531,158	115%
Entry Standard	48	15,275	33%	5	32,810	31%	–	–	–	–	–	–
Euronext	425	7,950	11%	196	52,145	18%	163	226,615	32%	233	7,561,750	83%
Eurolist	359	7,740	11%	189	53,500	19%	163	226,615	32%	233	7,561,750	83%
Alternext	66	6,080	11%	7	43,730	9%	–	–	–	–	–	–
LSE	1,149	1,796	23%	309	73,751	58%	200	533,060	86%	265	16,303,879	165%
Main market	126	6,352	24%	141	122,570	64%	161	657,915	82%	260	16,955,916	167%
AIM	1,023	1,564	23%	168	49,948	55%	39	225,766	100%	5	1,667,758	74%
OMX-Nordic list	210	23,876	48%	123	120,464	41%	97	493,230	53%	121	6,979,614	112%
Plus Segment	12	46,342	64%	9	81,345	27%	19	335,900	49%	2	862,932	30%
First North	60	26,691	82%	11	140,858	104%	2	2,165,337	140%	–	–	–
Stockholm												
SWX	49	3,777	20%	53	70,729	25%	57	305,669	34%	72	5,208,905	72%

Source: elaborations on Datastream and Borsa Italiana data. Exchange rates: ECB (as of 31 December 2007).

particularly low on the markets managed by Deutsche Börse, Euronext, LSE and SWX. STAR segment and BME are confirmed as the most liquid trading venues when we look at small caps. Liquidity differentials tend to decrease for mid-caps, although STAR continues to show a turnover that is larger than that of other segments and markets. The remarkable turnover of mid-caps traded on First North Stockholm appears to be more firm-specific given that only two companies are included in the sample. The average market capitalisation of large caps is different across markets, which weakens the robustness of any comparison in terms of turnover. The average market capitalisation of Borsa Italiana large caps is €8 billion compared to the €10 billion of Deutsche Börse and LSE and €11 billion of Euronext. Data from the UK and Nordic markets are inflated by the presence of reported trades not executed on the book, with the real risk that these trades are double-counted.

To sum up, the Italian and Spanish trading environments are the most liquid for mid- and small caps. The STAR segment in particular is seen to be the most liquid trading venue in Europe when we consider the entire €0–1 billion class. Alternative markets are mainly targeted at companies in the micro and small caps classes. A comparison across these markets shows that Mercato Expandi and First North Stockholm are most able to reconcile low listing and ongoing requirements with investor attractiveness in terms of liquidity. Despite this, alternative markets are in general notably less liquid than their respective main markets, the only exception being the German market for micro caps and Swedish market for small caps.

Turnover velocity is the appropriate measure to compare mid- and small caps liquidity with that of large ones. Turnover velocity allows us to normalise the turnover values with the size of the company. The analysis on turnover velocity confirms that liquidity is concentrated on large caps, although to varying degrees. The Italian market appears to be a highly liquid context for the trading of micro caps, which have a turnover velocity of 75 per cent. Subdividing further the micro cap class into two classes – €0–50 million and €50–100 million – we get a remarkable result. The smallest companies listed on Borsa Italiana have a turnover velocity of 88 per cent, only slightly less than the turnover velocity of large caps – 97 per cent. Even more remarkable is the liquidity of companies listed on the STAR segment with a market cap of <€50 million, which reach a median turnover velocity of 146 per cent.

Looking at the evolution of Italian market from 2002 and 2007, as summarised in Table 7.12, it is possible to identify a growing liquidity trend. In the context of a general increase in trading, the liquidity of

Table 7.12 Turnover velocity for the mid- and small caps – Italian markets (2002–7)

	2002	2003	2004	2005	2006	2007
STAR (%)	35.9	48.1	46.2	107.5	103.0	109.0
Standard (%)	36.8	38.8	36.8	81.5	65.6	86.1
Expandi (%)	6.1	8.6	9.3	15.8	25.9	35.9
Equity markets (%)	120.7	143.6	137.1	151.9	157.5	208.3
MIB Index	16,954	19,483	22,886	26,056	31,005	28,525
Var (%)	−23.7	14.9	17.5	13.9	19	−8.0

Source: elaborations on Borsa Italiana – R&D data; STAR and Standard data are restated to include since 2002 also MTAX (previously Nuovo Mercato) companies, which assignation to STAR and Standard segments has been effective from September 2005; Mercato Expandi started in December 2003, previously data are referred to Mercato Ristretto; MAC started in September 2007, giving the low number of trading days, MAC data have not been included.

mid- and small caps appears to have increased more than the whole market. This pattern is especially noticeable for the STAR segment after 2005, in the middle of a bull market. It will be interesting to see how liquidity changes across markets, segments and sizes in the course of the current bear market (starting on the second half of 2007). Preliminary evidence seems to suggest that with declining and turbulent markets, liquidity tends to flow back to larger companies.

Conclusions

Small and medium enterprises are usually characterised by less favourable access to external finance. In this framework equity markets play a crucial role. A company that goes public is able to raise new capital, both at the IPO and later. Being publicly traded allows the company to reduce information asymmetries and hence to tap new financing needs on better terms. Moreover, the market price conveys essential information that helps to steer and monitor management actions. A liquid secondary market makes it possible to invest and trade in these securities, lowering the firm's cost of capital. Stock exchanges have provided several options in order to favour the listing of small and medium enterprises. By segmenting main markets, stock exchanges offer small and medium companies adequate frameworks in terms of visibility and transparency. The introduction of alternative markets reduces the complexity and costs of going public, helping to bridge the gap between small companies and equity markets.

Looking at the IPO process, we highlighted that small firms are younger than large ones and issue, in relative terms, more primary shares, confirming that the main rationale for these firms is to raise new capital. The costs of going public differ considerably between large and small companies, being higher for small companies. Small companies try to contain these costs by frequently addressing only institutional investors by private placements. At the IPO, foreign institutional investors subscribe relatively fewer shares of small and medium Italian companies than of large ones. The greater uncertainty in valuation of SMEs is reflected in stronger under-pricing, albeit to a much lower extent than that recorded in the late 1990s by high-tech, innovative firms listed on European new markets. Venture capitalists and private equity funds are present in the share ownership of one in five small companies, a level similar to that of large enterprises. At the IPO, these investors significantly reduce their stake in the firm, but do not wholly exit from the capital.

The analysis of trading activity shows that small and medium caps are actually less liquid than large ones. The introduction of special segments with higher requirements tends to close the liquidity gap by means of higher transparency and corporate governance standards. Data on alternative markets show a lower liquidity compared to main markets, with some exceptions. Looking at Italian small and medium companies, we observed an asymmetrical effect of liquidity trends across sizes. The bull market had a relatively stronger effect on small caps liquidity than on large ones. The financial turmoil that started in the second half of 2007 is, although preliminary, showing a flow of liquidity from small caps to blue chip companies.

Appendix 7.1 The organisation of trading in the secondary market

Exchanges organise secondary markets in order to facilitate trading in financial instruments. The market model chosen is essential to maximise market quality and so reduce trading costs and improve the price discovery mechanism. Trading costs include not only explicit costs (for example, the exchange trading fees), but also implicit costs (as the bid–ask spread and price impact). Market models are defined by the combination of different trading characteristics (for example, trading phases, trading hours, order types, minimum trading lots, and so on). In this appendix, we compare order-driven with quote-driven markets and auction with continuous trading.

Order-driven vs. quote-driven

In order-driven markets, all traders can enter, modify and cancel orders on an order book. Orders are ranked and matched on the basis of priority rules (generally price–time priority). In quote-driven markets, only market makers can enter quotes on the trading system and non-market makers apply, generally by phone, the quotes of the chosen market maker without the need to respect priority rules (so-called preferencing). The main differences between order- and quote-driven markets are related to:

- *Transparency.* In order-driven markets it is possible to see orders entered by all the other traders and know all the trading possibilities (pre-trade transparency). In quote-driven markets non-market makers only know the quotes displayed by market makers. Conversely, market makers also know the intentions of the traders contacting them and the portfolio of these traders (post-trade transparency). This discrepancy creates an information asymmetry between market makers and non-market makers.
- *Risk of collusion.* The risk of collusion among market makers in quote-driven markets is a significant risk. Collusion usually results in higher bid–ask spreads.
- *Immediacy.* Market makers, by continuously displaying quotes, offer the opportunity to have immediate execution of trades. On order-driven markets, a similar result can be obtained by charging specific intermediaries to support liquidity. These intermediaries enter on the order book buy and sell orders within a maximum spread.

Call auction vs. continuous trading

There are two main phases during an auction. In the first, the pre-auction, traders can enter, modify and delete buy and sell orders; the trading platform collects orders and calculates a theoretical auction price, but no execution happens. In the second phase, which generally starts randomly, traders cannot enter, modify or delete orders and trades are executed at a single price, the auction price.

During continuous trading, traders can enter, modify or delete buy or sell orders and if price and volume conditions are respected, orders are matched immediately with orders on the opposite side of the book.

The main advantage of continuous trading is immediacy, whereas auctions allow a better price discovery, focusing liquidity in specific periods and obtaining meaningful prices.

In the same market it is possible to have both auction and continuous trading. Generally, to allow overnight orders to appear together on the book and to spread information to the market participants, trading starts with an auction. Furthermore, given the relevant uses of closing price, most of markets also close the trading day with an auction.

For mid- and small caps, the opportunity to concentrate liquidity in auctions is particularly valuable, giving their lower liquidity.

Acknowledgement

We would like to thank Luisella Bosetti, Valentina Coraggio, Luca Filippa and Alessandra Franzosi for their suggestions. The authors are responsible for any errors or omissions. The views expressed in this chapter do not necessarily reflect those of Borsa Italiana or the London Stock Exchange group.

8
The Role of the Public Sector

Elisabetta Gualandri and Paola Schwizer

Introduction

Small and medium-sized enterprises (SMEs) play an essential role in the economy internationally and above all in Europe, where over 20 million SMEs account for around two-thirds of jobs and half of turnover in the non-agricultural business sectors. SMEs' contribution to growth and employment, not to mention innovation, makes them key players in the achievement of the Lisbon Strategy goals (European Investment Bank, 2005). At the same time, restrictions on SMEs' access to external finance create undesirable obstacles to employment and growth.

While there is no indication of generalised market failure across Europe for the supply of finance to SMEs, the European Commission has, in a recent Communication, stressed the need for public action as a catalyst to the development of the markets at the European, national and regional levels in three specific areas (European Investment Bank, 2005, p. 6):

1 the improvement of the framework conditions for SME finance with, in particular, the development of financial markets in the new member states which suffer from a low level of equity investments and bank lending;
2 early stage finance, in particular through guarantees and micro-lending;
3 equity.

Innovative small and medium-sized enterprises (ISMEs) represent an extremely small proportion of SMEs overall in any country, but have a relevant role in creating new jobs and in enhancing technological development, with positive outcomes for economic growth. For these firms, financial constraints and serious equity gaps are observed even in the most developed countries due to market failures, which are particularly significant for this kind of business.

For these reasons, policy-makers are developing different types of intervention specifically focused on ISMEs at the national and international levels. This chapter analyses the best practices developed in different countries both inside and outside the EU, with the aim of identifying overall best practices on the basis of the concrete results achieved by different schemes, and specifying intervention criteria that could improve the effectiveness of private–public cooperation.

The chapter is organised as follows. The next section provides an analysis of the motivation for public sector intervention to bridge the equity gap facing innovative SMEs and a description of different types of scheme being developed by policy-makers at the national and international levels. Then we introduce the guiding lines of the EU approach. After that we outline the key elements of each country study in order to identify the best practices and pioneer schemes suitable for broader application. The countries surveyed are the US, Israel, UK, Germany, France, the Netherlands and Denmark. Summaries and important conclusions for the implementation and evaluation of public policies and incentive schemes for this sector are provided in the final section.

Government intervention: modes and motivations

As we have seen, there are two main reasons behind government measures to provide support for the birth and growth of innovative, and particularly technology-based, SMEs, and encourage entrepreneurial activity. First and foremost, these measures are a response to the market failures believed to generate an equity gap, especially during the initial stages of these firms' life cycle. As far as the European Commission is concerned, it is the existence of such market failures which justifies the introduction of public measures to supply or encourage the provision of risk capital in member states, by allowing such projects to be undertaken without breaching the regulatory framework on state aid. The concept of 'market failure' used for this purpose refers to situations in which a serious distortion in the allocation of resources is assumed to exist for two main reasons: imperfect, asymmetrical information, and deal costs which make the assessment costs too high in relation to the size of the investment required (European Commission, 2001).

Table 8.1 Public intervention measures to support the venture capital market

	Demand-side measures	**Supply-side measures**
Direct intervention	Public incubators	Public (-sponsored) venture capital funds
Indirect intervention	Promotion of enterprise and entrepreneurship	Downside protection scheme
	Management and skilled workforce	Upside leverage scheme
	Business incubators, science and technology parks and clusters	Fund's operating costs scheme
	Tax incentives	Exit schemes
		Tax incentives
		Business angels network

Source: European Investment Bank (2001, p. 49).

The second reason for policy-makers' intervention is the importance of the birth and development of these firms for economic growth overall as a source of benefits for society in general.[1]

Starting from these considerations, the role of public intervention in bridging the equity gap should form part of an action plan which defines how and when to act, and sets operational objectives and the rules of the game for the interactions between public and private players.[2] It is thus necessary to decide the type of instruments to be adopted on both the demand and supply sides, and the time horizon for the interventions planned. The concluding stage of this type of analysis needs to provide an assessment of the efficacy of public programmes in terms of the creation of enterprise and wealth.

There is general agreement that the role of government in the development of ISMEs must involve the promotion of the ideal context for the growth of the formal and informal underlying fundamental demand and supply of risk capital (Maula et al., 2007). The development of a private risk capital market for ISMEs requires the removal of any fiscal and legal obstacles, the fostering of a managerial culture and the creation of specific markets and/or segments for the listing of these kinds of firms, to simplify disinvestment by venture capital funds.

The possible forms of public intervention

Table 8.1 summarises the types of government intervention undertaken at the EU level and within the individual European states with the aim of reducing the equity gap for innovative and high-tech SMEs.[3] Forms of intervention are classified as direct, in which case public capital is used to establish venture capital funds and funds of funds and incubators, or indirect, involving schemes intended to foster and encourage the growth of the venture capital sector through measures targeting both the demand and supply sides (European Investment Bank, 2001). When developing financial intervention measures, it is important for policy-makers to consider the entire financing ladder and not only the instruments directly involving risk capital.

The aim of demand-side measures is to reduce the lack of entrepreneurial skills and the business culture gap which constitute a serious disadvantage for many small entrepreneurs. Direct measures focus on the creation of public incubators, while indirect programmes aim to create a social and economic climate hospitable to entrepreneurship (OECD, 2006a). They concentrate on developing a managerial cultural and specific know-how, defining measures for the protection of intellectual property and encouraging the development of business initiatives, incubators, technology parks and university spin-offs. Other possible measures are of a fiscal nature.

As far as the supply side is concerned, Jääskeläinen et al. (2004) identify three mechanisms generally used separately, involving: asymmetrical profit-sharing; investment timing in which the fact that the public funds enter first generates profit leverage for the private investors; and coverage of losses by the public partner (downside guarantee protection).

Direct intervention takes the form of the creation of venture capital funds or funds of funds using public resources or in partnership with private investors (so-called 'hybrid funds'). Target firms should belong to specific sectors (for example, high-tech, life sciences, biotechnology and so on) and/or be in specific life cycle stages, and suffer from a proven shortage of private investment funds ascertained with the aid of reliable equity gap measurement techniques. These measures should be of a temporary nature, function in line with market mechanisms and be managed by private managers. The guiding principle is risk-sharing, meaning that, apart from the preliminary seed stages, public funds should only be provided alongside private investment (financial intermediaries, informal investors and universities), combined with them in public–private partnership schemes (OECD, 2006a).

One interesting aspect of the ongoing debate concerns direct public intervention to develop the venture capital market and the possible contraindications (Leleux and Surlemont, 2003). Public intervention can have negative effects on the development of the venture capital market from two points of view: non-optimal allocation of resources and an increase, rather than a reduction, in the barriers to entry to this sector for private capital. The main causes of these problems are first that the funds are placed in the hands of public managers, who do not have sufficient experience in the selection of projects for investment, or the same incentive schemes as private managers. Second, and even more serious, the risk has been pointed out that private capital may be crowded out by public funds. This may occur if public capital, made available at lower cost, reduces the expected return on investment, so that the risk threshold applied to projects accepted for financing gradually rises. As a consequence, only the marginal projects would be left to private investors, creating what is known as a 'market for lemons' (OECD, 2006a). The aim of attracting new private operators to develop a thriving market for venture capital would thus not be fulfilled. However, there appears to be no empirical evidence of the occurrence of crowding out (Leleux and Surlemond, 2003).

On the supply side, indirect measures may adopt a variety of approaches. Some schemes involve less favourable terms for public partners with regard to meeting the costs of bankruptcies and profit distribution in operations undertaken in partnership with private investors. Other measures may offer subsidies to risk capital funds to cover a proportion of their administrative and/or management costs, while yet others aim to make it easier for funds to liquidate their holdings in firms, encourage the establishment of networks of business agents or provide tax-breaks for investors.[4]

In more general term, indirect schemes help to reduce the risk to private investors by transferring all or part of the potential costs of bankruptcy to the public sector (downside protection schemes). Measures of this kind are particularly suitable when the venture capital market is in its infancy, while at later stages in its development intervention models focusing on the potential profits for private investors (upside leverage schemes) become more common. In a mature market, various forms of risk/profit-sharing schemes are viewed as appropriate (European Commission, 2005a).

The EU approach

The large number of SMEs and their vital role in driving growth and providing competitiveness and employment, within the EU, have led to the introduction of specific regulatory measures and policies in the area of access to financial markets to encourage the SMEs' creation, favour their growth and ensure their strength. When drawing up its action plans, the European Commission has worked in three main directions with the aim of creating a favourable environment for SMEs' birth and growth: the encouragement of entrepreneurship, the establishment of an environment where innovation and change can flourish and the provision of guarantees that goods and services have free access to their respective markets.

Within this general framework, in 1998 the European Commission promoted a Risk Capital Action Plan (RCAP) with committed launching polices in the various EU states to support the creation of new high-tech enterprises and very small businesses.

This commitment was reinforced in 2000 by the Lisbon Council of Europe, with the so-called Lisbon Agenda, aiming to ensure that by 2010 the European economy can 'become the most dynamic and competitive knowledge-based economy in the world, capable of sustainable economic growth with more and better jobs and greater social cohesion' (European Council, 2000, point 5).

The RCAP has three main components: policies to aid the growth of venture capital; the reinforcement of public–private partnerships; and the transition from grants or subsidies to SMEs to programmes with rollover public funds, risk capital investments and the establishment of guarantee funds. The action plan includes regulatory measures intended to modernise and increase the flexibility of the EU member states' capital markets, to respond to the needs of both the demand and supply sides in the risk capital segment.

In 1999 the European Commission also launched its ambitious Financial Services Action Plan (FSAP), scheduled for completion and finalisation during 2005–10, with the aim of speeding up and simplifying financial integration and completing the construction of the single market in financial services.

The FSAP is a key document in the political process of constructing a common regulatory framework for the EU's financial markets, and will serve as a reference for new policy initiatives relating to the regulation of European capital markets and companies. With regard specifically to support for the foundation and growth of new firms, the main aims of the measures included in the FSAP are: the creation of less fragmented, more liquid national financial markets in which it is easier for SMEs to attract funds; and the establishment of a regulatory context suitable for firms' birth and growth.

Specific public measures to aid SMEs are mainly the province of the individual member states. Also in operation are EU-run measures intended to support the small and medium business sectors through the European Investment Bank Group, the financial arm of the EU. The

European Investment Bank (EIB) is an autonomous institution in which the shareholders are the EU member states; it facilitates access to SME finance through intermediate lending on competitive terms, for example as part of the multi-annual plan for enterprises and entrepreneurship. Its mission is to finance investment projects which contribute to the balanced development of the EU.

The European Investment Fund (EIF) is a financing body of the EU; it is owned by the EIB (62 per cent), the European Commission (30 per cent) and some 20 public and private financial institutions from across the EU-25 (8 per cent).

The EIF's mission is to support SMEs, increase their competitiveness and foster innovation and technology in Europe. To this end two main types of financial instruments are managed. The first consists of equity investments in regional and pan-European venture capital funds which support ISMEs, particularly in the high-tech sector, financing the seed, start-up and early growth stages. The second instrument consists of the provision of SME portfolio guarantees to banks granting loans to this kind of firm. In this way SMEs can benefit from the leverage effect of guarantees on the volume of loans which banks can make available to them.

The drafting of public programmes for the provision of risk capital begged the question of these programmes' compatibility with the regulations on state aid. The risks which may emerge are of three types: undesirable interference with competition due to the advantages enjoyed by the beneficiaries of public intervention; the risk of unnecessary use of public resources, since the beneficiary enterprises would have obtained funds in any case (known as 'dead weight' risk); and the risk of crowding out potential private investors (European Commission, 2001).

Before granting authorisation for measures to increase the availability of risk capital, the Commission requires proof of market failures, with thresholds set a priori at €500,000, €750,000 or €1 million, depending on the area concerned. In July 2006, a maximum ceiling of €1.5 million per investment instalment per firm within a twelve-month period was set.[5]

The measures adopted by member states are assessed for their ability to encourage private investments, and investment decisions must be made on the basis of commercial criteria, and the maximisation of profit in particular. All ideas of aid in the form of grants or subsidies are rejected in favour of the principles of market economics: this implies that when public funds are invested directly, a significant proportion (30–50 per cent) of the total capital must come from private sources and professional managers must be employed. The strategy therefore places a heavy emphasis on public–private partnerships, with risk-sharing or with incentives which reduce the level of risk undertaken by the private partners.

The approved forms of incentives are:

- the establishment of investment funds (risk capital funds), in which the state is a partner, investor or member, in some cases on less favourable terms than the other investors;
- subsidies to risk capital funds to cover a proportion of the administrative and management costs incurred;
- other financial instruments to benefit investors in risk capital or risk capital funds, to encourage them to make additional resources available for investments;
- the provision of guarantees to investors in risk capital or risk capital funds, covering a proportion of the losses incurred through their investments, or guarantees covering loans to risk capital investors/investment funds;
- fiscal incentives to encourage investors to invest in risk capital.

International best practices

This section presents a number of country case studies, examining public sector intervention intended to reduce the equity gap for ISMEs. The countries studied are: the US, Israel, the UK, Germany, France, the Netherlands and Denmark. Their basic approaches may vary widely within the schemes developed at international level (Box 8.1), but recently the policies adopted by all of them appear to be converging on direct intervention measures. The various types of public–private partnership launched have common features, at least in the following areas:

- *Aim*: development of a private market for venture capital.
- *Target*: identification of specific types of firms and life cycle stages.
- *Chosen instruments*: venture capital funds and funds of funds.
- *Schemes*: risk/profit-sharing (both equal shares and asymmetrical).

Below we outline the most significant aspects of the policies adopted in the various countries, before proceeding to a critical examination of the measures introduced.

Box 8.1   Intervention schemes developed at the international level[6]

1 Public–private partnerships on the supply side, with identification of the most suitable investment instruments: venture capital funds, venture capital funds of funds or public schemes offering private investors incentives and guarantees, to render investments less risky or increase the returns in the event of success.
2 Fiscal measures to encourage investments.
3 Regulatory measures intended to complete the equity markets, with reference to investor categories and suitable markets for the listing of ISMEs. Experience in the US in particular has shown that the venture capital industry benefits significantly from the large-scale involvement of pension funds, which typically invest in investment firms of this kind (Del Colle et al., 2006). The main measures introduced by the EU, within RCAP and FSAP, have been the prospectus directive, the pension funds directive, introduction of the IAS and regulations on corporate law and governance.
4 Provision of services to firms to help them overcome information asymmetries and the knowledge gap, to improve the business culture.
5 Actions aimed at stimulating new business initiatives, such as the creation of incubators, and facilitating university spin-offs.
6 Provision of innovative instruments such as semi-equity and mezzanine investment plans, with characteristics suited to this type of firm.

The United States

The US is the main point of reference for the measures subsequently introduced at the EU level, and in the domestic context in the UK, Israel and Finland.[7] Since their creation in the late 1950s, small business investment companies (SBICs) have played a fundamental role in developing the business of private venture capital investors in the US and are a keystone of the Federal government's strategy for reducing the equity gap.

1958 saw the approval of the Small Business Investment Act, establishing the Small Business Administration (SBA), with the aim of supplying managerial and financial aid to small enterprises. From the financial point of view, the aid takes the form of medium- and long-term loans,

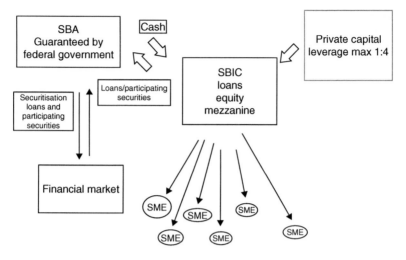

Figure 8.1 The structure of the SBIC Programme

as well as risk capital investments assisted by Federal guarantee systems. The SBICs, created as a result of this legislation and authorised by the SBA, are private venture capital companies, some of them bank-related, which enjoy leverage with the SBA in ratios of up to four times their own equity to enable them to finance small businesses. The SBA, covered by guarantees from the Federal government, then securitises these credits on the market.

The current operating structure of the so-called SBIC Programme, summarised in Figure 8.1, is of the upside leverage type and enables SBICs to provide small businesses with three types of funding: loans, mezzanine and risk capital. This structure derives from legislation passed in 1992, which allows SBICs not only to access SBA financing, but also to issue 'participating securities' (partnership interests which give entitlement to a share of profits, with a guaranteed minimum rate of interest) to be underwritten by the latter. These instruments allow the SBICs to postpone the payment of capital and interest until their operations generate sufficient cashflow to service the debt, while in the meantime the SBA can share in any profits. If the investments generate profits, the SBICs repay the debt and the interest, and then reimburse the private equity investors, so any earnings are shared between the SBA and the private investors. The share of the profits received by the SBA covers any failures to recoup funds granted to other SBICs, thus rendering the Federal programme self-financing. In the event of losses, private investors are not repaid until the SBA has been reimbursed; however, the leverage provided by the public funding allows potentially higher returns on the capital invested. These instruments, particularly well suited to financing risk capital investment in firms in the start-up and early stages, are also covered by Federal guarantee, and thus securitised by the SBA.

This innovation provided the basis for further growth in the number of SBICs, which in 2002 accounted for 58 per cent of venture capital investments in SMEs in the US (Small Business Administration, 2002), with a smaller average investment size than the rest of the venture capital industry, indicating their effectiveness in bridging the equity gap in this segment.

The schemes described above have been accompanied by specific programmes implemented with Federal funds to assist high-tech SMEs in their initial stages, achieving results described as above expectation (Maula et al., 2007). The Advanced Technology Program (ATP) and Small Business Innovation Research (SBIR) are R&D programmes intended to reinforce the development, on the basis of collaboration, of high-tech products with significant potential for economic growth (ATP) and their distribution (SBIR).

The SBIR programme, created by the 1982 Small Business Innovation Development Act, aims to encourage small firms to explore their technological potential and encourage the market distribution of the relative products. The programme, which receives 2.5 per cent of Federal R&D funds for small businesses, functions on a competitive basis. Each year, it sets areas of interest within which small businesses can submit applications, which are then assessed on the basis of their degree of innovation, technological merit and future market potential. The selected projects receive financial support in two stages: the start-up stage, in which up to $100,000 is allocated for six months, focuses on the feasibility of the idea/product, and enterprises which pass the review at the end of it are admitted to the second stage, in which the results of stage 1 are consolidated and a more in-depth verification of market potential is performed, with allocations of up to $750,000 for two years. In the third stage, production and sale, SBIR funds will be replaced by private capital or funds from other Federal agencies.

Israel

In Israel, the development of the venture capital industry during the 1990s made a strong contribution to the growth of innovative enterprises, especially in the ICT and high-tech sectors, thanks to a major expansion in the number of start-ups.[8] During this period, the Israeli government promoted a programme for the development of venture capital which in many respects reproduced the measures adopted in the US. The Yozma programme (1993–97) included not only a risk-sharing scheme, but also upside incentives, and generated outstanding results which led to the subsequent launch of other similar initiatives.

Yozma is a fund of funds established by the Israeli government in 1993, with capital of $100 million, to foster the growth of the private venture capital industry in Israel, partly by requiring the involvement of major foreign operators with a view to attracting their investments and exploiting their supply-side know-how. Yozma was obliged to invest 80 per cent of its capital in private venture capital funds and 20 per cent directly in high-tech businesses. The fund invested in ten funds only permitted to invest in business start-ups in Israel, acquiring 40 per cent of their capital ($8 million each). Overall, the fund attracted $150 million in investments from Israel and abroad, allowing it to make investments totalling $250 million in 200 start-ups.

Under the scheme, public and private investors were to bear any losses on the same basis, with the incentive for the private investor of a call option at a value equivalent to the capital revaluated to give a return of about 7 per cent per annum. The private partner in eight of these funds exercised its call option to purchase the public partner's holding after five years, in 1997. The return for the public investor depends on the price at which the call option is exercised. In this case the public shareholder does not step in to cover losses, but allows the private investor to multiply its return if the venture is successful, in the event that the value of the business is greater than that implicit in the call option price.

At the end of 2001 the venture capital funds created with the Yozma programme and other funds which had sprung from it, partly thanks to the managerial expertise acquired in the meantime, were managing resources worth $5 billion.

The Heznek Government Seed Fund has adopted a similar upside incentive scheme; it has a specific intervention plan, 50 per cent of the capital in which ($900 million) is held by the government. The government has granted the private investors a call option to purchase the public holding within five years at the initial price plus interest at a pre-set rate.

Following the example of the US, in Israel the programmes described above have also been accompanied by public measures on the demand side, especially in the R&D, to facilitate the early growth stage of high-tech businesses. The Tnufa A programme, for example, consists of subsidies of up to 85 per cent for pre-seed investments, up to a maximum of $50,000 per project. Technology incubators have also been created: for example, the Yozma programme has been accompanied by R&D Support and Technological Incubators Programmes on the demand side.

The United Kingdom

The UK is the European state with the best developed private equity and venture capital industries. The development of this sector dates from the 1980s, when it was encouraged by the Conservative administration's free market economic policies, which focused on the role of the markets as the driver for the growth of the economy.[9]

Public intervention schemes have been developed in close collaboration with the Small Business Service (SBS), an agency of the then Department of Trade and Industry and HM Treasury, renamed the Enterprise Directorate in July 2007, and now answerable to the Department for Business, Enterprise and Regulatory Reform (BERR), itself created on 28 June 2007 and discussed in greater detail below.

The measures introduced over time reflect a determined, well-informed, clearly structured approach, involving both the demand and supply sides of the venture capital fund market, on both national and regional bases, and prioritising collaboration with private investors. In the most recent years, the characteristics of UK government measures, in terms of target enterprises, regional competency and investment amount thresholds, often reflect an awareness of the research findings discussed in the previous section, concerning the existence, size and characteristics of the equity gap, and public reports analysing the problem. However, if even the UK, which has Europe's best-developed venture capital market, is compared with the US, the potential clearly emerges for further growth and development in this sector, in specific areas identified by recent studies of the equity gap: investments of relatively small amounts, in the early stages of the enterprise's life cycle.

To this end the main demand-side measures aim to compensate for the cultural and managerial skills gap, and provide incentives for enterprises, especially in disadvantaged contexts.

Government measures on the supply side respond to the specific aim of improving the conditions for the development of a private venture capital market. As well as fiscal incentives for informal investors and specific initiatives targeting young entrepreneurs, financial initiatives have been introduced with the aim of bridging the equity gap in various contexts and sectors, through the creation of venture capital funds with different levels of government participation. In all these schemes, the funds are managed by private operators, selected by public tender.

To guard more effectively against the direct involvement of the government or public sector employees, the government recently entrusted the supervision of all public projects in the field of private equity to an independent government agency established in 2006, the Capital for Enterprise Board, which is staffed by managers from the private equity sector, who are employed on the basis of professional criteria and paid by performance by means of incentive schemes.

At present, the main projects with direct involvement of public funds are:

- the UK High Tech Fund (fund of funds specialising only in early-stage investments in high-tech enterprises);
- Early Growth Funds (seven operating funds with investments not exceeding £100,000 each, in innovative business with high growth rates);
- Regional Venture Capital Funds (RVCFs) (nine funds, each operating in a different region, for start-up and early stage investments up to a ceiling of £250,000);
- Enterprise Capital Funds (ECFs) (founded in 2005), which will be discussed in greater detail below.

The RCVFs, and above all the recently added ECFs, are modelled to a large extent on the US SBICs, both from the operational point of view and with regard to the scheme of incentives adopted.

The ECFs were introduced in 2005 to overcome a clearly identified, well-documented market failure. The objective is to increase the availability of growth capital for SMEs affected by an equity gap identified by studies carried out in the early years of this century (HM Treasury – Small Business Service, 2003a) of between £250,000 and £2 million for high-growth SMEs. Application has been made to the European Commission to raise the ceiling to £3 million, after verification of compatibility with the regulations on state aid.

Public intervention takes two main forms: the first is the encouragement of an increased flow of private capital into SMEs, through an adjustment of the risk–return profile for private investors; the second is a reduction of the entry barriers for entrepreneurial risk capital managers through the introduction of a favourable leverage ratio, thus reducing the amount of private capital needed to make investment feasible (Department of Business, Enterprise and Regulatory Reform, 2007).

Government involvement consists of the provision of loans to private funds, in a similar way to the SBA, with a maximum leverage ratio of 2:1 in relation to the private capital invested, using the upside incentives approach adopted for the SBICs, with asymmetrical profit-sharing to attract private investors.[10] No downside protection is envisaged in the event of losses. The cost of the government loans is in line with the return on ten-year government bonds, and their repayment, together with that of the relative interest, takes priority over reimbursement of the risk capital. If a surplus profit is made, the public partner takes a share on the profit-sharing principle. Funds are created in annual rounds, with public tenders intended to involve the best private fund management teams. The first round in 2005 and the second in November 2006 received government funds of £50 million each; the third round, held in November 2007, received government investment of £60 million. Fund applications can be made by authorised or regulated professional investors or syndicates of business angels. For each round, the amount of the management commissions and the profit-sharing conditions for the public partner are specified, providing the government with guarantees that the ventures will break even over the long term.

With regard to the Regional Venture Capital Funds, studies have revealed a number of critical aspects (Mason and Harrison, 2003). While on the one hand the establishment of regional funds responds to venture capital funds' tendency to become actively involved in the businesses in which they invest, and therefore to prefer to invest in businesses to which they are geographically close, on the other hand these funds are criticised for not giving due consideration to the true potential demand for venture capital in some regions. Moreover, these funds have an investment ceiling of £250,000, a limit out of line with the findings of studies on the equity gap referred to earlier, which identify amounts between £250,000 and £1 million as critical. However, a second round of investments with the same ceiling is envisaged, and this may lay the criticism to rest.

A lively debate has developed on the subject of this public intervention and the methods adopted, with some fiercely critical comments, even though the UK is generally considered one of the world leaders in fostering business development (Mason and Harrison, 2003). The National Audit Office has recently criticised the procedures by which the intervention schemes are managed, pointing in particular to an excessive fragmentation of measures to support SMEs, which are run by several government agencies, with frequent changes in the responsibilities assigned to each, causing a lack of coherence in the overall plan of action. The National Audit Office bases its criticism on the fact that no fewer than 15 agencies and departments operate 265 programmes, theoretically involving about 3,000 measures for the support of SMEs. The Small Business Service has also been criticised for shortcomings in fulfilling its coordination function, while commentators acknowledge that the SBS directly manages projects worth only £170 million out of a total of £2.6 billion (Maula et al., 2007).

In June 2007, as already mentioned, the government renewed its strategy for enterprises and small and medium-sized businesses, by creating the BERR, under the aegis of which the Enterprise Directorate (formerly the SBS) operates. The overall objective is to ensure business success in an increasingly competitive world. This means raising productivity levels, increasing sustainable economic development and narrowing the gap in growth rates between regions. The regional development strategy is implemented in partnership with the Regional Development Agencies (RDAs), first launched in 1999, with the London Development Agency following in 2000. The RDAs have been created to contribute to government departmental objectives and the priorities identified in the Regional Economic Strategies.

Another interesting aspect of the measures adopted in the UK is the attention focused on informal investors or business angels, in the conviction that interventions to develop the venture capital market, while necessary, will not solve the problems at the bottom end of the market, where the sums required are smallest. The approach adopted consists mainly of fiscal schemes involving tax credits for investments made, and exemption from capital gains tax (Maula et al., 2007).

Germany

Germany provides one of the most significant examples of public intervention to reduce the equity gap and encourage the development of the venture capital market.[11] The various measures introduced over time have adopted both the indirect approach, in the form of downside protection and upside leverage schemes, and direct support for the development of the venture capital industry. In 2006, the public sector financed more than 10 per cent of the venture capital sector, as pointed out by the German Private Equity and Venture Capital Association e.V. (BVK, 2007).

Germany differs from the other countries in number of ways. The financing provided targets not only young, high-tech firms, but all SMEs with sales of less than €5 million (the so-called *Mittelstand*), in the belief that they are the true drivers of economic growth. SMEs account for about 95 per cent of Germany's 3.4 million firms, provide more than

70 per cent of jobs, generate more than half the country's taxable income and offer more than 80 per cent of apprenticeships. This sector is considered to have the highest potential for growth in profits and sales on the one hand, and the biggest equity gap (between €1 million and €5 million) on the other.

The supply structure is pyramidal, and hinges on one main lending institution, the Kreditanstalt für Wiederaufbau (KfW). 80 per cent of the KfW's capital is held by the Federal government and 20 per cent by the *Länder*. Alongside its direct intervention, the government is introducing measures intended to update the financial instruments used for equity financing to assist in the further development of the venture capital industry. This industry thus operates to a large extent under state patronage: investment firms are public organisations – the typical form is the *Mittelständische Beteiligungsgesellschaften* (MBG) – or function with public funds.

The supply side is structured on a regional basis. Unlike other countries such as the UK, in Germany the venture capital industry is not concentrated in one main financial centre, but is organised around five regional markets: Munich, Frankfurt, Berlin, Hamburg and the Rheinland (Schilder, 2006).

The indirect intervention programmes are manly run by the KfW, a reconstruction and development bank founded in 1948, with its roots in the Marshall Plan. In spite of the birth of similar organisations at the regional level starting in the 1970s, this bank has maintained and developed its key role in the coordination of public measures, its position reinforced by its merger in July 2003 with another public institution historically active in equity financing, the Deutsche Ausgleichsbank (DtA). The bank manages the European funds from the European Recovery Programme (ERP) and also supplies independent support, refinancing itself directly on the market (Hommel and Schneider, 2003). With assets of €360 billion at the end of 2006, the KfW is one of Germany's ten largest banks and operates in the venture capital sector under the KfW Mittelstandsbank brand.

Traditionally, the KfW operates through public–private partnerships and refinancing venture capital funds on favourable terms. The structure of the main programmes has remained unchanged over the years (see Figure 8.2), even though the KfW-Mittelstandsbank has worked to simplify the instruments used.[12]

With the support of the Federal Economy and Labour Ministry, the bank provides small high-tech firms with share capital for the development of innovative products, processes or services. The Ministry finances

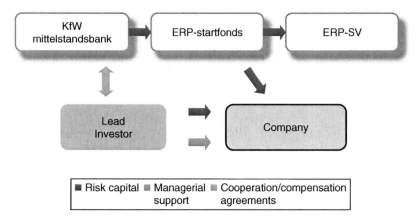

Figure 8.2 KfW – The structure of intervention and the key players

90 per cent of the investment and the KfW the rest. Target firms must be registered in Germany and have fewer than 50 employees, and annual sales or total assets of less than €10 million. The high-tech enterprise must not be more than five years old at the time of submission of the financing application. One particular product is ERP-Startfonds, for which all high-tech SMEs not more than six years old registered in Germany as GmbHs (limited liability companies) are eligible to apply. More than half the firm's capital must be owned by the entrepreneur, who must also manage the company himself. The KfW Mittelstandsbank also offers entrepreneurs grants of up to €150,000 to finance all the expenses involved in establishing a new high-tech company. KfW aid is available only if a private investor ('Leadinvestor') contributes the same amount as the KfW and also becomes involved in the management of the firm. As well as capital, the Leadinvestor is therefore also required to provide technological, financial and managerial expertise. This role may be filled by venture capital firms (accredited with the KfW), other companies (strategic partners) or business angels (whose involvement must be approved by the KfW on a case-by-case basis). Public funds are only forthcoming if the private investor fulfils the requirements of due diligence; the private partner is therefore required to gather information and perform a feasibility study on the investment project, for which it is then reimbursed.

The banks operates as a silent partner in exchange for a fixed rate of interest at the minimum market levels. Venture capital investors benefit from the leverage effect on their investment; moreover, in the event of bankruptcy, half of the private investor's loss will be covered by public funds. These terms have made the Germany venture capital market particularly attractive over time.

In 2004 €250 million was allocated for five years. The ceiling on individual investments is €3 million (€1.5 million for first investments). The maximum duration of the investment is ten years.

In the area of direct intervention, in 2004 the Economy and Labour Ministry launched the first public fund, the management of which was assigned to the European Investment Fund, managed by the EIB. The new financial instrument, ERP-EIF Dachfonds, has assets of €500 million for investment in risk capital funds mainly investing in seed and early stage high-tech enterprises registered in Germany. The Ministry has made a commitment of €250 million, matched by the same amount from the EIF. This programme also finances venture capital funds which provide high-tech enterprises with follow-on financing for their growth and expansion stages.

In terms of target sectors, the preference is for the areas in which German firms are particularly strong, such as information and communications technology, life sciences, energy including renewables, and in particular the support technologies which provide the link between traditional and innovative technologies.

Dachfonds allows a maximum investment period of five years and a disinvestment period of up to ten years. However, after its first two years in operation, the fund has already distributed profits to its investors further to disinvestment in a company in the portfolio of one of the six funds in which the Dachfonds initially invested.

This new financial instrument, intended to replace the existing system of state subsidies, has become a benchmark in Europe, and the European Commission has urged the EIF to submit proposals for the creation of other similar instruments in the various member states.

The German government has recently encouraged the development of technological incubators and networks of business angels (Kolbeck and Wimmer, 2003). One example of an incubator is the IZET Innovation Centre,[13] created by the Gesellschaft für Technologieförderung Itzehoe GmbH, a non-profit company founded by the city of Itzehoe and the Steinburg district. It offers enterprises professional infrastructure, a flexible support service and expert advice. Technology transfers take place with the nearby Fraunhofer-Institut für Silicon Technologie (ISIT) and other universities and research institutes.

In 1998 the IZET became a partner in the North German electronic commerce competence centre. It provides training in corporate design, business activities and financing strategies, with a special focus on the means by which risk capital can be raised. The IZET operates through a regional network of ten incubators in the Schleswig-Holstein *Länder*, and also participates in European R&D transfer and standardisation projects, in association with other technology centres across the whole of the EU.

The Usine project is particularly significant. It adopts the pre-incubation approach, very effective in managing the initial stages of the commercial exploitation of scientific achievements, since it allows the potential entrepreneur to gain experience in the management of his enterprise before it is actually established. The incubator assigns the potential entrepreneur a cost and earnings centre, within which all the activities relating to the future enterprise are carried out.

With regard to business angel networks, the Economy Ministry, together with the German Stock Exchange and the KfW, has sponsored the Business Angels Netwerk Deutschland (BAND), which has created a sort of electronic catalogue ('business angels forum') in which professionals and SMEs can register their areas of expertise and development targets respectively. Entrepreneurs in each *Land* can use search engines to find the know-how and type of investor best suited to their businesses' needs.

France

In France, the government's interest in the venture capital market is longstanding and has led to a large number of interventions, with a complex structure.

After measures of various kinds intended to promote and encourage the development of SMEs and innovation in the 1960s and 1970s, in the early 1980s a series of measures created a legal, fiscal and institutional framework intended to promote the risk capital financing of SMEs, especially innovative enterprises (Dubocage and Rivaud-Danset, 2002a). Apart from the establishment of the Second Marché (1983), a market for the listing of SMEs, the main measures involved the creation of:

- Fonds Communs de Placement à Risque (FCPRs), open-ended venture capital funds;
- SOFARIS (1982), an agency which provides guarantees for loans to, and risk capital investments in, SMEs by financial intermediaries;
- Sociétés de Capital à Risque (SCRs), venture capital firms.

In spite of these measures, it was not until the mid-1990s, due in part to the improved economic situation, that a sharp increase in venture capital investments in firms in the early stages of their life cycles was recorded.

From the second half of the 1990s, additional, far-reaching measures were launched to create legal, fiscal and institutional conditions more favourable to innovation and the relative business ventures, with direct and indirect intervention on both the demand and the supply sides of the risk capital market, focusing on different stages in the business life cycle (Dubocage and Rivaud-Danset, 2002a; 2002b). In particular, 1996 saw the creation of the Nouveau Marché, based on the the the US NASDAQ, followed in 1997 by the launch of the Fonds Communs de Placement Innovation (FCPIs), granting tax incentives to private investors provided funds invest at least 60 per cent of their capital in unlisted innovative French companies. Then, in 1998, the Fonds Publics pour le Capital Risque (FPCR) were founded. They allow the direct investment of public capital in venture capital funds on a public–private partnership basis; they are discussed in greater detail below.

One typical feature of the French system is the role played in industrial policy by large public bodies, which have modified their modes of intervention over time in response to the changing objectives of industrial policy (Landi and Rigon, 2006). Intervention on the supply side of the SME investment market is in the hands of the Caisse de Dépots et Consignations (CDC), a large public bank founded in 1816, which is directly involved in the venture capital market and in public intervention schemes. The CDC recently created CDC Enterprises, a wholly-owned subsidiary, to promote initiatives aimed at encouraging the development of venture capital funds investing in young companies with high growth potential and/or a high-tech content (Finlombarda, 2005).

Among its operations, CDC Enterprise manages the FPCRs, funds of funds modelled on Israel's Yozma, established to invest in venture capital funds specialising in innovative and high-tech firms, especially in the start-up stages, on a risk-sharing basis. At least 50 per cent of each investment must be covered by private capital on exactly the same conditions as the public funds assigned. Financing for the funds is provided by the CDC, the French government and the European Investment Fund (European Investment Bank, 2005). Between 2000 and September 2004, investments were made in 11 funds, which in turn invested in 83 businesses. Originally, the aim was to encourage the development of new investment teams, but in fact half the investments have been managed by well-established teams.

The Netherlands

The Netherlands differs from the other country cases examined in some major respects. In the Netherlands, SMEs play a central role in the economy: out of 768,000 businesses, 99 per cent are SMEs, accounting for 50 per cent of total sales and providing 60 per cent of jobs. Their small size is considered ideal for favouring product innovation, an objective on which public and private capital converges. Dutch SMEs operate with a low level of leverage, and the problem of the equity gap is therefore on a much smaller scale. Banks and investment firms often hold shares in small enterprises, thanks in part to the greater degree of openness to the market found among Dutch entrepreneurs. However, the Dutch government continues to stimulate the growth of the entrepreneurial system through the provision of direct financing to SMEs, credit and equity guarantee schemes, and action plans to support the venture capital industry (European Commission, 2004b).

Of the programmes implemented with the aim of limiting the equity gap, the Participation Guarantee Order Scheme (PPM), active during 1981–95 and intended for private venture capital funds investing in early stage businesses, has become particularly important over the years. Under this programme, which together with the German BTUs and the France's SOFARIS has gradually acquired importance at the European level in development of the venture capital market, the Dutch government covered 50 per cent of funds' losses, up to a maximum ceiling. In total, about €400 million was invested in 900 businesses up to 1994. Since then, the relative weight of the programme has gradually decreased in proportion to the independent growth of the venture capital market.

Over time the PPM Scheme has been replaced by three funds financed by public–private capital – the Techno-Starter funds. Each fund has capital of about €4.5 million. One third consists of public financing, convertible into an endowment fund if a profit is generated; the other two-thirds consist of private investment. Unlike the PPM, the funds are able to specialise their managers in specific industrial sectors. Special projects have also been run with similar mechanisms in the ICT sector, such as the public–private twinning fund, accompanied by an incubator, and the biotechnology industry. Tax incentives have been introduced for private investors investing in start-ups, who are able to deduct any losses incurred from their taxable income.

In 2005, after a further review of its innovation policy by the Dutch Economy Ministry, a framework TecnoPartner Seed Capital Scheme, which incorporates the previous funds and opens the way to new financial instruments, was introduced. The programme, which confirms the principles of collaboration between the public and private sectors, is equally financed by private venture capital funds and funds of funds financed by public money. Allocations of €240 billion are planned by

2015. As part of this scheme, the Ministry has also begun to finance the incubators and business angel networks created by private initiatives started in the 1990s.

The Netherland aims to surpass the EU average and rank among the EU's leading states by 2010 in four indicators: the proportion of innovative firms in the manufacturing sector compared to the total number of firms; the proportion of innovative firms involved in cooperation and innovative compared to the total number of innovative firms, and the sales generated by new or significantly updated products in the manufacturing sector as a percentage of the total sales in the sector (European Commission, 2005b).

Denmark

Danish innovation policy is changing rapidly (European Commission, 2006d). Innovation as an area of policy is steadily gaining ground in the public and political debate. In general, the Danish innovation system is perceived to be strong and fairly effective, with a number of competitive strengths and few serious weaknesses (Christensen et al., 2005). The political and institutional environment, policy towards private enterprise, foreign investment policy, financing and the highly developed infrastructure and institutions, a skilled labour force and a sophisticated financial sector are all contributing to this strength. Furthermore, the Danish system currently enjoys strong macro-structural conditions. The economy is quite strong. There is a trade surplus, inflation is low, public debt has been reduced, public budgets are balanced, savings are at a satisfactory level, the currency is stable and interest rates are in line with European trends (European Commission, 2006d).

However, even though the general picture is positive, there is still room for improvement at both the macro and micro levels. Danish regulations are perceived to weaken competition, the tax system is seen by some as skewing economic incentive structures and the labour market could be further strengthened (Christensen, 2000). Together, improvements to these factors could potentially create better foundations for innovation and a more dynamic system. In addition, overall R&D investments are still modest compared to the Barcelona objective (and the best performers).

The Danish innovation governance system is currently in the early stages of implementing a wide-ranging reform and restructuring process, and it is a major challenge to successfully implement the many reforms and thereby create a well-functioning, coherent, coordinated national innovation system. The recent reforms have targeted the university sector, the public research institutions, the technology service system, the advisory and funding structures and the regional system, to mention only the most important (European Commission, 2006d). At the same time, new strategies and action plans have been formulated regarding national and regional growth, collaboration between the public and private spheres, knowledge development, strategic research, and so on. In addition, a new set of very ambitious innovation-related objectives have very recently been launched in accordance with the Government Foundation outlining the objectives of the present government.

In Denmark an analysis of the Danish venture capital market has estimated that there are around 1,000 potential business angels willing to invest on average 1 million DKK per year (Christensen, 2000; 2004). This would bring their total annual investments to approximately 1 billion DKK, representing almost 25 per cent of all venture capital investments. However, this potential has not been realised, owing largely to the lack of linkages between potential investors and firms seeking finance. Danish business angels tend to invest locally, prefer co-investment with other angels, and co-operate to a limited extent with venture capital funds (Christensenn et al., 2005). Some studies indicate that problems may also stem from a low proportion of entrepreneurs in Denmark due largely to high levels of taxation (Jensen and Vinergaard, 2002). Other studies underline that small firms are not aware of financing sources and find the venture market confusing (Christensenn, 2000; 2004).

Since the late 1980s, the Danish government has introduced a number of direct and indirect intervention schemes to encourage the venture capital industry and reduce the equity gap for high-growth young firms, with varying degrees of success. Public involvement in the birth of innovative instruments such as technological incubators and business angel networks is more recent but particularly significant.

The main government measures supporting the venture capital sector have led to the establishment of the following funds:

- *Danish Development Finance Corporation (Dansk Udviklingsfinansiering, DUF)*, founded in 1988 for the equity financing of small enterprises. The initial investment amounted to 500 million DKK (€67 million). The investors were pension funds (44 per cent), banks, building societies, insurance companies and private firms (44 per cent) and the Central Bank (12 per cent). The government provided guarantees covering the losses incurred by risk capital investors. This venture was wound up at the end of the 1990s, with the sale of the portfolio to an asset management company.

- *Business Development Fund (Erhvervsudviklingsfonden)*, founded in 1992 to finance high-tech start-up projects or existing young enterprises. The capital initially allocated was 2 billion DKK (€270 million), intended for the purchase of bonds. The fund shared the downside risk, but only received a fixed interest rate in the event of success. In the event of insolvency, the fund cancelled the debt and acquired the rights to the project. The fund suffered losses of more than 60 per cent of the capital invested on more than 900 projects financed.
- *Equity Guarantee Programme (Udviklingsselskaber)*, launched in 1994. Established by the Ministry of Trade and Industry, with funds of 1 billion DKK to stimulate the development of a venture capital market. The programme provided partial guarantees for losses on investments in new enterprises from the seed and start-up stages to the early growth stage, using a model similar to the Dutch PPM. Initially, the guarantees covered 50 per cent of the losses incurred from investments in firms with fewer than 250 employees and assets of less than 50 million DKK, with a maximum ceiling of 50 million DKK for each individual venture capital firm. In 2002, the guarantee was reduced to 10 per cent for five years. During the first two years, 1 billon DKK was allocated to the programme; 815 million DKK was made available to 13 venture capital funds. In 1997, the year in which the Danish Parliament decided to extend the programme for an additional two years, the funds had in turn provided guarantees for 400 million DKK covering investments in about 100 firms. The programme has gradually been run down since 2000.
- *Vaekstfonden (Business Development Fund)*, established in 2000. The successor to the Business Development Fund and the Equity Guarantee Programme. It operates as a private venture capital company, with public guarantees, with capital of 300 million DKK. It is one of the key players on the Danish venture capital market. Between 1992 and 2007 it co-financed more than 3,500 Danish companies, with a total of 6.5 DKK billion invested. It operates as a fund of funds in the private equity sector, mainly in the north of the country. It engages in seed financing in innovative and high-tech sectors, and supplies mezzanine credit to a wide spread of sectors. The targets are: R&D activities, in both small and large companies; internationalisation projects and development projects with business development finance guarantees and skill development projects. Companies with up to 250 full-time employees and a total turnover of up to 290 million DKK are eligible for these loans, provided that no more than 25 per cent of the company's share capital is owned by companies not meeting these

criteria. It is part of a broader project intended to facilitate access to international venture capital and encourage the birth in Denmark of an internationally competitive private equity industry. The forms of intervention are:

- *Equity capital (seed financing)*: short-term loans and acquisition of capital stakes of up to 25 per cent.
- *Equity guarantees*: guarantees covering 50 per cent of the losses of the venture capital company (form of intervention gradually being phased out).
- *Loans and loan guarantees*: for the financing of high-tech projects.

The fund is still in operation.

The Danish government has also provided incentives for pension funds to invest in unlisted firms. The last few years have seen strong growth in the sector, which has become the main private equity investment channel.

Technological incubators (*Innovationsmiljøer*) have also been financed partly by the government and partly by private capital. During 1998–2004, incubators financed by the Ministry of Science, Technology and Innovation invested about 534 million DKK in SMEs in the form of pre-project (experimentation) loans and equity. During the same period, financing of more than 1 billion DKK was received from private investors. At present there are eight main incubators, managed by universities or accredited research centres: DTU – Innovation A/S; HIH Development; Østjysk Innovation A/S; NOVI Innovation A/S; Syddansk Innovation A/S; Teknologisk Innovation; HIH Development A/S; and CAT-Symbion Innovation A/S. Its satisfaction with the incubators' work led the Danish government to refinance the individual projects until 2004. The individual incubators have been operating as financially independent projects ever since.

In 2000, VækstFonden founded the Danish Business Angels Network (DBAN) and the Regional Business Angels Network (RBAN). The DBAN and RBAN were founded around the incubators and research centres. They currently have more than 200 and 63 members respectively. The minimum investment for membership of the network is £500,000 per annum for each business angel. The DBAN has established a web portal to help to bring investors and entrepreneurs together. Other initiatives have been organised together with the Danish Venture Capital Association (DVCA).

The activities of business angels have not yet been developed to their full potential. The barriers to the development of the business angel system lie in information asymmetries between investors and firms, the prevalence of small local circuits, the limited degree of cooperation with venture capital funds and the high tax rate.

Conclusions

The main aim of public intervention intended to bridge the equity gap for ISMEs is to develop a private risk capital market, with a particular focus on venture capital.

This survey has highlighted various possible modes of public intervention and the contexts in which each is most likely to be effective. The findings may be of assistance to policy-makers defining the procedures for public intervention to reduce the equity gap, with regard to compatibility with EU regulations on state aid and the most appropriate way of constructing a real plan of action, including direct and indirect measures on both the demand and the supply sides of the risk capital market.

A survey of the international best practices clearly indicates that measures involving only the supply of risk capital are not sufficient; intervention is also needed on the demand side.[14] For the most problematic areas, there is evidence that public measures to stimulate the private growth of the venture capital industry and the relative managerial expertise are of only limited efficacy. To be more effective, policies must include actions intended to create background conditions which encourage more able, better-skilled entrepreneurs to enter key innovative sectors, such as the high-tech sector. Fiscal measures have an important role to play here. Action plans must consider the entire financing ladder in order to identify the measures best suited to the specific needs and life cycle stages of the target firms. In all cases, public intervention which includes financial involvement must be compatible with market mechanisms, comply with normal business principles and involve risk-sharing with the private sector. Policies which use public capital to allow entrepreneurs access to funding at lower costs and thus reduce the rates of return for investors are to be avoided. This will prevent public funds from crowding out private investors.

Public intervention requires the creation of tools for assessing the efficacy and efficiency of the policies implemented, which allow monitoring of their overall impact on the economy in terms of both the birth and growth of innovative enterprises (European Commission, 2005a; OECD, 2006a).

The assessment of public intervention policies serves two ends. First, it allows the verification essential before new programmes are launched in the individual countries, with the aim of maximising the return achieved through the use of scarce resources. Second, it helps to spread good practices in other countries, even if the economic and financial structures, as well as the cultural and business contexts, are different.

At present, although there is a general awareness of the need to implement suitable assessment processes, relatively little has been achieved, partly due to problems of methodology.[15] There are many participants in the theoretical debate concerning the use of incentives, and a great deal of disagreement with regard to possible conclusions, which may be inevitable since the type of assessment involved is counterfactual, setting out to answer the question of what would have happened if no incentives had been available.

More work is thus required in this area to allow public programmes to be assessed from two main points of view. The first is an assessment of the measures' success in achieving the stated objectives: an evaluation must be made of the quality and efficacy of public programmes in terms of the creation of wealth and businesses. With reference specifically to incentive programmes for venture capital, periodic monitoring is needed of the rate of creation of new firms capable of operating independently, without any direct public aid, generating a return on investments in relation to risk in line with the market's requirements (Maula et al., 2007). The second area concerns the possible negative repercussions of public intervention in terms of the inefficient allocation of investments or distortion of competition, which may lead to the crowding out of private investors already described, with the paradoxical outcome of raising rather than lowering the barriers to entry to the private venture capital industry.[16]

Since the issue of evaluation of the impact of government action is crucial for the success of incentive models, the OECD (2006d) has been asked by OECD and non-OECD governments to take the lead in establishing international benchmarks, as well as in measuring the size of SMEs' financing gaps. The objective is to facilitate comparison of the relative performance of national markets in providing finance and bridging the equity gap for ISMEs.

Notes

Chapter 1   Innovation and Economic Growth

1. For a review of Schumpeter's theoretical works, see Acs and Audretsch (1988).
2. For a review of the perspective to this theme of the neo-Schumpeterian approach, see Giuliani (2002).
3. For a review of the main effects of entrepreneurship on regional development, see Fritsch (2008).
4. For Germany, see Audretsch and Keilbach (2002); for the UK, Hart and Hanvey (1995); for Spain, Callejon and Segarra (1999); for Sweden, Foelster (2000); for the Netherlands, Stel and Suddle (2008); and for Portugal, Baptista et al. (2008).
5. The key references on the role of smallness in the process of innovative activities are Acs and Audretsch (1990) and Audretsch (1995).
6. The Community Innovation Survey (CIS) is conducted every four years by EU member states and monitors Europe's progress in the area of innovation.
7. For further details, see Rivaud-Danset (2002) and Florio (2003).
8. For a recent survey, see Romani and Pottelsberghe (2004).
9. See NVCA (2002b), NVCA and Global Insight (2004; 2007), EVCA (1996; 2001) and BVCA (2007).

Chapter 2   Access to Finance of Innovative SMEs

1. For a recent surveys of the theoretical literature on financial constraints of SMEs, see Beck and Demirguc-Kunt (2006) and Hall (2002; 2005).
2. For further details, see Landi and Rigon (2006), and also this volume, chapter 1.
3. For further details, see Canovi et al. (2007).
4. See Myers (1984), Myers and Majluf (1984) and Hughes and Cosh (1994).
5. '[T]he imitation of a new invention requires expenditure of between 50 and 75 per cent of the cost originally incurred' (Hall, 2005, p. 3).
6. '[I]n practice fifty per cent or more of the R&D portion of this investment is the wages and salaries of highly educated scientists and engineers' (Hall, 2005, p. 4).
7. See, among others, Petersen and Rajan (1994) and Berger and Udell (1995).
8. 'The fact that high-growth, high-risk new ventures often obtain angel finance/or venture capital before they obtain significant amounts of external debt suggests that the moral hazard problem may be particularly acute for these firms' (Berger and Udell 1998, p. 9).
9. See Seward (1990), Dewatripoint and Tirole (1994) and Kaplan and Stromberg (2003).
10. For an analysis, see chapter 5.
11. For further details on the small ticket problem, see Berger and Udell (1998) and Petrella (2001).
12. Chapter 8 provides a detailed discussion of this topic.

Chapter 3   Equity Gap and Innovative SMEs

1. For an in-depth account of the debate, see Cressy (2002).
2. For further details, see Akerlof (1970), Leland and Pyle (1977), Diamond (1984) and Jenses and Meckling (1976).
3. See Report of the Committee on Finance and Industry (1931) (the Macmillan Report).
4. See HM Treasury – Small Business Service (2003a), Bracchi (2006) and Gervasoni (2006).
5. See: Bank of England (2001), Hall (2002), Landi and Rigon (2006) and Magri (2007).
6. See OECD (2004) and Del Colle et al. (2006).
7. See European Commission (2001), Bank of England (2001), Carpenter and Petersen (2002), HM Treasury – Small Business Service (2003a; 2003b), OECD (2004; 2006a), European Commission (2005a), Landi and Rigon (2006) and Maula et al. (2007). Empirical evidence that in Italy, as has been clearly demonstrated for the US, venture capital operators tend to finance young, small and higher-risk firms, and those with greater information asymmetries in general, is provided by Del Colle et al. (2006).
8. On this, see Rajan and Zingales (2001) and European Commission (1995).
9. For a summary of the theoretical debate, see Cressy (2002).
10. On the debate see in particular HM Treasury – Small Business Service (2003a), Harding (2002), Harding and Cowling (2006), European Commission (2005a) and OECD (2006a).
11. See: HM Treasury – Small Business Service (2003a) and OECD (2006a).
12. See Harding (2002), Harding and Cowling (2006), HM Treasury – Small Business Service (2003a; 2003b), OECD (2006a) and Lawton (2002).
13. See: Harding (2002) and OECD (2006a, p. 10 and Annex).
14. See: HM Treasury – Small Business Service (2003b, p. 24).

Chapter 4   An Original Equity Requirement Estimation Model

1. Models 1 and 2 were originally developed by Canovi et al. (2007).
2. See Cavallo et al. (2002). In the Italian intermediate industry and services census, a distinction is made between the high-tech sector with high-tech content, the high-tech manufacturing sector with medium technology content, high-tech service sectors with high-tech content and high-tech service sectors with medium technology content. In terms of classification of economic activities, the high-tech manufacturing sector with high-tech content corresponds to the following codes: 24.4 (Manufacture of pharmaceutical, medicinal chemicals and botanical products); 30 (Manufacture of office machinery and computers); 32 (Manufacture of radio, television and communication equipment and apparatus); 33 (Manufacture of medical, precision and optical instruments, watches and clocks); 35.3 (Manufacture of aircraft and spacecraft). The high-tech service sectors with high-tech content are the following: 72.2 (Software consultancy and supply); 72.60 (Other computer-related activities); 73.1 (Research and experimental development on natural sciences and engineering).

3. We excluded from our sample medium and large firms as defined in the European Commission Recommendation (2003a). In the Recommendation companies with sales below the €2 million threshold are defined as micro enterprises and those between €2 million and €10 million as small enterprises, while medium-sized enterprises are defined as those having sales volumes between €10 and €50 million. Large companies are those with sales volumes above €50 million. Thus we excluded from our sample companies with sales in 2006 in excess of €20 million.

4. This implied the exclusion from the sample only of companies with negative growth in sales.

5. Standard deviation = 105.5.

6. See, for instance, Biais and Gollier (1997).

7. The range is from a value of −€232.1 k for small enterprises in the manufacturing sector to €4,201.7 k for small enterprises in the service sector. The evidence that some values are negative should not be surprising since the equity requirement has been computed in residual terms; if the other forms of coverage are larger than the additional financial requirement, then the last form of coverage calculated, the equity requirement, is negative.

Chapter 5   The Intermediaries in the Risk Capital Industry

1. According to some studies, it emerges that business angels often invest in 'local' projects which are easy to get to so that they can visit the investee company more often, thereby reducing the degree of information asymmetry.

2. In Europe, one of the most important steps in the development of non-profit development activities has been the trial project run by the European Community General Directorate for Regional Policies, which has allowed the creation of the first business innovation centres with the aim of encouraging investments in disadvantaged areas of EU member states. For details, see European Commission (2003d).

3. See chapter 3.

4. In this section the terms venture capital and private equity are used interchangeably since the operating cycle of a risk capital operator has the same features in all cases.

5. See Gervasoni and Sattin (2000), Caselli and Gatti (2002) and Timmons and Bygrave (1992).

Chapter 6   Size and Evolution of the Risk Capital Industry

1. On the US market, under the NVCA definition, expansion financing operations are broken down into expansion and later stage financing categories. In this stage the capital is provided for companies that have reached a fairly stable growth rate; that is, companies that are not growing as fast as the rates attained in the expansion stages. These companies are expected to have a positive cashflow; they may or may not be actually profitable, but they are more likely to be so than in previous stages of development (NVCA, 2007).

2. A similar result with regard to the countries considered would have been obtained if the figure for capital committed during 2005 and 2006 had been used.
3. For details about exit possibilities, see EVCA (2007b).

Chapter 7 The Role of Equity Markets

1. It is important to stress that although a liquid and efficient equity market is a prerequisite for the development of these intermediaries, it is by no means a sufficient condition. The legal and governance system and political institutions that foster a cultural framework favourable to entrepreneurship are as important. For details, see Black and Gilson (1998) and Becker and Hellman (2005).
2. Levine (2005) offers an in-depth survey of the finance–growth nexus.
3. Levine and Zervos (1998) examine the distinct role of stock market and banking development on economic growth.
4. Euronext is the company that manages the equity markets in Paris, Amsterdam, Brussels and Lisbon and the London derivatives market, Liffe.
5. OMX is the company that manages the Nordic equity markets of Copenhagen, Helsinki, Stockholm and Reykjavik and the Baltic markets of Riga, Vilnius and Tallin.
6. For an in-depth study, see Schwartz and Francioni (2004).
7. Directors, substantial shareholders, employees with a holding or interest of more than 0.5 per cent of AIM securities and their families.
8. According to Prospectus Directive the obligation to redact a prospectus applies when securities are admitted to trading on an EU regulated market or if the offer is made to more than 100 persons and the aggregate value of securities being offered is greater than €2.5 million.
9. The large weight of Mercato Expandi on total market capitalisation is in part the result of two large financial institutions belonging to the former Mercato Ristretto.
10. For a review of the theory and the practice of going public, see Jenkinson and Ljunqvist (2001); other notable surveys are Ritter (1998), Ljungqvist (2007) and Ritter and Welch (2002). For a comprehensive empirical analysis of the evolution of IPOs in the Italian market since the mid-1980s, see Delle Vedove et al. (2005). Franzosi e Pellizzoni (2005) provide a detailed study on the effect of going public on Italian small caps.
11. Empirical evidence suggests that seasoned equity offerings are less frequent than expected. Eckbo (2007) provides a detailed analysis. Rigamonti (2007) shows that in the Italian context, about only one out of five firms re-enter the market with a seasoned offering within three years of the IPO.
12. There are many ways in which an institutional investor may show interest, each with a different information value for the underwriter: limit bids, strike bids, step-up bids.
13. Ibbotson (1975) is one of the earliest studies.
14. For a survey on under-pricing, see Ljungqvist (2007).
15. For further details on this subject, see chapters 5 and 6.

16. For a detailed analysis on the change and the evolution of ownership of Italian companies that listed through IPOs between 1985 and 2005, see Rigamonti (2007).
17. In particular turnover velocity is calculated as the number of shares traded during 2006 and number of listed shares at 2006 year-end. For companies listed during the year, turnover velocity is annualised.

Chapter 8   The Role of the Public Sector

1. See in particular: European Commission (2005a), OECD (2004; 2006a), Lawton (2002), Dubocage and Rivaud-Danset (2002a; 2002b) and Maula et al. (2007).
2. See European Commission (2005a) and Maula et al. (2007). With particular reference to measures involving venture capital, see McGlue (2002).
3. For a survey of public intervention at the international level, see in particular OECD (2004), European Commission (2005a) and Maula et al. (2007). A more specific analysis, covering only some contexts, is provided by Finlombarda (2005).
4. For supply-side incentive schemes in the context of forms of public–private partnerships for the development of venture capital funds and an assessment of their efficacy, see Jääskeläinen et al. (2004).
5. See: European Commission (2001; 2006e).
6. See: OECD (2006a) and HM Treasury – Small Business Service (2003a; 2003b).
7. For the US case study, see in particular HM Treasury – Small Business Service (2003a), McGlue (2002), European Investment Bank (2001), Mayoral et al. (2003) and Maula et al. (2007).
8. For the Israeli experience, see in particular European Investment Bank (2001), Mayoral et al. (2003), Modena (2003), Avnimelech and Teubal (2004), Finlombarda (2005) and Maula et al. (2007).
9. For a UK case study, see in particular HM Treasury – Small Business Service (2003a), Bank of England (2001 and 2004), Finlombarda (2005) and Maula et al. (2007).
10. See European Commission (2004a), Small Business Service (2004) and Maula et al. (2007).
11. For the public intervention policy in Germany, see Sunley et al. (2005), Plagge (2006) and Schilder (2006).
12. The traditional programmes established to support the growth of the *Länder* of the former East Germany are Beteiligungskapital für kleine Technologieunternehmen (BTU), DtA-Technologie-Beteiligungsprogramm, Förderung und Unterstützung von technologieorientierten Unternehmensgründungen. The most recent (introduced in November 2004) are known as ERP-Startfonds.
13. Institut für Mittelstandsforschung (IfM), 'Unternehmensgrößenstatistik 2003/2004'.
14. Jääskeläinen et al. (2004) produced a simulation with the Monte Carlo method to verify the capacity of public measures to stimulate the private development of venture capital, with various types of incentives: upside leverage schemes, where private investors take a larger share of the profit,

different entry timing with later entry for private investors to increase their return, downside protection schemes to reduce private investors' losses.

15. See in particular European Commission (2005a). With specific reference to venture capital measures, see McGlue (2002). Bronzini and de Blasio (2006) have developed an empirical analysis of the Italian context with reference to the efficacy of investment incentives.

16. A pan-European empirical study developed by Leleux and Surlemond (2003) for the period 1990–96 finds no evidence of crowding out, but nor does it find proof that public intervention is capable of creating a risk capital market for private investors starting from nothing, although it is shown to be beneficial to the venture capital industry as a whole.

References

Acs, Z. J. and D. B. Audretch (1988) 'Testing the Schumpeterian Hypothesis', *Eastern Economic Journal* 14, 2: 129–40.

Acs, Z. J. and D. B. Audretch (1990) *Innovation and Small Firms*, Cambridge: Cambridge University Press.

AIFI (2007) *AIFI Yearbook 2007*, Italian Private Equity & Venture Capital Association, Roma: Bancaria Editrice.

Akerlof, G. (1970) 'The Market for "Lemons": Quality Uncertainty and the Market Mechanism', *Quarterly Journal of Economics* 84, 3: 488–500.

Amihud, Y. and H. Mendelson (1986) 'Asset Pricing and the Bid–Ask Spread', *Journal of Financial Economics* 17, 2: 223–49.

Anton, J. J. and D. A. Yao (1998) 'The Sale of Intellectual Property: Strategic Disclosure, Property Rights, and Incomplete Contracts', Philadelphia: The Wharton School, University of Pennsylvania.

Audretsch, D. B. (1995) *Innovation and Industry Evolution*, Cambridge, MA: MIT Press.

Audretsch, D. B. (2007) 'Entrepreneurship Capital and Economic Growth', *Oxford Review of Economic Policy* 23, 1: 63–78.

Audretsch, D. B. and M. P. Feldman (2004) 'Knowledge Spill-overs and the Geography of Innovation', in J. V. Henderson and J. F. Thisse (eds.), *Handbook of Regional and Urban Economics*, North-Holland: Elsevier, pp. 2713–39.

Audretsch, D. B. and M. Keilbach (2002) 'Entrepreneurship Capital and Economic Performance', ZEW Discussion Paper 02-76.

Audretsch, D. B. and R. Thurik (2002) 'Linking Entrepreneurship to Growth', OECD Science, Technology and Industry Working Papers, 2081/2, Paris: OECD Publishing.

Audretsch, D.B., E. Santarelli and M. Vivarelli (1999) 'Start-up Size and Industrial Dynamics: Some Evidence from Italian Manufacturing', *International Journal of Industrial Organization* 17, 7: 965–83.

Avnimelech, G. and M. Teubal (2004) 'Venture Capital Start-up Co-evolution and the Emergence & Development of Israel's New High-Tech Cluster', *Economics of Innovation and New Technology* 13, 1: 33–60.

Aylward, A. (1998) 'Trends in Venture Capital Financing in Developing Countries', IFC Discussion Paper 36, Washington, DC: World Bank.

Bank of England (2001) *The Financing of Technology-Based Small Firms*, London, February.

Bank of England (2004) *Finance for Small Firms – An Eleventh Report*, London, June.

Baptista, R., V. Escária and P. Madruga (2008) 'Entrepreneurship, Regional Development and Job Creation: the Case of Portugal', *Small Business Economics* 30, 1: 49–58.

Beck, T. and A. Demirguc-Kunt (2006) 'Small and Medium-Sized Enterprises: Access to Finance as a Growth Constraint', *Journal of Banking and Finance* 30, 11: 2931–43.

Becker, R. M. and T. F. Hellmann (2005) 'The Genesis of Venture Capital – Lessons from the German Experience', in V. Kanniainen and C. Keuschnigg (eds),

Venture Capital, Entrepreneurship, and Public Policy, Cambridge, MA: MIT Press, pp. 33–67.

Benveniste, L. M. and P. A. Spindt (1989) 'How Investment Bankers Determine the Offer Price and Allocation of New Issues', *Journal of Financial Economics* 24, 2: 343–61.

Berger A. and G. Udell (1995) 'Relationship Lending and Lines of Credit in Small Firms Finance', *The Journal of Business* 68, 3: 351–81.

Berger A. and G. Udell (1998) 'The Economics of Small Business Finance: the Roles of Private Equity and Debt Market in the Financial Growth Cycle', *Journal of Banking and Finance* 22, 6–8: 613–73.

Bestre, H. (1985) 'Screening vs Rationing in Credit Markets with Imperfect Information', *American Economic Review* 75, 4: 850–55.

Bhattacharya, S. and J. R. Ritter (1985) 'Innovation and Communication: Signaling with Partial Disclosure', *Review of Economic Studies* 50, 2: 331–46.

Biais, B. and C. Gollier (1997) 'Trade Credit and Credit Rationing', *Review of Financial Studies* 10, 4: 903–37.

Bizzarri, L. (2006) 'Il finanziamento delle imprese innovative', Convegno AIDEA 2006 'Finanza e industria in Italia', Roma, 28–29 settembre.

Black, B. S. and R. J. Gilson (1998) 'Venture Capital and the Structure of Capital Markets: Banks versus Stock Markets', *Journal of Financial Economics* 47, 3: 243–77.

Bottazzi, L. and M. Da Rin (2002) 'Venture Capital in Europe and the Financing of Innovative Companies', *Economic Policy* 17, 34: 229–69.

Bottazzi, L., M. Da Rin and F. Giavazzi (2001) 'Research, Patent and Financing of Ideas: Why is the EU Potential so Low?', Working Paper for the Group of Economic Analysis of the European Commission.

Bracchi, G. (2006) 'L'impatto del private equity sullo sviluppo economico', AIFI convegno annuale 2006, Milano.

Brealey, R.A., S. C. Myers, A. J. Marcus and R. Brealey (2003) *Fundamentals of Corporate Finance*, New York: McGraw-Hill/Irwin.

Bronzini, R. and G. de Blasio (2006) 'Qual'è l'effetto degli incentivi agli investimenti? Una valutazione della legge 488/92', *Temi di discussione*, Banca d'Italia n. 582, marzo.

Brugnoli, C. (2003) *La nuova impresa innovativa: ambiente, formazione, gestione e finanziamento*, Torino: G. Giappichelli Editore.

BVCA (2007) *The Economic Impact of Private Equity in the UK*, Research Study undertaken by IE Consulting.

BVK (2007) *BVK Yearbook 2007*, Berlin.

Bygrave, W. D. and J. A. Timmons (1992) *Venture Capital at the Crossroads*, Cambridge, MA: Harvard Business School Press.

Callejon, M. and A. Segarra (1999) 'Business Dynamics and Efficiency in Industries and Regions: The Case of Spain', *Small Business Economics* 13, 4: 253–71.

Canovi, L., A. G. Grasso and V. Venturelli (2007) 'Il fabbisogno di capitale di rischio delle Pmi innovative in Italia', *Banca Impresa Società* 26, 2: 309–34.

Cardullo, M. W. (1999) *Technological Entrepreneurism: Enterprise Formation, Financing and Growth*, Baldock: Research Studies Press.

Carlin, W. and C. Mayer (2003) 'Finance, Investment, and Growth', *Journal of Financial Economics* 69, 1: 191–226.

Carpenter, R. E. and B. C. Petersen (2002) 'Capital Market Imperfections, High-Tech Investment, and New Equity Financing', *The Economic Journal* 112, 477: F54–F72.

Carree, M. A. and A. R. Thurik (2003) 'The Impact of Entrepreneurship on Economic Growth', in J. A. Zoltan and D. B. Audretsch (eds.), *Handbook of Entrepreneurship Research*, Boston, MA: Kluwer, pp. 437–71.

Cary, L. (1999) *The Venture Capital Report, Guide to Venture Capital in the UK & Europe*, Venture Capital Report, London.

Caselli, S. (2001) *Corporate banking per le piccole e medie imprese*, Roma: Bancaria Editrice.

Caselli, S. and S. Gatti (2002) *Venture Capital in the Euro System: Market Structure, Strategies and Management*, Milano: Newfin, Università Bocconi.

Cavallo, C., M. Lazzeroni, A. Patrono and A. Piccaluga (2002) 'Rapporto Annuale dell'Osservatorio sulle imprese high tech della Provincia di Pisa', typecript.

Chew, D. (2007) 'Private Equity: Past, Present, and Future. An interview with Steve Kaplan', *Journal of Applied Corporate Finance* 19, 3: 8–16.

Christensen, J. L. (2000) 'Effects of Venture Capital on Innovation and Growth', Division of Economic Analysis, Danish Ministry of Trade and Industry, Copenhagen.

Christensen, J. L. (2004) 'Changes in Danish Innovation Policy: Responses to the Challenges of a Dynamic Business Environment', in Biegelbauer and Borras (eds.), *Innovation Policy in Europe and the USA*, London: Ashgate.

Christensen, J. L., B. Dalum, B. Gregersen, B. Johnson, B. Lundvall and M. Tomlinson (2005) 'The Danish Innovation System', Department of Business Studies, Aalborg University, Denmark, Seoul: Workshop 7–9 March.

Committee on Finance and Industry (1931) *Macmillan Report*, Cmd. 3897. London: HMSO.

Committee on Small Business House of Representatives (2006) 'Bridging the Equity Gap: Examining the Access to Capital for Entrepreneurs, Act of 2006', Washington, DC: US Government Printing Office.

Conroy, R. M. and R. S. Harris (2007) 'How Good are Private Equity Returns?' *Journal of Applied Corporate Finance* 19, 3: 96–108.

Cornelli, F. and D. Goldreich, (2001) 'Bookbuilding and Strategic Allocation', *Journal of Finance* 56, 6: 2337–69.

Cornelli, F. and D. Goldreich (2003) 'Bookbuilding: How Informative is the Order Book?' *Journal of Finance* 58, 4: 1415–43.

Cressy, R. (2002) 'Funding Gaps: a Symposium', *The Economic Journal* 112, 477: F1–16.

Cruickshank, D. (2000) *Competition in UK Banking. A Report to the Chancellor of the Exchequer*, London: The Stationery Office.

Cumming, D. and U. Walz (2004) 'Private Equity Returns and Disclosure around the World', LSE Working Paper N. 9, RICAFE, April.

Cumming, D., D. Siegel and M. Wright (2007) 'Private Equity, Leveraged Buy-outs and Governance', *Journal of Corporate Finance* 13, 4: 439–60.

Dantas Machado, C. and K. Raade (2006) 'Profitability of Venture Capital Investment in Europe and United States', Economic Paper No. 245, European Commission Directorate for Economic and Financial Affairs, Brussels, March.

De Meza D. and D. Webb (1987) 'Too Much Investment: A Problem of Asymmetric Information?' *Quarterly Journal of Economics* 102, 2: 281–92.

Del Colle, D. M., P. Finaldi Russo and A. Generale (2006) 'The Causes and Consequences of Venture Capital Financing. An Analysis Based on a Sample of Italian Firms', *Temi di discussione*, Banca d'Italia, no. 584, March.

Delle Vedove, F., G. Giudici and P. A. Randone (2005) 'The Evolution of Initial Public Offerings in Italy', BIt Notes 14, Borsa Italiana.

Department for Business Enterprises and Regulatory Reform (2007) *Enterprise Capital Funds Bidding Process*, London: BERR.

Dewatripoint, M. and J. Tirole (1994) 'A Theory of Debt and Equity: Diversity of Securities and Manager-Shareholder Congruence', *Quarterly Journal of Economics* 109, 4: 1027–54.

Diamond, D. W. (1984) 'Financial Intermediation and Delegated Monitoring', *Review of Economic Studies* 51, 3: 393–414.

Diamond, D. W. (1991) 'Monitoring and Reputation: The Choice between Bank Loans and Directly Placed Debt', *Journal of Political Economy* 99, 4: 688–721.

Dubocage, E. and D. Rivaud-Danset (2002a) 'Government Policy on Venture Capital Support in France', *Venture Capital: An International Journal of Entrepreneurial Finance* 4, 1: 25–43.

Dubocage, E. and D. Rivaud-Danset (2002b) 'The Development of Venture Capital in Europe. The Role of Public Policy', University of Paris Nord 13, December.

Eckbo, B. E. (2007), *Handbook in Corporate Finance*, North-Holland: Elsevier.

Engel, D. (2002) 'The Impact of Venture Capital in Firm Growth: An Empirical Investigation', ZEW Discussion paper 02-02.

European Central Bank (2007) 'Corporate Finance in the Euro Area', Occasional Paper Series 63, Frankfurt A/M, June.

European Commission (1995) *Green Paper on Innovation*, December, Brussels.

European Commission (1998) 'Risk Capital: a Key to Job Creation in the European Union', Commission Communication of 31 March 1998, SEC(1998) 552 final, Brussels.

European Commission (1999) 'Implementing the Framework for Financial Markets: Action Plan' Commission Communication of 11 May 1999, COM (1999) 232 final, Brussels.

European Commission (2001) 'State Aids and Risk Capital', *Official Journal of the European Communities* (2001/C 235/03), Brussels.

European Commission (2002) 'Productivity: The Key to Competitiveness of European Economies and Enterprises', Communication from the Commission to the Council and the European Parliament, COM (2002) 262 final, Brussels.

European Commission (2003a) 'European Commission Recommendation, 6 May 2003', OJ L 124, 20/05/2003, Brussels.

European Commission (2003b) 'Communication from the Commission to the Council and the European Parliament, Access to Finance of Small and Medium-Sized Enterprises', 1.12.2003, COM(2003) 713, Brussels.

European Commission (2003c) 'Benchmarking Business Angels', Enterprise Directorate-General European Commission, Final Report, November, Brussels.

European Commission (2003d) 'Creating an Entrepreneurial Europe. The Activities of the European Union for Small and Medium-sized Enterprises (SMEs)', Commission Staff Working Paper, COM(2003) 58, Brussels.

European Commission (2004a) 'State Aids – United Kingdom, Aid C 17/04 (ex N 566/03) – Enterprise Capital Funds', *Official Journal of the European Communities*, (2004/C 225/02): C225/222-C225/227), Brussels.

European Commission (2004b) *Progress Report on the Implementation of the Charter of Small and Medium Sized Enterprises in the Netherlands*, Brussels.

European Commission (2005a) *Best Practices of Public Support for Early Stage Equity Finance*, Final Report of the Expert Group, Directorate-General for Enterprise and Industry, September, Brussels.

European Commission (2005b) *Report on the Implementation of the European Charter for Small Enterprises in the Member States of the European Union*, Brussels.

European Commission (2006a) 'Expert Group Report on Removing Obstacles to Cross-border Investments by Venture Capital Funds', European Commission DG Enterprise and Industry, Brussels.

European Commission (2006b) 'Implementing the Community Lisbon Programme: Financing SME Growth – Adding European Value', COM (2006) 439, Brussels.

European Commission (2006c) 'Report of the Alternative Investment Expert Group on Managing, Servicing and Marketing Hedge Fund in Europe', European Commission Internal Market and Services DG, Brussels.

European Commission, (2006d) Enterprise Directorate-General, *Annual Innovation Policy Trends and Appraisal Report* (Denmark), Brussels.

European Commission, (2006e) 'Risk Capital: Community Guidelines on State Aid to Promote Risk Capital Investments in Small and Medium-sized Enterprises', *Official Journal of European Communities* C 194, 18.08.2006, Brussels.

European Council (2000) 'Presidency Conclusion' Lisbon European Council, 23-24 March.

European Investment Bank (2001) *Financing Innovative Firms through Venture Capital*, February, Luxemburg.

European Investment Bank (2005) *Towards a New Strategy for the EIB Group*, Internal document, June, Luxemburg.

Eurostat (2007) 'European Business: Facts and Figures'. European Communities, Luxembourg.

EVCA (1996) *The Economic Impact of Venture Capital in Europe*, in collaboration with Coopers & Lybrand Corporate Finance, European Private Equity & Venture Capital Association, Zaventem, Belgium.

EVCA (1999) *Private Equity Fund Structures in Europe*, European Private Equity & Venture Capital Association, Zaventem, Belgium.

EVCA (2001) *Policy Priorities for Private Equity: Fostering Long-Term Economic Growth*, EVCA White Paper, European Private Equity & Venture Capital Association, Zaventem, Belgium.

EVCA (2005) *EVCA Yearbook 2005*, European Private Equity & Venture Capital Association, Zaventem, Belgium.

EVCA (2007a) *EVCA Yearbook 2007*, European Private Equity & Venture Capital Association, Zaventem, Belgium.

EVCA (2007b) *Guide on Private Equity and Venture Capital for Entrepreneurs*, Special Paper, November, Belgium.

Fama, E. (1985) 'What's Different about Banks', *Journal of Monetary Economics*, 15, 1: 29–39.

Financial Services Authority (2006) 'Private Equity: a Discussion of Risk and Regulatory Engagement', Discussion Paper, November, London

Finlombarda (2005) *Finanza e innovazione. Quarto quaderno sui casi di finanza innovativa per la creazione di techno start-up*, Milano.

Finocchiaro, A. (2000) 'Quale finanza per lo sviluppo e l'innovazione in Europa?', Report by the Deputy Governor of the Bank of Italy, Bellagio, July.

Florio, A. (2003) 'Il finanziamento delle imprese innovative. Quale ruolo per il sistema bancario?', Politecnico di Milano, Dipartimento di Ingegneria Gestionale.

Foelster, S. (2000) 'Do Entrepreneurs Create Jobs?', *Small Business Economics* 14, 2: 137–48.

Franzosi, A. and E. Pellizzoni (2005), 'Gli effetti della quotazione. Evidenza dalle mid- & small caps italiane', BIt Notes 13, Borsa Italiana.

Fritsch, M. (2008) 'How Does New Business Formation Affect Regional Development? Introduction to the Special Issue', *Small Business Economics* 30, 1: 1–14.

Gervasoni, A. (2006) 'Lo sviluppo del mercato italiano del venture capital al servizio della competitività del sistema imprenditoriale', Convegno AIDEA 2006 'Finanza e industria in Italia', Roma, 28–29 settembre.

Gervasoni, A. and F. L. Sattin (2000) *Private Equity e Venture Capital. Manuale di investimento nel capitale di rischio*, Milano: Guerini e Associati.

Giuliani, E. (2002) 'Cluster Absorptive Capability: an Evolutionary Approach for Industrial Clusters in Developing Countries', in Druid Summer Conference on Industrial Dynamics of the New and Old Economy – Who is Embracing Whom? Copenhagen/Elsinore, 6–8 June.

Goergen, M., A. Khurshed, J. A. McCahery and L. Renneboog (2003) 'The Rise and Fall of the European New Markets: On the Short and Long-run Performance of High-tech Initial Public Offerings', ECGI Working Paper Series in Finance, 27.

Gompers, P. A. (1995) 'Optimal Investment, Monitoring and the Staging of Venture Capital', *Journal of Finance* 50, 5: 1461–89.

Gompers, P. A. (1997) 'Ownership and Control in Entrepreneurial Firms: an Examination of Convertible Securities in Venture Capital Investments', Working Paper, Cambridge, MA: Harvard Business School.

Gompers, P. A. and J. Lerner (1998) 'What Drives Venture Capital Fund-raising?' *Brookings Papers on Economic Activity: Macroeconomics*: 149–92.

Gompers, P. A. and J. Lerner (2001) 'The Venture Capital Revolution', *Journal of Economic Perspectives* 15, 2: 145–68.

Gompers, P. A. (1998) 'Resource Allocation, Incentives and Control: The Importance of Venture Capital in Financing Entrepreneurial Firms', in Z. J. Acs, B. Carlsson and C. Karlsson *Entrepreneurship, SMEs, and the Macroeconomy*, Cambridge: Cambridge University Press.

Gompers, P. A. and J. Lerner (2006) *The Venture Capital Cycle*, Cambridge, MA: MIT Press.

Gorman, M. and W. A. Sahlman (1989) 'What do Venture Capitalists Do?' *Journal of Business Venturing* 4, 4: 231–48.

Graham, T. (2004) *Graham Review of the Small Firms Loan Guarantee, Recommendations*, September.

Greenbaum, S. I. and A. V. Thakor (1995) *Contemporary Financial Intermediation*, Chicago: Dryden Press.

Gualandri, E. and P. Schwizer (2008) 'Bridging the Equity Gap: il caso della PMI innovative', *Studi e Note di Economia*, no. 1.

Gualandri, E. and V. Venturelli (2007) 'Assessing and Measuring the Equity Gap and the Equity Requirements for Innovative SMEs', Proceedings of Seventh International Business Research Conference, Sydney, 3–6 December.

HM Treasury and Small Business Service (2003a) *Bridging the Finance Gap. A Consultation on Improving Access to Growth Capital for Small Business*, April.

HM Treasury and Small Business Service (2003b) *Bridging the Finance Gap: Next Steps in Improving Access to Growth Capital for Small Businesses*, December.

Hall, B. H. (2002) 'The Financing of Research and Development', *Oxford Review of Economic Policy* 18, 1: 35–51.

Hall, B. H. (2005) 'The Financing of Innovation', typescript, December.

Handa P. and R. A. Schwartz (1996) 'How Best to Supply Liquidity to a Securities Market', *The Journal of Portfolio Management* 22, 2: 44–51.

Harding, R. (2002) 'Plugging the Knowledge Gap: International Comparison of the Role for Policy in the Venture Capital Market', *Venture Capital: An International Journal of Entrepreneurial Finance* 4, 1: 59–76.

Harding, R. and M. Cowling (2006) 'Assessing the Scale of the Equity Gap', *Journal of Small Business and Enterprise Development* 13, 1: 115–32.

Harding, R., D. Brooksbank, M. Hart, D. Jones-Evans, J. Levie, M. O'Reilly, and J. Walker (2005) *Global Entrepreneurship Monitor*, United Kingdom.

Hart, M. and E. Hanvey (1995) 'Job Generation and New and Small Firms: Some Evidence from the Late 1980s', *Small Business Economics* 7, 2: 97–109.

Hellmann, T. and M. Puri (2000) 'The Interaction between Product Market and Financing Strategy: The Role of Venture Capital', *Review of Financial Studies* 13, 4: 959–84.

Hellmann, T. and M. Puri (2002) 'Venture Capital and the Professionalization of Startup Firms: Empirical Evidence', *Journal of Finance* 57, 1: 169–97.

Himmelberg, C. P. and B. C. Petersen (1994) 'R&D and Internal Finance: a Panel Study of Small Firms in High-Tech Industries', *Review of Economic and Statistics* 76, 1: 38–51.

Hommel, U. and H. Schneider (2003) 'Financing the German Mittelstand', EIB Papers, 8, 2: 52–89.

Hughes, A. (1993) 'The "Problems" of Finance for Smaller Businesses', in M. Dimsdale M. and M. Prevezer (eds.), *Capital Markets and Company Success*, Oxford: Oxford University Press.

Hughes, A. and D. J. Cosh (1994) *Finance and the Small Firm*, London: Routledge.

Ibbotson, R. G. (1975) 'Price Performance of Common Stock New Issues', *Journal of Financial Economics* 2, 3: 235–72.

Itzel, E., N. Rökaeus, E. Höglund and M. Lundh (2004) 'Differences between Business Angels and Venture Capitalists', Stockholm School of Entrepreneurship.

Jääskeläinen M., M. Maula and G. Murray G. (2004) 'Performance of Incentive Structure in Publicly and Privately Funded Hybrid Venture Capital Funds', in S. A. Zahra, C. G. Brush, P. Davidsson, J. O. Fiet, P. G. Greene, R. T. Harrison, M. Lerner, C. Mason, D. G. Meyer, J. Sohl and A. Zacharakis (eds.), *Frontiers of Entrepreneurship Research*, Babson College, Babson Park, pp. 668–81.

Jeng, L. and P. Wells (2000) 'The Determinants of Venture Capital Funding: Evidence Across Countries', *Journal of Corporate Finance* 6, 3: 241–89.

Jenkinson, T. and A. Ljungqvist (2001) *Going Public: The Theory and Evidence on How Companies Raise Equity Finance*, Oxford: Oxford University Press.

Jensen, M. and W. Meckling (1976) 'Theory of the Firm: Managerial Behaviour, Agency Costs and Ownership Structure', *Journal of Financial Economics* 3, 4: 305–60.

Jensen, N. W. and C. Vinergaard (2002) 'Growth Improving Focus for the Danish Venture Capital Market', Working Paper, Copenhagen Business School.

Kaplan, S. N. and L. Zingales (1997) 'Do Investment–Cashflows Sensitivities Provide Useful Measures of Financing Constraints?', *Quarterly Journal of Economics* 112, 1: 168–215.

Kaplan, S. N. and L. Zingales (2000) 'Investment–Cashflows Sensitivities are not Valid Measures of Financing Constraints', *Quarterly Journal of Economics* 115, 2: 707–12.

Kaplan, S. N. and P. Stromberg (2003) 'Financial Contracting Theory Meets the Real World: An Empirical Analysis of Venture Capital Contracts', *Review of Economic Studies* 70, 2: 281–315.

Kaplan, S. N. and A. Schoar (2005) 'Private Equity Performance: Returns, Persistence, and Capital Flows', *Journal of Finance* 60, 4: 1791–1823.

Kenney, M., K. Han and S. Tanaka (2002) 'The Globalization of Venture Capital: The Cases of Taiwan and Japan', paper presented at the International Conference on Financial systems, corporate investment in innovation and venture capital jointly organised by UNU/INTECH and EU-DG Research at Brussels, 7–8 November.

KfW Bankengruppe (2003) 'Eigenkapital für den "breiten" Mittelstand', Frankfurt, January.

Kolbeck, C. and R. Wimmer (2003) *Finanzierung für den Mittelstand*, Wiesbaden: Gabler.

Kortum, S. and J. Lerner (1998) 'Does Venture Capital Spur Innovation?' NBER Working Paper Series, Working Paper 6846, 674-692.

Landi, A. (2005), 'Imprenditorialità e accesso alla finanza', University of Modena and Reggio Emilia, February.

Landi, A. and A. Rigon (eds.) (2006) *Finanza e sviluppo delle PMI in Europa: ruolo delle banche e dell'intervento pubblico*, Roma: Bancaria Editrice.

Lawton, T. C. (2002) 'Missing the Target: Assessing the Role of Government in Bridging the European Equity Gap and Enhancing Economic Growth', *Venture Capital: An International Journal of Entrepreneurial Finance* 4, 1: 7–17.

Leland, H. E. and D. H. Pyle (1977) 'Informational Asymmetries, Financial Structure and Financial Intermediation', *Journal of Finance* 32, 2: 371–87.

Leleux, B. and B. Surlemont (2003), Public versus Private Venture Capital: Seeding or Crowding out? A pan-European Analysis', *Journal of Business Venturing* 18, 1: 81–104.

Levine, R. (2005) 'Finance and Growth: Theory and Evidence', in P. Aghion and S. Durlauf (eds.), *Handbook of Economic Growth*, North-Holland: Elsevier.

Levine, R. and S. Zervos (1998) 'Stock Markets, Banks and Economic Growth', *American Economic Review* 88, 3: 537–58.

Ljungqvist, A. (2007) 'IPO Under-pricing', in B. Espen Eckbo (ed.), *Handbook in Corporate Finance*, North-Holland: Elsevier.

Lucas, R. (1993) 'Making a Miracle', *Econometrica* 61, 2: 251–72.

Magri, S. (2007) 'The Financing of Small Innovative Firms: The Italian Case', *Temi di discussione*, Banca d'Italia, no. 640, September.

Martin, R., C. Berndt, B. Klagge and P. Sunley (2005) 'Spatial Proximity Effects and Regional Equity Gaps in the Venture Capital Market: Evidence from Germany and the United Kingdom', *Environment and Planning* 37, 7: 1207–31.

Mason, C. M. and R. T. Harrison (2003) 'Closing the Regional Equity Gap? A Critique of the Department of Trade and Industry's Regional Venture Capital Funds Initiative', *Regional Studies* 37, 8: 855–68.

Maula, M. and M. Mäkelä (2003) 'Cross-border Venture Capital', in A. Hyytinen and M. Pajarinen (eds.), *Financial Systems and Firm Performance: Theoretical and Empirical Perspectives*. Helsinki: Taloustieto, pp. 269–91.

Maula, M., G. Murray and M. Jääskeläinen (2007) 'Public Financing of Young Innovative Companies in Finland', MTI 03, Ministry of Trade and Industry, Helsinki.

Mayer, C., K. Schoors and Y. Yafeh (2004) 'Sources of Funds and Investment Activities of Venture Capital Funds: Evidence from Germany, Israel, Japan and the United Kingdom', *Journal of Corporate Finance* 11, 3: 586–608.

Mayoral, R. H., T. L. Eldert and G. Struck (2003) *Comparative Review of Legal and Regulatory Frameworks Supporting Venture Capital*, Report prepared for Millennia Consulting.

McGlue, D. (2002) 'The Funding of Venture Capital in Europe: Issues for Public Policy', *Venture Capital: An International Journal of Entrepreneurial Finance* 4, 1: 45–58.

Megginson, W. (2004) 'Toward a Global Model of Venture Capital?' *Journal of Applied Corporate Finance* 16, 1: 8–26.

Mittelstandsforschung – IfM (2004), *Unternehmensgrößenstatistik 2003/2004*, Bonn.

Modena, V. (2003) *Proposte per la creazione di fonti efficaci di capitali di rischio in Italia*, Milano: Franco Angeli.

Modigliani, F. and M. Miller (1958) 'The Cost of Capital, Corporate Finance, and the Theory of Investment', *American Economic Review* 48, 3: 261–97.

Mottura, P. (1987) 'Condizioni di equilibrio della strategia d'impresa', *Finanza Marketing e Produzione*, 1, Marzo.

Munck, N. H. and K. Mortensen (2003) 'Homogeneous Liquidity Pattern across Equity Markets', OMX Exchanges Focus Series.

Murray, G. C. (2007) 'Venture Capital and Government Policy', in H. Landstom (ed.), *Handbook of Research in Venture Capital*, London: Edward Elgar.

Myers, S. C. (1984) 'The Capital Structure Puzzle', *Journal of Finance* 39, 3: 575–92.

Myers, S. C. and N. C. Majluf (1984) 'Corporate Financing and Investment Decisions When Firms Have Information that Investors Do not Have', *Journal of Financial Economics* 13, 2: 187–221.

NVCA (2002a) *NVCA Yearbook 2002*, Arlington, VA: NVCA.

NVCA (2002b) *Venture Capital as a Key Factor Powering U.S. Economic Growth*, Press Release, June 26, Washington, DC.

NVCA (2007) *NVCA Yearbook 2007*, Arlington, VA: NVCA.

NVCA and Global Insight (2004) *Venture Impact 2004. Venture Capital Benefits to the U.S. Economy*, Washington, DC.

NVCA and Global Insight (2007) *Venture Impact. The Economic Importance of Venture Capital Backed Companies to the U.S. Economy*, Washington, DC.

Nye, D. and N. Wasserman (1999) 'Patterns of VC Evolution: Comparing the Israeli and Indian Venture Capital Industries', *Journal of Private Equity* 3, 1: 26–48.

OECD (2004) *Financing Innovative SMEs in a Global Economy*, published paper from the 2nd OECD Conference of Ministers Responsible for Small and Medium Sized Enterprises (SMEs), Promoting Entrepreneurship and Innovative SMEs in a Global Economy, Istanbul, Turkey, 3–5 June.

OECD (2005) 'Oslo-Manual – Guidelines for Collecting and Interpreting Innovation Data', 3rd edn., Paris: OECD.

OECD (2006a) *The SME Financing Gap (Vol. I): Theory and Evidence*, Vol. 2006, No. 19, October, Paris: OECD.

OECD (2006b) *The SME Financing Gap (Vol. II): Proceedings of the Brasilia Conference, 27-30 March 2006*, Vol. 2007, No. 5, June, Paris: OECD.

OECD (2006c) *The OECD Brasilia Action Statement for SME & Entrepreneurship Financing*, the OECD Conference on Better Financing for Entrepreneurship and SME Growth, Brazil: OECD.

OECD (2006d) *Policy Brief*, November, Paris: OECD.

Pagano, M., F. Panetta, and L. Zingales, (1998), 'Why Do Companies Go Public? An Empirical Analysis', *Journal of Finance* 53, 1: 27–64.

Paleari, S., D. Piazzalunga, R. Redondi, F. Trabucchi, and S. Vismara (2007) 'Academic EurIPO – Fact Book 2007'.

Petersen, M. A. and R. G. Rajan (1994) 'The Benefits of Firm–Creditor Relationships: Evidence from Small Business Data', *Journal of Finance* 49, 1: 3–37.

Petrella, G. (2001) 'Sistemi finanziari e finanziamento delle imprese innovative: profili teorici ed evidenze empiriche dall'Europa', Quaderni ref., no. 4, May.

Petrella, G. (2005), 'Are Euro Area Small Caps an Asset Class? Evidence from Mean–Variance Spanning Tests', *European Financial Management* 11, 2: 229–253.

Plagge, A. (2006) *Public Policy for Venture Capital*, Wiesbaden: Deutscher Universitätsbuchverlag.

Queen, M. (2002) 'Government Policy to Stimulate Equity Finance and Investor Readiness', *Venture Capital: An International Journal of Entrepreneurial Finance* 4, 1: 1–5.

Rajan, R. G. and L. Zingales (1998) 'Financial Dependence and Growth', *American Economic Review* 88, 3: 559–86.

Rajan, R. and L. Zingales (2001) 'Financial Systems, Industrial Structure and Growth', *Oxford Review of Economic Policy* 17, 4: 467–82.

Ramakrishan, R. T. S. and A. V. Thakor (1984) 'Information Reliability and the Theory of Financial Intermediation', *The Review of Economic Studies* 51, 3: 415–32.

Rigamonti, S. (2007) 'Evolution of Ownership and Control in Italian IPO Firms', BIt Notes 17, Borsa Italiana.

Ritter, J. R. (1998) 'Initial Public Offerings', *Contemporary Finance Digest*.

Ritter, J. R. and I. Welch (2002) 'A Review of IPO Activity, Pricing and Allocations', *Journal of Finance* 57, 4: 1795–1828.

Rivaud-Danset, D. (2002) 'Innovation and New Technologies: Corporate Finance and Financial Constraints', International Conference Financial Systems, Corporate Investment in Innovation and Venture Capital, jointly organised by the European Commission-DG Research and the Institute for New Technologies of the United Nations University, 7–8 November, Brussels.

Romani, A. and B. Pottelsberghe van (2004) 'The Economic Impact of Venture Capital', Deutsche Bundesbank, Discussion Paper Series 1: Studies of the Economic Research Centre, 18.

Romer, P. (1986) 'Increasing Returns and Long-Run Growth', *Journal of Political Economy* 94, 5: 1002–37.

Rossignoli, B. (1991) 'Flusso dei fondi e fabbisogno finanziario. Elementi per la programmazione e il controllo', in C. Bisoni and B. Rossignoli (eds.), *Letture di finanza aziendale*, Milano: Giuffrè Editore.

Sahlman, W. A. (1988) 'Aspects of Financial Contracting in Venture Capital', *Journal of Applied Corporate Finance* 1, 2: 23–36.

Sahlman, W. A. (1990) 'The Structure and Governance of Venture-Capital Organizations', *Journal of Financial Economics* 27, 2: 473–521.

Schilder, D. (2006) 'Public Venture Capital in Germany – Task Force or Forced Task?' Freibergworkingpapers, no. 12.

Schumpeter, J. (1934) *The Theory of Economic Development*, Cambridge, MA: Harvard University Press.

Schwartz, R. A. and R. Francioni (2004) *Equity Markets in Action: the Fundamentals of Liquidity, Market Structure and Trading'*, New York: John Wiley & Sons.

Seward, J. K. (1990) 'Corporate Financial Policy and the Theory of Financial Intermediation', *Journal of Finance* 45, 2: 351–77.

Small Business Administration (2002) *Small Business Investment Company Program, Fiscal Year 2002*, Special Report, June 15.

Small Business Service (2004) *Pathfinder Enterprise Capital Funds: Draft Guidance for Applicants*, London.

Stel, van A. and K. Suddle (2008) 'The Impact of New Firm Formation on Regional Development in the Netherlands', *Small Business Economics* 30, 1: 31–47.

Stiglitz, J. (1985) 'Credit Markets and the Control of Capital', *Journal of Money Credit and Banking* 17, 2: 133–52.

Stiglitz J. E. and A. Weiss (1981) 'Credit Rationing in Markets with Imperfect Information', *American Economic Review* 71, 3: 393–410.

Sunley, P., B. Klagge, C. Berndt and R. Martin (2005) 'Venture Capital Programmes in the UK and Germany: In What Sense Regional Policy?' *Regional Studies* 39, 2: 255–73.

Sweeting, R. C. and C. F. Wong (1997) 'A UK 'Hands-off' Venture Capital Firm and the Handling of post-investment Investor–Investee Relationships', *Journal of Management Studies* 34, 1: 125–52.

Szego, B. (2002) 'Il venture capital come strumento per lo sviluppo delle piccole e medie imprese: un'analisi di adeguatezza dell'ordinamento italiano', *Banca d'Italia, Quaderni di ricerca giuridica*, No. 55.

TEKES (2005) 'Business Cycle Effects on Start-up Finance in Finland', *Technology Review*, 172/2005, Helsinki.

Timmons, J. A. and W. D. Bygrave (1986) 'Venture Capital's Role in Financing Innovation for Economic Growth', *Journal of Business Venturing* 1, 2: 161–76.

Trotta, A. (2001) *Finanza innovativa per le piccole imprese. Le prospettive di sviluppo dell'Informal Venture Capital Market in Italia*, Padova: CEDAM.

Vesper, K. H. (1993) *New Venture Mechanics*, New York: Prentice Hall Business.

Wall, J. (1998) 'Better Exits', EVCA Special Paper, Zaventem, Belgium.

Williamson, O.E. (1988) 'Corporate Finance and Corporate Governance', *Journal of Finance* 43, 3: 567–91.

Wilson, J. W. (1985) *The New Venturers. Inside the High Stakes World of Venture Capital*, Menlo Park, CA: Addison-Wesley.

Wright, M., S. Pruthi and A. Lockett (2005) 'International Venture Capital Research: From Cross-country Comparisons to Crossing Borders', *International Journal of Management Reviews* 7, 3: 135–65.

Index